TExES 158 Physical Education EC-12
Teacher Certification Exam

By: Sharon Wynne, M.S.
Southern Connecticut State University

"And, while there's no reason yet to panic, I think it's only prudent that we make preparations to panic."

XAMonline, INC.
Boston

To obtain permission(s) to use the material from this work for any purpose including workshops or seminars, please submit a written request to:

XAMonline, Inc.
21 Orient Ave.
Melrose, MA 02176
Toll Free 1-800-509-4128
Email: info@XAMonline.com
Web www.xamonline.com
Fax: 1-781-662-9268

Library of Congress Cataloging-in-Publication Data

Wynne, Sharon A.
Physical Education EC-12 158: Teacher Certification / Sharon A. Wynne. -2nd ed.
ISBN 978-1-58197-620-5
1. Physical Education EC-12 158   2. Study Guides.   3. TexES
4. Teachers' Certification & Licensure.   5. Careers

Disclaimer:
The opinions expressed in this publication are the sole works of XAMonline and were created independently from the National Education Association, Educational Testing Service, or any State Department of Education, National Evaluation Systems or other testing affiliates.

Between the time of publication and printing, state specific standards as well as testing formats and website information may change that is not included in part or in whole within this product. Sample test questions are developed by XAMonline and reflect similar content as on real tests; however, they are not former tests. XAMonline assembles content that aligns with state standards but makes no claims nor guarantees teacher candidates a passing score. Numerical scores are determined by testing companies such as NES or ETS and then are compared with individual state standards. A passing score varies from state to state.

Printed in the United States of America
TExES: Physical Education EC-12 158
ISBN: 978-1-58197-620-5

TEXAS SUBJECT AREA TEST – *Physical Education*

ABOUT THE TExES:

For each TExES (Texas Examinations of Educator Standards) examination, XAMonline has prepared a test framework based on the state subject area competency objectives set forth by the State of Texas. Each test framework consists of a set of test domains, competencies, and skills. Collectively, these objectives establish the general set of knowledge that each applicant should possess to achieve certification. All individuals seeking an initial Texas teaching license must pass the TExES subtest that matches the type of license they are seeking. All TExES examinations are criterion referenced, meaning, each test measures an examinee's knowledge in relation to an established standard of competence rather than in relation to the performance of other examinees.

TEST ADMINISTRATION:

On each test date, prospective teachers can take the TExES Physical Education test in either the morning or afternoon session. Each session is five hours long.

The TExES Physical Education EC-12 test consists of 90 multiple-choice questions, 80 scored questions and 10 nonscorable, pilot questions.

While many TExES examinations have free response or essay questions, the Physical Education test **does not**, and consists entirely of multiple-choice questions.

SCORE REPORTS:

Each score report will indicate whether an individual has passed their respective test. Score reports also include a description of each individual's performance on the major content subareas of the test. The scoring scale for each test ranges from 100 to 300, with 240 representing the minimum passing score.

TEST STRUCTURE

The ETS, the designer of the TExES examinations, describes the test structure as follows:

Domain Number	Domain Title	Approximate Percentage of Test	Approximate Number of Scorable Questions
I	Movement Skills and Knowledge	38%	30
II	Health-Related Physical Fitness	31%	25
III	The Physical Education Program	31%	25

Table of Contents

DOMAIN III.   THE PHYSICAL EDUCATION PROGRAM

Great Study and Testing Tips!

What you study in order to prepare for the subject assessments is the focus of this study guide, but equally important is *how* you study.

You can increase your chances of truly mastering the information by taking some simple but effective steps.

Study Tips:

1. Some foods aid the learning process. Foods such as milk, nuts, seeds, rice, and oats help your study efforts by releasing natural memory enhancers called CCKs (*cholecystokinin*) composed of *tryptophan*, *choline*, and *phenylalanine*. All of these chemicals enhance the neurotransmitters associated with memory. Before studying, try a light, protein-rich meal of eggs, turkey, and fish. All of these foods release the memory enhancing chemicals. The better the connections, the more you comprehend.

Likewise, before you take a test, stick to a light snack of relaxing and energy boosting foods. A glass of milk, a piece of fruit, or some peanuts release various memory-boosting chemicals and help you to relax and focus on the subject at hand.

2. Learn to take great notes. A by-product of our modern culture is that we have grown accustomed to getting our information in short doses (e.g. TV news sound bytes or USA Today style newspaper articles).

Consequently, we've subconsciously trained ourselves to assimilate information better in neat little packages. If your notes are scrawled all over the paper, it fragments the flow of the information. Strive for clarity. Newspapers use a standard format to achieve clarity. You can make your notes much clearer by using proper formatting. A very effective format is the *"Cornell Method."*

Take a sheet of loose-leaf lined notebook paper and draw a line all the way down the paper about 1-2" from the left-hand edge.

Draw another line across the width of the paper about 1-2" up from the bottom. Repeat this process on the reverse side of the page.

Look at the highly effective result. You have ample room for notes, a left hand margin for special emphasis items or inserting supplementary data from the textbook, a large area at the bottom for a brief summary, and a little rectangular space for just about anything you want.

3. <u>Get the concept then the details.</u> Too often, we focus on the details and don't gather an understanding of the concept. However, if you simply memorize only dates, places, or names, you may well miss the whole point of the subject.

A key way to understand things is to put them in your own words. If you are working from a textbook, automatically summarize each paragraph in your mind. If you are outlining text, don't simply copy the author's words.

Rephrase them in your own words. You remember your own thoughts and words much better than someone else's, and subconsciously tend to associate the important details to the core concepts.

4. <u>Ask Why?</u> Pull apart written material paragraph by paragraph and don't forget the captions under the illustrations.

Example: If the heading is "Stream Erosion", flip it around to read, "Why do streams erode?" Then answer the questions.

If you train your mind to think in a series of questions and answers, not only will you learn more, but it also helps to lessen the test anxiety because you are used to answering questions.

5. <u>Read for reinforcement and future needs.</u> Even if you only have 10 minutes, put your notes or a book in your hand. Your mind is similar to a computer; you have to input data in order to have it processed. *By reading, you are creating the neural connections for future retrieval.* The more times you read something, the more you reinforce the learning of ideas.

Even if you don't fully understand something on the first pass, *your mind stores much of the material for later recall.*

6. <u>Relax to learn, so go into exile.</u> Our bodies respond to an inner clock called biorhythms. Burning the midnight oil works well for some people, but not everyone.

If possible, set aside a particular place to study that is free of distractions. Shut off the television, cell phone, and pager and exile your friends and family during your study period.

If silence really bothers you, try background music. Studies show that light classical music played at a low volume aids in concentration.

Music without lyrics that evokes pleasant emotions is strongly suggested. Try just about anything by Mozart which can relax you.

7. Use arrows not highlighters. At best, it's difficult to read a page full of yellow, pink, blue, and green streaks.

Try staring at a neon sign for a while and you'll soon see my point. The plethora of colors obscures the message.

A quick note, a brief dash of color, an underline, and an arrow pointing to a particular passage is much clearer than a multitude of highlighted words.

8. Budget your study time. Although you shouldn't ignore any of the material, *allocate your available study time in the same ratio that topics may appear on the test.*

Testing Tips:

1. Get smart, play dumb. Don't read anything into the question. Don't assume that the test writer is looking for something other than what is asked. Stick to the question as written and don't read extra things into it.

2. Read the question and all the choices *twice* before answering. You may miss something by not carefully reading and re-reading both the question and the answers.

If you really don't have a clue as to the right answer, leave it blank the first time through. Go on to the other questions, as they may provide a clue as to how to answer the skipped questions.

If later on, you still can't answer the skipped ones . . . *Guess.*
The only penalty for guessing is that you *might* get it wrong. One thing is certain; if you don't put anything down, you will get it wrong!

3. Turn the question into a statement. Look at the way the questions are worded. The syntax of the question usually provides a clue. Does it seem more familiar as a statement rather than as a question? Does it sound strange?

By turning a question into a statement, you may be able to spot if an answer sounds right, and it may trigger memories of material you've read.

4. Look for hidden clues. It's actually very difficult to compose multiple-choice questions without giving away part of the answer in the options presented.

In most multiple-choice questions, you can often readily eliminate one or two of the potential answers. This leaves you with only two real possibilities, and automatically your odds go to fifty-fifty with very little work.

5. Trust your instincts. For every fact that you have read, you subconsciously retain something of that knowledge. On questions that you aren't certain about, go with your basic instincts. **Your first impression on how to answer a question is usually correct.**

6. Mark your answers directly on the test booklet. Don't bother trying to fill in the optical scan sheet on the first pass through the test.

Just be very careful to mark your answers correctly when you eventually transcribe them to the scan sheet.

7. Watch the clock! You have a set amount of time to answer the questions. Don't get bogged down trying to answer a single question at the expense of 10 questions you can more readily answer.

DOMAIN I.   MOVEMENT SKILLS AND KNOWLEDGE

COMPETENCY 1.0   PRINCIPLES OF MOTOR DEVELOPMENT AND MOTOR LEARNING

SKILL 1.1   Demonstrate knowledge of principles and stages of motor development.

The development of motor skills in children is a sequential process. We can classify motor skill competency into stages of development by observing children practicing physical skills. The sequence of development begins with simple reflexes and progresses to the learning of postural elements, locomotor skills, and, finally, fine motor skills. The stages of development consider both innate and learned behaviors.

STAGES OF MOTOR LEARNING

Stage 1 – Children progress from simple reflexes to basic movements such as sitting, crawling, creeping, standing, and walking.

Stage 2 – Children learn more complex motor patterns including running, climbing, jumping, balancing, catching, and throwing.

Stage 3 – During late childhood, children learn more specific movement skills. In addition, the basic motor patterns learned in Stage 2 become more fluid and automatic.

Stage 4 – During adolescence, children continue to develop general and specific motor skills and master specialized movements. At this point, factors including practice, motivation, and talent begin to affect the level of further development.

SKILL 1.2   Know motor learning principles, processes, and concepts and use this knowledge to promote students' acquisition and refinement of motor skills.

In addition to a thorough knowledge of the motor development process, physical education instructors must understand the principles of learning and information transfer to facilitate student progress. Important concepts include practice, feedback, observational learning, and self-assessment.

PRACTICE

Frequent, structured practice of motor skills enhances skill development in children. Without practice and instruction, natural ability and talent dictates the extent of motor skill development.

FEEDBACK

Feedback, or input from the tutor or educator, forms an extremely vital part of any learning process. Just as positive feedback works as a motivator enabling an athlete to improve and surge ahead with renewed interest, negative feedback also helps an athlete recognize and correct his or her mistakes.

When performers learn a skill, the skill goes into their short-term memory and receives positive feedback. The skill may eventually go into their long-term memory, creating memory that is more permanent. That is how positive feedback works to encourage the performer and helps in making the performer remember every aspect of the performance.

Negative feedback helps athletes, whether novice or experienced, become conscious of their mistakes. They can use this negative feedback to improve their shortcomings. Without feedback, an athlete is not likely to improve his or her technique and will lose motivation.

There are different types of feedback and it is always important for the performer to receive the right type. Some examples of feedback include the following:

Intrinsic feedback – information received by the athlete as a direct result of producing a movement through the kinesthetic senses – e.g. feeling from muscles, joints, and balance.

Extrinsic feedback – information not inherent in the movement itself but which improves intrinsic feedback (this is also known as augmented feedback). There are two main categories: knowledge of performance and information about the technique and performance. The coach can provide extrinsic feedback verbally or visually via video. Extrinsic feedback enables the athlete to establish a kinesthetic reference for the correct movement.

Research also indicates that the stage when an athlete receives feedback is as important as the content of the feedback. Negative feedback might be boring for the beginner. However, if a performer is elite, then knowledge of results is very important. In addition, during the cognitive stage, positive feedback is essential to make sure that the athlete learns a skill successfully. Thus, feedback plays an extremely important role in any learning process, as it facilitates learning to a great extent.

SELF-ASSESSMENT

Self-assessment is a powerful tool in motor skill development. Requiring students to assess their own skills and abilities encourages students to reflect upon their current skill level and take control of the development process.

OBSERVATIONAL LEARNING

Many physical education instructors believe that observational learning is the most effective method of learning motor skills. Visual observation of proper skill performance by an instructor or peer is generally more effective in promoting skill development than verbal instructions.

SKILL 1.3   Demonstrate knowledge of principles and components of perceptual-motor development and their relationship to motor performance.

Perceptual-motor development refers to one's ability to receive, interpret, and respond successfully to sensory signals coming from the environment. Because many of the skills acquired in school rely on the child's knowledge of his body and its relationship to the surroundings, good motor development leads directly to perceptual skill development. Development of gross motor skills lead to successful development of fine motor skills, which in turn help with learning, reading, and writing. Adolescents with perceptual-motor coordination problems are at risk for poor school performance, low self-esteem, and inadequate physical activity participation. Without a successful intervention, these adolescents are likely to continue avoiding physical activity and experience frustration and teasing from their peers. Children with weak perceptual-motor skills may be easily distracted or have difficulty with tasks requiring coordination. They spend much of their energy trying to control their bodies, exhausting them so much that they physically cannot concentrate on a teacher-led lesson. Unfortunately, perceptual-motor coordination problems do not just go away and they don't self-repair.

Practice and maturity are necessary for children to develop greater coordination and spatial awareness. Physical education lessons should emphasize activities that children enjoy doing, are sequential, and require seeing, hearing, and/or touching. Discussing with students the actual steps involved in performing a fundamental skill is a great benefit. Activities and skills that can be broken down and taught in incremental steps include running, dribbling, catching or hitting a ball, making a basket in basketball, and setting a volleyball. Recommended strategies include introducing the skill, practicing in a variety of settings with an assortment of equipment, implementing lead-up games modified to ensure practice of the necessary skills, and incorporating students into an actual game situation.

CONCEPT OF BODY AWARENESS APPLIED TO PHYSICAL EDUCATION ACTIVITIES

Body awareness is a person's understanding of his or her own body parts and their capability of movement.

Instructors can assess body awareness by watching students play a game of "Simon Says" and asking the students to touch different body parts. You can also instruct students to make their bodies into various shapes, such as, from straight to round to twisted, to fit into different sized spaces.

In addition, you can instruct children to touch one part of their body to another and to stamp their feet, twist their neck, clap their hands, nod their heads, wiggle their noses, snap their fingers, open their mouths, shrug their shoulders, bend their knees, close their eyes, bend their elbows, or wiggle their toes

CONCEPT OF SPATIAL AWARENESS APPLIED TO PHYSICAL EDUCATION ACTIVITIES

Spatial awareness is the ability to make decisions about an object's positional changes in space (i.e. awareness of three-dimensional space position changes). Developing spatial awareness requires two sequential phases: 1) identifying the location of objects in relation to one's own body in space, and 2) locating more than one object in relation to each object and independent of one's own body. Plan activities using different size balls, boxes, or hoops and have children move towards and away; under and over; in front of and behind; and inside, outside, and beside the objects.

CONCEPTS OF SPACE, DIRECTION, AND SPEED RELATED TO MOVEMENT CONCEPTS

Effort Awareness is the knowledge of balance, time, and force and how they relate to athletic movements and activities. Research shows that space, direction, and speed are interrelated with movement concepts. Students who understand these concepts will move with confidence and avoid collisions.

A student or player incorporates movement concepts such as space, direction, speed and vision to understand and perform a sport. For instance, a player will determine the appropriate personal space while playing soccer or basketball.

For a player, the concepts are all interconnected. The player has to understand how to maintain or change pathways with speed. This means the player has the ability to change motion and perform well in space or the area that the players occupy on the field.

SKILL 1.4 Analyze the impact of various factors on motor development and relate developmental changes to motor performance.

A variety of influences affects a student's physical performance and fitness level:

Societal – We cannot separate students from the societies in which they live. The general perceptions around them about the importance of fitness activities will necessarily have an effect on their own choice regarding physical activity. We should consider the "playground to PlayStation" phenomenon and the rising levels of obesity among Americans negative societal influences on motor development and fitness.

Psychological – Psychological influences on motor development and fitness include a student's mental well-being, perceptions of fitness activities, and level of comfort in a fitness-training environment (both alone and within a group). Students experiencing psychological difficulties, such as depression, will tend to be apathetic and lack both the energy and inclination to participate in fitness activities. As a result, their motor development and fitness levels will suffer. Factors like the student's confidence level and comfort within a group environment, related to both the student's level of popularity within the group and the student's own personal insecurities, are also significant. It is noteworthy, though, that in the case of psychological influences on motor development and fitness levels, there is a more reciprocal relationship than with other influences. While a student's psychology may negatively affect their fitness levels, proper fitness training has the potential to positively affect the student psychologically, thereby reversing a negative cycle.

Economic – The economic situation of students can affect their motor development and fitness because lack of resources can detract from the ability of parents to provide access to extra-curricular activities that promote development, proper fitness training equipment (ranging from complex exercise machines to team sport uniforms to something as simple as a basketball hoop), and even adequate nutrition.

Familial – Familial factors that can influence motor development and fitness relate to the student's home climate concerning physical activity. A student's own feelings toward physical activity often reflect the degree to which caregivers and role models (like older siblings) are athletically inclined and have a positive attitude towards physical activity. It isn't necessary for the parents to be athletically inclined, so much as it is important for them to encourage their child to explore fitness activities that could suit them.

Environmental and Health – Genetic make-up (i.e. age, gender, ethnicity) has a big influence on growth and development. Various physical and environmental factors directly affect one's personal health and fitness. Poor habits, living conditions, and afflictions such as disease or disability can impact a person in a negative manner. A healthy lifestyle with adequate conditions and minimal physical or mental stresses will enable a person to develop towards a positive, healthy existence. A highly agreed upon motor development theory is the relationship between one's own heredity and environmental factors.

RELATIONSHIP OF MOTOR DEVELOPMENT TO PHYSICAL, COGNITIVE, PSYCHOSOCIAL, AND EMOTIONAL DEVELOPMENT

Instructors should place students in rich learning situations, regardless of previous experience or personal factors, which provide plenty of positive opportunities to participate in physical activity. For example, prior to playing a game of softball, have students practice throwing by tossing the ball to themselves, progress to the underhand toss, and later to the overhand toss. Studies show that physical activity leads to improved motor development in children. Physical activity also enables various other progressions that shape the mind and personality of an individual. Such developments, which are the result of physical activity, include cognitive, psychosocial, and emotional growth.

Very often, we ignore the close relationship shared by motor development and the other aspects of development. Motor development, which starts with the proper nutrition, deeply affects the other aspects of development in an individual. Children acquire a vast range of motor development skills such as grasping, crawling, walking, running, and even speaking during the early stages of their lives. Gradually, such motor skills further develop leading to participation in sport and play activities that promote confidence in children and allow them to develop responsibility, deep emotions, and social etiquette. Through participation in sports, children learn to cooperate and develop competitive skills that will aid them in adulthood.

Studies reveal that the different types of play in childhood link motor development with the other aspects of development. Different kinds of play or physical activity such as cognitive play, social play, physical play, and emotional play, help in the overall development of a child.

Simple motor skills such as repeatedly hitting the ground with a shovel or building sand castles help in developing thinking and cognitive skills. Social play helps children to play with their peers cooperatively, to develop their motor skills, and to develop a sense of social togetherness. Motor activities greatly influence physical development as well. They help in providing the foundation for a normal and healthy physical education program suitable for all children. Research also shows that free play among peers leads to significant cognitive developments (such as improvement of reasoning abilities).

The manner in which children hop, jump, skip, run, climb, and play greatly facilitates their motor and physical development and helps to build other aspects of their personality. Children accomplish this development through their constant interaction with surrounding elements, environments, and persons.

Thus, motor skill development, which encompasses all motor movements by children, is strongly related to the physical, social, and emotional development of children.

SKILL 1.5   Apply knowledge of techniques for evaluating motor skills, detecting errors in motor performance, and providing positive corrective feedback.

ERRORS IN SKILL PERFORMANCE

Because performing a skill has several components, determining why a participant is performing poorly may be difficult. Instructors may have to assess several components of a skill to determine the root cause of poor performance and appropriately correct errors. **An instructor should have the ability to identify performance errors by observing a student's mechanical principles of motion during the performance of a skill. Process assessment** is a subjective, observational approach to identifying errors in the form, style, or mechanics of a skill.

APPROPRIATE OBJECTIVE MEASUREMENTS OF FUNDAMENTAL SKILLS

Instructors should use **product assessments**, quantitative measures of a movement's end result, to evaluate objectively fundamental skills. How far, how fast, how high, or how many are the quantitative measures of product assessments.

A **criterion-referenced test** (superior to a standardized test) or a **standardized norm-referenced test** can provide valid and reliable data for objectively measuring fundamental skills.

SKILL ASSESSMENT INFORMATION USED TO CORRECT ERRORS IN SKILL PERFORMANCE

Instructors can use criterion-referenced standards to diagnose weaknesses and correct errors in skill performance because such performance standards define appropriate levels of achievement. However, instructors can also use biomechanical instructional objectives. The following list describes the skill assessment criteria in several representative activities:

- Archery - measuring accuracy in shooting a standardized target from a specified place.

- Bowling - calculating the bowling average attained under standardized conditions.

- Golf - the score after several rounds.

- Swimming - counting the number of breaststrokes needed to swim 25 yards.

After assessing student skill performance, the instructor should design drills or tasks that will develop the weakest component of the student's performance. For example, an instructor notices that a group of students attempting to shoot basketball free throw shots cannot get the ball to the basket because they do not use their legs to add power to the shot. The instructor should use this observation to construct drills that encourage leg use and develop strength.

FEEDBACK

In addition to the information in Skill 1.2, we will also introduce a few key feedback tools and techniques. First, videotape is an invaluable feedback tool. Videotaping a student performing a motor skill allows the student to view, first-hand his or her own performance and recognize errors that are not visible from the performer's perspective. Second, kinesthetic feedback is the physical guidance of a student through a motor skill by an instructor. For example, an instructor might guide a student's arms through the process of swinging a baseball bat. Kinesthetic feedback is particularly effective when teaching young children. Finally, instructors can use verbal and nonverbal cues in teaching sport skills and strategy. For example, "follow through" is a common phrase used by tennis coaches in instructing students. Conversely, if the instructor swings the racket the correct way to demonstrate a proper follow through, he uses a nonverbal cue.

COMPETENCY 2.0   **PRINCIPLES AND PRACTICES FOR DEVELOPING, COMBINING, AND INTEGRATING MOTOR SKILLS**

SKILL 2.1   **Recognize characteristics and elements of locomotor, nonlocomotor, manipulative, and rhythmic skills.**

LOCOMOTOR SKILLS

Locomotor skills move an individual from one point to another.

1. **Crawling** - A form of locomotion where the person moves in a prone position with the body resting on or close to the ground or on the hands and knees.

2. **Creeping** - A slightly more advanced form of locomotion in which the person moves on the hands and knees.

3. **Walking** - with one foot contacting the surface at all times, walking shifts one's weight from one foot to the other while legs swing alternately in front of the body.

4. **Running** - an extension of walking that has a phase where the body is propelled with no base of support (speed is faster, stride is longer, and arms add power).

5. **Jumping** - projectile movements that momentarily suspend the body in midair.

6. **Vaulting** - coordinated movements that allow one to spring over an obstacle.

7. **Leaping** - similar to running, but leaping has greater height, flight, and distance.

8. **Hopping** - using the same foot to take off from a surface and land.

9. **Galloping** - forward or backward advanced elongation of walking combined and coordinated with a leap.

10. **Sliding** - sideward stepping pattern that is uneven, long, or short.

11. **Body Rolling** - moving across a surface by rocking back and forth, by turning over and over, or by shaping the body into a revolving mass.

12. **Climbing** - ascending or descending using the hands and feet with the upper body exerting the most control.

NONLOCOMOTOR SKILLS

Nonlocomotor skills are stability skills where the movement requires little or no movement of one's base of support and does not result in change of position.

1. **Bending** - movement around a joint where two body parts meet.
2. **Dodging** - sharp change of direction from original line of movement such as away from a person or object.

3. **Stretching** - extending/hyper-extending joints to make body parts as straight or as long as possible.
4. **Twisting** - rotating body/body parts around an axis with a stationary base.

5. **Turning** - circular moving the body through space releasing the base of support.
6. **Swinging** - circular/pendular movements of the body/body parts below an axis.

7. **Swaying** - same as swinging but movement is above an axis.

8. **Pushing** - applying force against an object or person to move it away from one's body or to move one's body away from the object or person.

9. **Pulling** - executing force to cause objects/people to move toward one's body.

MANIPULATIVE SKILLS

Manipulative skills use body parts to propel or receive an object, controlling objects primarily with the hands and feet. Two types of manipulative skills are receptive (catch + trap) and propulsive (throw, strike, kick).

1. **Bouncing/Dribbling** - projecting a ball downwards.

2. **Catching** - stopping momentum of an object (for control) using the hands.

3. **Kicking** - striking an object with the foot.

4. **Rolling** - initiating force to an object to instill contact with a surface.

5. **Striking** - giving impetus to an object with the use of the hands or an object.

6. **Throwing** - using one or both arms to project an object into midair away from the body.

7. **Trapping** - without the use of the hands, receiving and controlling a ball.

RHYTHMIC SKILLS

Rhythmic skills include responding and moving the body in time with the beat, tempo, or pitch of music. To develop rhythmic skills, instructors can ask students to clap their hands or stomp their feet to the beat of the music. Dancing and gymnastics requires high levels of rhythmic competency. As with all physical skills, development of rhythmic skills is a sequential process.

SKILL 2.2   Demonstrate knowledge of characteristics and elements of manipulative skills and mature motor patterns.

ANALYSIS OF BASIC MOVEMENT PATTERNS: OVERHAND THROW, UNDERHAND THROW, KICK

Overhand Throw

The overhand throw consists of a sequence of four movements: a stride, hip rotation, trunk rotation, and forward arm movement. The thrower should align his body sideways to the target (with opposite shoulder pointing towards the target). The overhand throw begins with a step or stride with the opposite foot (i.e. left foot for a right-handed thrower). As the stride foot contacts the ground, the pivot foot braces against the ground and provides stability for the subsequent movements. Hip rotation is the natural turning of the hips toward the target. Trunk rotation follows hip rotation. The hips should rotate before the trunk because the stretching of the torso muscles allows for stronger muscle contraction during trunk rotation. Following trunk rotation, the arm moves forward in two phases. In the first phase the elbow is bent. In the second phase, the elbow joint straightens and the thrower releases the ball.

Development of the overhand throwing motion in children occurs in three stages: elementary, mature, and advanced. In the elementary stage, the child throws mainly with the arm and does not incorporate the other body movements. The signature characteristic of this stage is striding with the foot on the same side of the body as the throwing arm (i.e. placing the right foot in front when throwing with the right hand). In the mature stage, the thrower brings the arm backward in preparation for the throw. Use of body rotation is still limited. Children in the advanced stage incorporate all the elements of the overhand throw. The thrower displays an obvious stride and body rotation.

Underhand Throw

The thrower places the object in the dominant hand. When drawing the arm back the triceps straighten the elbow and, depending on the amount of power behind the throw, the shoulder extends or hyperextends using the posterior deltoid, latissimus dorsi, and the teres major. At the time of drawback, the thrower takes a step forward with the leg opposite of the throwing arm. When coming back down, the thrower moves the shoulder muscles (primarily the anterior deltoid) into flexion. When the object in hand moves in front of the body, the thrower releases the ball. The wrist may be firm or slightly flexed. The thrower releases the object shortly after the planting the foot and the biceps muscle contracts, moving the elbow into flexion during follow through.

Kick

In executing a kick, the object needs to be in front of the body and in front of the dominant leg. The kicker steps and plants with the opposite leg while drawing the kicking leg back. During draw back, the hamstring muscle group flexes the knee. When the kicker plants the opposite foot, the hips swing forward for power and the knee moves into extension using the quadriceps muscle group. The contact point is approximately even with the plant foot and a comfortable follow through completes the action.

IDENTIFYING MATURE AND IMMATURE MOTOR PATTERNS

In all physical activity or training, there are certain fundamental movement skills that involve patterns necessary for the development of the body. We define them as the foundation movements or precursor patterns to the more specialized complex skills that are useful in all types of sports, dance, and play.

Fundamental movement skills form an indispensable part of all physical activity and physical education. Such basic movement skills are extremely important for children in their early years. These particular skills include running, stopping, changing direction, starting, hopping, skipping, and rolling.

These fundamental movement skills play an important role in the physical well-being of all growing children and are important for adults as well. These skills create the framework of every physical activity and sport.

Physical education instructors should be able to identify mature and immature motor patterns. For example, when observing an overhand throw, there are certain universal characteristics of immature throwing patterns. These include stepping with the foot on the same side of the body as the throwing arm, using only the elbow to propel the object, and facing the target throughout the throwing process. Conversely, characteristics of a mature overhand throwing pattern include leading with the foot opposite the throwing hand, using the entire body and arm to propel the ball, and starting the throwing motion facing perpendicular to the target.

SKILL 2.3 **Demonstrate knowledge of activities, strategies, safety practices, and equipment for promoting students' development of locomotor, nonlocomotor, body control, manipulative, and rhythmic skills.**

Motor-development learning theories that pertain to a general skill, activity, or age level are important and necessary teacher background information for effective lesson planning. Motor-skill learning is unique to each individual but does follow a general sequential skill pattern, starting with general gross motor movements and ending with specific or fine motor skills. Teachers must begin instruction at a level where all children are successful and proceed through the activity to the point where frustration for the majority is hindering performance. Students must learn the fundamentals of a skill, or subsequent learning of more advanced skills becomes extremely difficult. Instructors must spend enough time on beginning skills so they become second nature. Teaching in small groups with enough equipment for everyone is essential. Practice sessions that are too long or too demanding can cause physical and/or mental burnout. Teaching skills over a longer period of time, but with slightly different approaches, helps keep students' attentive and involved as they internalize the skill. The instructor can then teach more difficult skills while continuing to review the basics. If the skill is challenging for most students, allow plenty of practice time so they retain it due to learning in depth before having to use it in a game situation.

Visualizing and breaking the skill down mentally is another way to enhance the learning of motor movements. Instructors can teach students to "picture" the steps involved and see themselves executing the skill. An example is teaching dribbling in basketball. Start teaching the skill with a demonstration of the steps involved in dribbling. Starting with the first skill, introduce key language terms and have students visualize themselves performing the skill. A sample-progression lesson plan to teach dribbling could begin with students practicing while standing still. Next, add movement while dribbling. Finally, introduce how to control dribbling while being guarded by another student.

KNOWLEDGE OF ACTIVITIES FOR BODY MANAGEMENT SKILL DEVELOPMENT

Sequential development and activities for locomotor skills acquisition

Sequential Development = crawl, creep, walk, run, jump, hop, gallop, slide, leap, skip, step-hop.

- **Activities to develop walking skills** include walking slower and faster in place; walking forward, backward, and sideways with slower and faster paces in straight, curving, and zigzag pathways with various lengths of steps; pausing between steps; and changing the height of the body.

- **Activities to develop running skills** include having students pretend they are playing basketball, trying to score a touchdown, trying to catch a bus, finishing a lengthy race, or running on a hot surface.

- **Activities to develop jumping skills** include alternating jumping with feet together and feet apart, taking off and landing on the balls of the feet, clicking the heels together while airborne, and landing with a foot forward and a foot backward.

- **Activities to develop galloping skills** include having students play a game of Fox and Hound, with the lead foot representing the fox and the back foot the hound trying to catch the fox (alternate the lead foot).

- **Activities to develop sliding skills** include having students hold hands in a circle and sliding in one direction, then sliding in the other direction.

- **Activities to develop hopping skills** include having students hop all the way around a hoop and hopping in and out of a hoop reversing direction. Students can also place ropes in straight lines and hop side-to-side over the rope from one end to the other and change (reverse) the direction.

- **Activities to develop skipping skills** include having students combine walking and hopping activities leading up to skipping.

- **Activities to develop step-hopping skills** include having students practice stepping and hopping activities while clapping hands to an uneven beat.

Sequential development and activities for nonlocomotor skill acquisition

Sequential Development = stretch, bend, sit, shake, turn, rock and sway, swing, twist, dodge, and fall.

- **Activities to develop stretching** include lying on the back and stomach and stretching as far as possible; stretching as though one is reaching for a star, picking fruit off a tree, climbing a ladder, shooting a basketball, or placing an item on a high self; waking and yawning.

- **Activities to develop bending** include touching knees and toes then straightening the entire body and straightening the body halfway; bending as though picking up a coin, tying shoes, picking flowers/vegetables, and petting animals of different sizes.

- **Activities to develop sitting** include practicing sitting from standing, kneeling, and lying positions without the use of hands.

- **Activities to develop falling skills** include first collapsing in one's own space and then pretending to fall like bowling pins, raindrops, snowflakes, a rag doll, or Humpty Dumpty.

MANIPULATIVE SKILL DEVELOPMENT

Sequential Development = striking, throwing, kicking, ball rolling, volleying, bouncing, catching, and trapping.

- **Activities to develop striking** begin with the striking of stationary objects by a participant in a stationary position. Next, the person remains still while trying to strike a moving object. Then, both the object and the participant are in motion as the participant attempts to strike the moving object.

- **Activities to develop throwing** include throwing yarn/foam balls against a wall, then at a big target, and finally at targets decreasing in size.

- **Activities to develop kicking** include alternating feet to kick balloons/beach balls, then kicking them under and over ropes. Change the type of ball as proficiency develops.

- **Activities to develop ball rolling** include rolling different size balls to a wall, then to targets decreasing in size.

- **Activities to develop volleying** include using a large balloon and, first, hitting it with both hands, then one hand (alternating hands), and then using different parts of the body. Change the object as students progress (balloon, to beach ball, to foam ball, etc.)

- **Activities to develop bouncing** include starting with large balls and, first, using both hands to bounce and then using one hand (alternate hands).

- **Activities to develop catching** include using various objects (balloons, beanbags, balls, etc.) to catch and, first, catching the object the participant has thrown him/herself, then catching objects someone else threw, and finally increasing the distance between the catcher and the thrower.

- **Activities to develop trapping** include trapping slow and fast rolling balls; trapping balls (or other objects such as beanbags) that are lightly thrown at waist, chest, and stomach levels; trapping different size balls.

RHYTHMIC SKILL DEVELOPMENT

Dancing is an excellent activity for the development of rhythmic skills. In addition, any activity that involves moving the body to music can promote rhythmic skill development.

Dance concepts and forms

Students of dance acquire many skills during their course of study. The student identifies and demonstrates movement elements in dance performance and uses correct body alignment, strength, flexibility, and stamina (for more demanding performances). Crucial to any form of dance is the concept of coordination in the performance of technical movements. Technical movements must look as though they are easy to perform. The dancer must perform technical dance skills with artistic expression including musicality and rhythm. As the student progresses, he or she will perform more extended movement sequences and rhythmic patterns. The student will then have the experience to introduce his or her own style into the performance. The student will also be able to use improvisation to solve movement problems and adjust choices based on the movement responses of other dancers in the ensemble. Through continued experience, he or she will become a skillful, seasoned dancer whose technique and ability will transcend any form of dance.

Instructors can create rhythmic activities by putting on music with a strong beat and asking students to dance to the beat. Additionally, the instructor should ask students to listen to the beat and move accordingly (e.g. stomping their feet or clapping their hands in time with the beat). It is important for children to learn to move to various sounds and use their bodies to mimic the beat. Another idea is to have the students take turns beating on a coffee can while trying to keep movements in sync with the rhythm. In more structured dance forms, technique or skill comes into play. For instance, in ballet, dancers must have good flexibility, body control, and coordination. Ballet dancers must also have a sense of rhythm, an understanding of music, good turnout and alignment, and a sense of balance and counterbalance. These skills take many years to acquire and, once acquired, take many more years to master and maintain. Ballet dancing may express a mood, tell a story, or simply reflect a piece of music and is the most classical of all dance forms. Other types of music may have similar requirements in terms of a sense of musicality and rhythm. For example, tap dance requires a greater degree of footwork and modern is comparable to ballet, but more flowing and less rigid.

SKILL 2.4   Know how to select and use developmentally appropriate techniques and activities to promote students' integration and refinement of locomotor, nonlocomotor, body control, manipulative, and rhythmic skills.

Locomotor skills are movements that take an individual from one place to another. Walking and running are the simplest examples of locomotor skills. Skipping, jumping, leaping, hopping, and sliding are other locomotor skills that physical educators teach their students.

Trainers adopt various strategies to incorporate the locomotor, nonlocomotor, and object control skills into their workout schedule. These skills are very effective in making students stronger and healthier.

Initially, instructors try to combine those locomotor skills into their training schedule in an easy-to-follow manner. Combining running and sliding or running and jumping will play a huge part in making children understand the fundamentals of locomotor skills.

Once they become familiar with the procedure, physical educators can show students how to balance and transfer weight through using various locomotor skills. However, the teacher should demonstrate how to control locomotor movements at proper speeds and forces. Shot put, tumbling, and give-and-go are some examples of how to teach students the nuances of locomotor skills.

We can apply the same strategies to nonlocomotor skill instruction. First, the students should learn the basics of every skill from simple nonlocomotive movements such as 360-degree turns and lifting weights, to complex movements like tug-of-war and scissors kicks. It is important for the instructor to maintain a smooth transition. This makes comprehension as unproblematic as possible. Locomotor and nonlocomotor skills make children agile and physically fit. It is the job of a physical educator to make learning and practicing the skills more enjoyable and entertaining.

COMBINATIONS OF OBJECT CONTROL SKILLS

Object control skills help students remain fit and agile. These skills also help students to become better performers. Physical educators will often combine a number of object control skills to enhance a child's reflexes.

Catch and throw is an ideal example of integrating such skills. This type of skill requires a high level of concentration and nimbleness. A combination of object control skills is always at the heart of any physical activity.

Object control skills make all the difference in successful athletic performance. An ideal combination of these skills keeps students healthy and satisfied.

INTEGRATION STRATEGIES

Physical education instructors should develop innovative strategies to help students learn the nuances of locomotor, nonlocomotor, and object control skills. Physical education instructors should also present these skills in an entertaining manner for students.

If a teacher starts a training schedule with simple activities, they are more likely to keep the students interested. Once students develop interest, teachers should introduce complex activities such as running and catching, pivoting and throwing, and running and jumping.

The above progression strategy is a widely accepted method for combining locomotor, nonlocomotor, and object control skills. The moment students start taking interest in their physical activities, the job becomes easier for the teachers as well as the students. Finally, traditional sports activities are a perfect venue for the application of combined skills.

SPORTS AND GAMES

All sports require the application of motor skills in complex forms. For example, the motor skills required to play tennis include running, jumping, striking, and volleying. In addition, tennis players must combine these skills. For example, a player often has to strike the ball while running or jumping. To play any sport at a high level, athletes must master many motor skills and develop the ability to combine those skills to master sport-specific movements.

> **SKILL 2.5   Recognize and analyze key elements in combinations of motor skills, demonstrations of agility and balance, and dance steps and sequences.**

Combinations of motor skills, demonstrations of agility (the ability of the body to change direction quickly) and balance, and dance steps and sequences all involve the same key elements of body awareness (proprioception/kinesthesia) and control. Some specific elements include pivot and throw, and a variety of movement sequences that combine traveling, rolling, balancing, and weight transfer.

Pivot and throw are both skills that grow out of the individual's awareness and control of his body's positioning and weight distribution, both at rest and, especially, in motion. To properly execute this movement sequence (i.e., changing direction and continuing to move, maintaining fluid movement throughout the execution), the actor must efficiently distribute his body weight, and manage his weight distribution properly throughout the execution of the pivot. Poor execution will put the individual off-balance, preventing him from continuing the chain of movement without stumbling.

Movement sequences that combine traveling, rolling, balancing, and weight transfer, as with the pivot and throw skills described earlier, rely on the individual's awareness and control of his body's positioning and weight distribution. In order to travel across a space, execute rolls, balancing techniques, and the requisite weight transfers linked to those actions, the athlete must have a keen sense of where their weight is currently distributed, and how to move it in the desired direction with maximum efficiency.

SKILL 2.6 **Demonstrate knowledge of techniques and activities for refining and improving motor skills in games, sports, and dance activities and for adjusting movements, techniques, and tactics based on feedback and critical evaluation.**

SEE ALSO Skill 1.2

CUES FOR RHYTHMIC SKILL DEVELOPMENT

Effective cues to facilitate rhythmic-skills acquisition include walking, clapping, and devising games. Instructors can also teach children to find individual memory cues and methods for creating and responding to rhythm.

Walking is an excellent activity for facilitating rhythmic-skills acquisition, because every student knows how to do it, and the footfalls create a steady rhythm that isn't too fast for students to follow. Practice reciting poems and singing songs with the beats falling on the footfalls. Similarly, the class can create a beat by clapping steadily.

Instructors can devise games that help children act out the sounds on a beat, enforcing the acquisition of rhythmic skills. Instructors can also teach students to devise their own memory cues (e.g. mnemonic devices) and methods for creating and responding to rhythm. These can include dances and actions devised by students and ways of representing auditory patterns.

RHYTHMIC SKILL IMPROVEMENT TECHNIQUES

Instructors can accommodate different learning styles and characteristics by applying techniques like body percussion and the creation of charts and song mappings. These techniques merge different learning styles and senses to help students better grasp the rhythmic-skills content.

Body percussion (i.e. loudly but gently slapping different parts of the body, mostly the outer limbs) is another way of creating a rhythm that students can learn to maintain and copy. A benefit of this technique is that it implements tactile and kinesthetic stimuli into the skill acquisition process, catering to more kinesthetically oriented learners.

Charts and song mapping are both techniques that help children connect with the sounds that correspond to the beats in a rhythm, by writing them out or drawing them visually. This connects with more visually oriented learners.

Simple technology that instructors can use to facilitate rhythmic-skills acquisition includes rhythm-keeping devices like metronomes that students can use as a sensory baseline for the beat of the rhythm that they are learning. More advanced technology includes software that simulates rhythmic activity and asks the student to respond at correct intervals.

USE OF TECHNOLOGY

Physical educators can use various technological tools to analyze student performance, fitness, and performance. Two important and interrelated technological tools are videotape and movement analysis software.

Videotape

Videotaping students participating in skill performance and fitness activities allows students and teachers to analyze technique closely. Instructors can identify and point out errors in form to the students. This visual reinforcement enhances the learning process. In addition, periodic videotaping allows instructors to monitor progress in skill performance and fitness over time.

Movement analysis software

Movement analysis software helps students and instructors analyze movement patterns captured on digital video cameras in great detail. For example, movement analysis software can distill the individual characteristics of a person's gate. Such high detailed analysis allows instructors and students to study individual patterns of movement, individual movement styles, and strategies for peak performance. Movement analysis software helps identify key elements of a movement that need improvement and helps track progress in development, maturation, and error correction.

COMPETENCY 3.0   MOVEMENT CONCEPTS AND BIOMECHANICAL PRINCIPLES

SKILL 3.1   Apply knowledge of movement concepts related to time, space, direction, level, force, and flow and kinesthetic awareness concepts such as direction and relationships to objects.

SEE ALSO Skill 1.3

CONCEPT OF EFFORT QUALITIES APPLIED TO PHYSICAL EDUCATION

Effort qualities are the qualities of movement that apply the mechanical principles of balance, time, and force).

Balance - activities for balance include having children move on their hands and feet, lean, move on lines, and balance and hold shapes while moving.

Time - activities using the concept of time can include having children move as fast as they can and as slow as they can in specified, timed movement patterns.

Force - activities using the concept of force can include having students use their bodies to produce enough force to move them through space. They can also paddle balls against walls and jump over objects of various heights.

CONCEPTS OF EQUILIBRIUM AND CENTER OF GRAVITY APPLIED TO MOVEMENT

When body segments move independently, body mass redistributes, changing the location of the body's center of gravity. Segments also move to change the body's base of support from one moment to the next to cope with imminent loss of balance.

The entire center of gravity of the body shifts in the same direction of movement of the body's segments. As long as the center of gravity remains over the base of support, the body will remain in a state of equilibrium. The more the center of gravity is situated over the base, the greater the stability. A wider base of support and/or a lower center of gravity enhances stability. To be effective, the base of support must widen in the direction of the force produced or opposed by the body. Shifting weight in the direction of the force in conjunction with widening the base of support further enhances stability.

Constant interaction of forces that move the body in the elected direction results in dynamic balance. The smooth transition of the center of gravity changing from one base of support to the next produces speed.

CONCEPT OF FORCE APPLIED TO MOVEMENT

Force is any influence that changes the state of motion of an object. We must consider the objective of movement.

Magnitude of Force – force must overcome the inertia of the object and any other resisting forces for movement to occur.

For linear movement, force applied close to the center of gravity requires a smaller magnitude of force to move the object than does force applied farther from the center of gravity.

For rotational movement, force applied farther from the center of gravity requires a smaller magnitude of force to rotate the object than does force applied closer to the center of gravity.

For objects with a fixed point, force applied anywhere other than through the point of fixation results in object rotation.

Energy – the capacity to do work. (The more energy a body has the greater the force with which it can move something [or change its shape] and/or the farther it can move it).

Movement (mechanical energy) has two types:

1. Potential energy (energy possessed by virtue of position, absolute location in space or change in shape).

>   **A. Gravitational potential energy** - potential energy of an object that is in a position where gravity can act on it.

>   **B. Elastic (strain) potential energy** - energy potential of an object to do work while recoiling (or reforming) after stretching, compressing, or twisting.

2. Kinetic energy (energy possessed by virtue of motion that increases with speed).

Force Absorption - maintaining equilibrium while receiving a moving object's kinetic energy without sustaining injury or without losing balance while rebounding. The force of impact is dependent on an object's weight and speed. The more abruptly kinetic energy is lost, the more likely injury or rebound occurs. Thus, **absorbing force requires gradually decelerating a moving mass by utilization of smaller forces over a longer period**. Stability is greater when the force is received closer to the center of gravity.

Striking resistive surfaces - the force of impact per unit area decreases when the moving object's area of surface making contact increases and the surface area that the object strikes increases.

Striking non-resistive surfaces - the force of impact decreases if the moving object's area of surface making contact decreases because it is more likely to penetrate.

The more time and distance that motion stops for a moving object to strike any surface, the more gradually the surface absorbs the force of impact, and the reaction forces acting upon the moving object decrease.

Equilibrium returns easily when the moving body (striking a resistive surface) aligns the center of gravity more vertically over the base of support.

Angular force against a body decreases when the distance between a contacting object and the body decreases and the contact occurs closer to the center of gravity. Also, widening the base of support in the direction of the moving object increases stability.

CONCEPT OF LEVERAGE APPLIED TO MOVEMENT

First-class lever - the axis is between the points of application of the force and the resistance.

First-class lever systems

Second-class lever - the force arm is longer than the resistance arm (operator applies resistance between the axis and the point of application of force).

Second-class lever systems

Third-class lever - the force works at a point between the axis and the resistance (resistance arm is always longer than the force arm).

Third-class lever systems

Muscle force is applied where muscles insert on bones.

With a few exceptions, the body consists primarily of third-class levers, with bones functioning as the levers and contracting innervated muscles acting as the fulcrums or by gravity acting on various body masses. As a result, the human body favors speed and range of motion over force.

Because most human body levers are long, their distal ends can move rapidly. Thus, the body is capable of swift, wide movements at the expense of abundant muscle force.

The human body easily performs tasks involving rapid movement with light objects. Very heavy tasks require a device for the body to secure an advantage of force.

Sports instruments increase body levers, thereby increasing the speed of an object's imparting force. However, the use of sports instruments requires more muscle force.

The body's leverage rarely includes only one part of the body (a simple, singular lever). Movement of the body is an outcome of a system of levers operating together. However, levers do function in sequence when the force produced by the system of levers is dependent on the speed at the extremity. Many levers function simultaneously for a heavy task (e.g. pushing).

SKILL 3.2   Relate biomechanical principles to various movement activities.

MECHANICAL PRINCIPLES OF MOTION APPLIED TO PHYSICAL EDUCATION ACTIVITIES

1. **Inertia** - tendency of a body or object to remain in its present state of motion; an object will stay in a prescribed straight path and will move at its given speed unless some force acts to change it.

2. **Projecting objects for vertical distance** - the forces of gravity and air resistance prevent vertically projected objects from continuing at their initial velocities. The downward, resistive force of gravity slows a projectile directed upward until it halts (at the peak of vertical path). At this point, the downward force of gravity becomes an incentive force that increases the speed of the object until it confronts another force (the earth or other external object) that slows the object until it stops. When the object stops ascending and begins to descend, gravity alters the object's direction of motion. Air resistance (of still air) always opposes the object's motion. Therefore, an ascending object's air resistance is downward and a descending object's air resistance is upward. An increase in velocity increases air-drag force that decreases the magnitude of the drag as the object moves upward, slowing in velocity. The magnitude of the drag increases as the object moves faster and faster downward. Moreover, the direction and magnitude of the object's acceleration, due to the force of gravity, are constant while direction and magnitude of changes, due to air resistance, are dependent on the object's speed and direction.

An object travels the highest when projected with the greatest velocity, and the object's weight affects neither gravity's upward deceleration nor its downward acceleration. The object's weight, however, is a factor in calculating the net force acting on the object's vertical movement through the air.

- **Projecting the body for vertical distance** - for these activities (e.g. vertical leaping), the height of reach of the hand from the ground is the significant factor. The following three factors determine the body's reach height: 1) the center of gravity's vertical velocity, 2) the center of gravity's height from the ground at takeoff, and 3) the vertical distance of the fingertips relative to the center of gravity at the peak of the jump.

- **Projecting for vertical distance with a horizontal component** - for these activities (e.g. high jumping), a running approach to the point of takeoff produces some horizontal velocity even with a 100% vertical takeoff.

- **Projecting for horizontal distance** - a body will continue to travel horizontally until an external force, usually the ground, halts it. Gravity stops vertical movement while ground friction eventually stops horizontal velocity, preventing any additional horizontal distance. "Air time" increases when the initial upward vertical velocity component is greater. There is a tradeoff between maximum "air time" (determined by vertical velocity) and maximum horizontal distance (determined by horizontal velocity).

- **Horizontal projections where takeoff and landing heights are equal** - maximum horizontal distance occurs when the projection angle is 45-degrees.

- **Horizontal projections where takeoff and landing heights are uneven** – the height of an object's center of gravity depends on a performer's height and his/her location in relation to the ground upon release or impact of the object. The greater the object's travel time forward, the farther the object's distance before landing. Hence, a taller performer has an automatic advantage over a shorter performer who throws with the same projection velocity. In addition, the greater the difference between takeoff and landing heights, the smaller the optimum angle of release - given equal projection velocities.

Projecting objects for accuracy:

- **Vertical plane targets** - accuracy is easiest when using a trajectory that is perpendicular to the target as it coincides with the target face. As projection distance increases, a more curved parabolic path is required.

- **Horizontal plane targets** - the more vertically the projectile arrives at the target (as close to 90 degrees as possible), the greater the likelihood of successfully hitting the target and preventing the object from rolling or sliding away from the target area.

Projecting the body for accuracy - for moving or positioning the body (or its segments) to achieve an ideal/model performance by body maneuvers, the performer projects his body's center of gravity to an imaginary target point in space.

Projecting objects for accuracy when speed may enhance the performance - the performer must increase the angle of projection for slower projection speeds (must consider participant's height).

- **Acceleration** - the movement response (acceleration) of a system depends not only on the net external force applied, but also depends on the resistance to movement change (inertia).

If an object's acceleration is proportional to the applied force, greater force produces greater acceleration. An object's acceleration is inversely proportional to its mass (the greater the mass, the less the acceleration).

- **Angular acceleration** (rate that an object's angular speed or direction changes) - angular acceleration is great when there is a large change in angular velocity in a short amount of time. A rigid body (or segment) encounters angular acceleration or deceleration only when a net external torque is applied. When torque stops, the body reaches and maintains a new velocity until another torque occurs. Acceleration is always in the direction of the acting torque, and the greater the torque, the greater the angular acceleration.

- **Linear acceleration** (time rate of change in velocity) - an object's magnitude of acceleration is significant if there is a large change of velocity in a small amount of time. When the same velocity changes over a longer period, acceleration is small. Acceleration occurs only when force is applied. When the force stops, the object/body reaches a new and the object/body continues at the new speed until that a force changes that speed or direction. In addition, the direction of acceleration is the same direction as the applied net force. A large force produces a large acceleration. A small force produces a modest acceleration.

- **ero/Constant Acceleration** (constant velocity) - there is no change in a system's velocity when the object/body moves at a given velocity and encounters equal, opposing forces. Hence, velocity is constant since no force causes acceleration or deceleration.

- **Acceleration caused by gravity** - a falling object/body continues to accelerate at the rate of 9.8 m/sec. (32 ft/sec.) throughout its fall.

- **Radial acceleration (direction change caused by centripetal force)** - centripetal force is aimed along an illusory line (the circular path) at any instant. Therefore, it is the force responsible for change of direction. The bigger the mass, the greater the centripetal force required. A tighter turn magnifies direction change (radial acceleration), so friction must increase to offset the increased acceleration. Maximum friction (centrifugal force) reduces speed. A combination of the variables mass, radius of curvature, speed of travel, and centripetal force cause radial acceleration.

Action/Reaction - every action has an equal and opposite reaction.

- **Linear motion** - the larger the mass, the more it resists motion change initiated by an outside force.

Body segments exert forces against surfaces they contact. These forces and the reaction of the surfaces result in body movement. For example, a runner propels himself forward by exerting a force on the ground (as long as the surface has sufficient friction and resistance to slipping). The force of the contact of the runner's foot with the ground and the equal and opposite reaction of the ground produces movement. A canoe paddler or swimmer exerts a backward force by pushing the water backwards, causing a specific velocity that is dependent on the stroke's force - as well as the equal and opposite force made by the water pushing forward against the canoe paddle or arm moving the canoe or swimmer forward.

Every torque (angular motion) exerted by one body/object on another has another torque equal in magnitude and opposite direction exerted by the second body/object on the first. Changing angular momentum requires a force that is equal and opposite of the change in momentum.

Performing actions in a standing position requires the counter pressure of the ground against the feet for accurate movement of one or more parts of the body.

SKILL 3.3   Identify techniques and activities for promoting students' understanding and application of movement concepts and biomechanical principles.

Instructors can promote student understanding and application of movement concepts and biomechanical principles by using techniques that showcase a particular movement or action along with strategies for improvement. Sample applications of movement concepts and biomechanical principles include moving in pathways or at different levels, and adjusting throwing techniques by using principles of rotation and force application.

Moving in pathways means that students execute the training motions slowly, ensuring that the path of movement remains along the most efficient possible track (both to cut down wasted movement and to use muscles most effectively).

Adjusting throwing techniques by using principles of rotation and force application involves analyzing the action of the throw and focusing on discrete elements of the action, one at a time, that the student can improve by applying biomechanical processes (in terms of angle of rotation and muscular force application). Instructors can facilitate this process by recording student movements with a video camera and reviewing the film in slow motion with student. Ideally, instructors should ask the student to identify the areas that he or she believes need improvement before the instructor begins to make suggestions.

SKILL 3.4   Know how to use movement concepts and biomechanical principles to analyze movement skills, promote the acquisition and refinement of specific movements and sports skills, improve body mechanics for safe and efficient movement, and appreciate the aesthetics of creative and skilled movements.

SEE ALSO Skill 8.4 (Posture and Body Mechanics)

We can use movement concepts and biomechanical principles to analyze movement skills by first examining the movement skill in detail (often with the assistance of recording equipment that allows play back in slow motion), and then breaking down the motions involved. For each motion, we should note the angle through which the joints move and the direction of force that the muscles apply. We can check this information against our knowledge of movement concepts and biomechanical principles. Finally, we can modify the motion to ensure that the joints move and the muscles apply force in the most efficient way.

Instructors can facilitate student acquisition and refinement of specific movements and sports skills by applying this same knowledge to the teaching and training process. Instructors should teach students both the correct way to execute the movement and the biomechanical principles that facilitate the movement. In effect, this helps students understand why they should not be perform the movement in ways that are incorrect (because the body cannot perform the movement as effectively in that way). This helps the student self-monitor their own progress, and focus on the elements that need improvement.

Instructors can encourage improvement of body mechanics for safe and efficient movement by giving students an understanding of what the underlying biomechanical principles really are. When students understand the way their bodies work, it is easier for them to modify their movement activities "on the fly" to correspond to more healthy and efficient movement. For example, when lifting a television, the knowledge of correct spinal alignment and weight distribution for lifting purposes can help students deduce the best way to perform the lift.

ENJOYMENT OF AESTHETIC AND CREATIVE ASPECTS OF SKILLED PERFORMANCE

Physical education instructors should instill in their students a respect for and appreciation of the aesthetic and creative aspects of skilled performances. Dance, gymnastics, and figure skating are examples of performance activities that have an obvious creative and expressive element. In addition, all sports require creativity and have aesthetic elements. For example, the ball control of an expert soccer player, the touch, control, and power of a professional tennis player, and the elegance and grace of a basketball player soaring for a slam-dunk are all aesthetically pleasing and awe inspiring to the trained eye. To truly appreciate the complexity and difficulty of skilled performances, one must have sufficient knowledge and understanding of the activity. Thus, the role of physical education is to introduce students to various physical activities so they can understand the aesthetic elements.

SKILL 3.5 Recognize and analyze similar movement concepts and elements in various movement patterns and sports skills.

There are similar movement concepts and elements in a variety of movement patterns and sports skills. While the activities may differ, the human bodies that execute them are all the same functionally, and will apply pressure and effort most efficiently in a small number of ways. We will examine two sample similarities, though there are many more to consider. The similarities that we will examine are between the seemingly unrelated worlds of professional team sports, weight lifting, and martial arts.

The first sample similarity is the parallel between swinging a bat in baseball and swinging a sword or staff in weapon-based martial arts such as Iaido. In both cases, the practitioner must focus on the target (opponent or incoming baseball), maintain proper form, move with the entire body (energy deriving from the hips and shoulders), and focus the impact of the strike on a single point (again, the opponent or incoming baseball).

The second sample similarity is the parallel between performing a squatting, power-lifting exercise in a weight-room and executing a Judo hip-throw. In both cases, proper form is critical, centering on executing the lifting motion by bending the knees and bearing the brunt of the weight with the legs (and not the back). Proper form and lifting with the legs avoids undue strain on the knees by bending them to unhealthy angles.

COMPETENCY 4.0   INDIVIDUAL, DUAL, AND TEAM SPORTS AND ACTIVITIES

SKILL 4.1   Demonstrate knowledge of techniques, skills progressions, conditioning programs, rules, safety practices, offensive and defensive strategies, and types and uses of equipment for individual, dual, and team sports and activities.

INDIVIDUAL AND DUAL SPORTS AND ACTIVITIES – OVERVIEW

Archery – Skills that students study in archery classes include proper care for their equipment, properly stringing the bow, drawing, and shooting with accuracy (including compensating for distance, angle, and wind).

Safety practices in archery include respectful handling of the equipment (which is potentially dangerous) and ensuring that students only draw bows when pointed at a (non-living) target. Finally, instructors should keep students away from the path between firing students and their targets at all times.

Proper equipment for archery classes include a bow and arrows, which can vary greatly in technical complexity and cost, and a target.

Badminton – Students in a badminton class will have to master the strokes as basic skills and should learn at least some of them by name (e.g. types of serves, net shot, net kills, drive, push, lift). Students should also know which strokes are appropriate from which areas of the court.

Bocce ball – Requires a flat, level playing surface (packed dirt, gravel or grass are ideal). The instructor divides students into two teams of one, two, or four players each. Each team gets four balls, divided equally among the players. A player from the starting team stands behind the foul line (10 feet from the throwing end of the court) and throws the small ball ("pallina") toward the opposite end of the playing surface. The player then throws one of the larger balls ("boccia"), trying to get it as close to the pallina as possible without touching it. Players from the opposing team take turns throwing their balls until one of the balls stops closer to the pallina than the starting player's ball. If they fail to do so, the starting team tries to outdo its first attempt. Teams continue to take turns in this manner until they have thrown all the balls. The team with closest ball gets a point. This game emphasizes throwing skills (coordination, gross and fine motor skills).

Bowling – Skills that students will learn in bowling classes include learning to select a ball of comfortable weight and appropriate for the shot they need to make, properly controlling the ball so it hits the pins they are aiming for, and learning the dynamics of pin interaction to plan the proper angle of entry for the ball.

Safety practices in bowling include wearing proper footwear, handling the balls cautiously, and preventing horseplay (to avoid situations where a heavy bowling ball may drop inopportunely and cause injury).

Equipment needed for a bowling class includes proper footwear, a bowling ball, pins, and a lane.

Cross-country running – Much like track and field, cross-country running will teach the students proper running form, the ability to pace their energy expenditure relative to the length of the course, and the ability to adapt their running technique to the terrain.

Cross-country running strategy focuses on adapting energy expenditure relative to the length of the course and psychological training to minimize responsiveness to physical exhaustion. Runners should familiarize themselves with a course before running it.

Safety practices, like other running sports, focus on proper attention to warm-ups and cool-downs and remaining attentive to the course, which may be quite rugged. Because cross-country running often takes place in fairly remote, natural settings, it is important to coordinate the availability of first aid.

Equipment required for cross-country running includes proper footwear and water to prevent dehydration on longer runs.

Frisbee Golf – Skills that students will acquire in a Frisbee golf class include methods of throwing the Frisbee (primarily forehand, side arm, and backhand throws). Students will also gain an intuitive sense for the physics governing the movement of the Frisbee (e.g. stability and speed range).

Frisbee golf strategy focuses on gauging distances and the amount of force and angle of throw required to land the disc in the target.

Frisbee golf safety practices involve ensuring that students don't wander in areas where a disc is in play, as this may result in injury. Instructors should also instruct students to remain alert and not throw the disc if they perceive there is a possibility that they might hit an individual.

Equipment needed for Frisbee golf include a proper disc (though you can substitute a regular Frisbee for school purposes), target nets, and a playing area large enough to accommodate the game without excessive risk of the Frisbee flying irretrievably out of bounds.

Golf – The most fundamental skills for students to learn when studying golf include the correct way to execute a golf swing with proper posture and how to judge distance for shot selection correctly. Further, students should learn specific shots and their names (e.g. tee shot, fairway shot, bunker shot, putt).

Strategy in golf centers on properly gauging distances and required force to control the ball to the best extent possible.

Safety practices in golf, especially with students, involve ensuring that the course is clear and there are no students nearby when players are swinging. Instructors should also remind students that golf clubs are not toys, and that misuse can result in injury.

Equipment necessary for a golf class includes a proper set of clubs and golf balls (a golf course or open area for hitting balls is also necessary).

Handball – Skills that students will learn in a handball class will include catching and accurately throwing the ball, taking steps while bouncing it (similar to basketball's dribble), and quick analysis of the playing situation to determine who the best target is for a pass.

Strategy in handball centers on staying one step ahead of the opposing team. Keep them guessing and have multiple contingencies for given situations, so that game play doesn't become predictable (and easier to counter). Specific tactics can include types of shots that are harder for the opponent to hit, and shots that will put the ball out of play (when it is advantageous to do so).

Pickleball – Skills that students will learn in pickleball classes include manipulation of the ball with the racket and the variety of strokes.

Pickleball strategy is similar to tennis. Students should learn to vary their strokes to keep their opponents guessing, with the goal of reaching the frontcourt in a net volley position first. This places the students in the best position to win the point.

Table Tennis (Ping Pong) – Skills that students will study when learning table tennis include the variety of grips (e.g. penhold, shakehand, V-grip), and the various types of offensive and defensive strokes. Students will also learn to gauge the force needed to manipulate the ball properly.

Strategies for success in table tennis involve manipulating and minimizing the opponent's ability to return a shot – this includes learning to hit to the opponent's weak side, putting a spin on the ball so as to make its movement less predictable, and setting the opponent up to receive a shot that he cannot return.

Tennis – Skills that students will learn when studying tennis include the proper grips of the racket and stroke techniques, which they should know by name (e.g. flat serve, topspin serve, twist serve, forehand, backhand, volley, overhead).

Shuffleboard – Depending on whether students are playing deck shuffleboard or table shuffleboard, they will learn to manipulate the discs, either with or without sticks.

Strategy requires students to properly gauge and apply the force needed to propel the disc accurately to a particular spot on the playing area.

Safety practices in shuffleboard include properly instructing and monitoring students to avoid horseplay, which may result in injury caused by the playing equipment.

Equipment needed for a shuffleboard class include a disc with which to play, the equipment to manipulate the disc (this will vary depending on whether the shuffleboard game is played on a deck or on a table), and the appropriate playing area.

Track and field – In track and field practice, students will acquire proper running form, the ability to pace their energy expenditure relative to the length of the track, and the ability to manipulate objects in field events.

Track and field strategy focuses on learning to pace energy expenditure relative to the length of the track and analyzing the psychological interaction with other racers and competitors.

Safety practices in track and field include adhering to proper warm up and cool down procedures to prevent injury and handling field equipment (e.g. discus, javelin, shot) with care.

Equipment that is important to track events is minimal, with the only important requirement being appropriate footwear. Field events require specialized equipment. For example, throwing events require a discus, shot, or javelin. Jumping events require a landing area and height or length measuring device.

COMBATIVE ACTIVITIES – OVERVIEW

Basic knowledge of wrestling includes knowledge of basic techniques (familiarity with pins, reversals, and positioning transitions), drills for practicing technique (e.g. students can drill shooting and sprawling, drill reversals from pinned positions, etc.), and terminology (naming the techniques, e.g. shoot, sprawl, half nelson, full nelson, etc.).

Basic knowledge of self-defense includes familiarity with basic striking techniques (punches and kicks), blocks and evasions, knowledge of major vital points on the body (eyes, nose, ears, jaw, throat, solar plexus, groin, knees, in-step), knowledge of basic escape techniques (from chokes, grabs and bear-hugs) and some situational training (to prevent 'freezing' in a real-life encounter). Martial arts (e.g. judo, karate) are common forms of self-defense that physical education instructors can teach to students.

Fencing – Fencing practice will impart to students proficiency in proper fencing form, techniques (for example parries and strikes), and an awareness of open target areas on their opponents. Students will also acquire efficient movement skills.

Fencing strategy focuses on minimizing the number and size of vulnerable target areas on the body, while maneuvering (with the feet, body, and foil) to maximize the vulnerability of opponent target areas in order to score a point.

Safety practices include proper attention to full protective gear, proper form, and careful monitoring of students in practice. Instructors should remind students frequently that they should not take frustrations out on training partners.

Equipment required for fencing practice includes the full gamut of protective gear (suit and helmet), appropriate footwear, and, of course, the fencing foil or saber. Higher technology suits that record points are also available, but are not required.

In-class focus should be placed on strategies for conflict recognition (based on developing an understanding of threat factors, like individuals in a hostile frame of mind), avoidance (physically avoiding potentially dangerous situations), and diffusion (overview of the psychology of confrontations, evaluation of the motivations behind a hostile encounter, understanding of the way body language and eye contact can impact the situation).

TEAM PASSING SPORTS – OVERVIEW

Basketball – The fundamental skills of basketball include passing, dribbling, and shooting. As students' skills improve, they may begin to specialize in playing a specific position (point guard, shooting guard, small forward, power forward or center).

Touch/Flag Football – Skills that students will practice include running and passing – tackling is not relevant in touch or flag football situations. As students improve, they may begin to specialize in playing specific positions (e.g. quarterbacks or receivers). They may also become more involved in the study and implementation of strategy.

The main goal of offensive strategy in football is to move closer to the opposing team's end zone, to the point where the ball is close enough to score either a touchdown or a field goal. The aim of defensive strategies is to prevent this same movement towards the end zone by the opposition. Both offensive and defensive strategies make important use of concepts of time management and the possibility of "running out the clock". Formations are central to football strategy, both on offense and on defense, and students should become familiar with simple formations for both.

Lacrosse – Lacrosse players must master the skills of catching and throwing the ball with their sticks and cradling (the motion that allows players to run with the ball in their stick).

Lacrosse strategy has many parallels with other team sports like basketball, soccer, and field hockey. In all of these sports, the team of players has to maneuver to outflank and outsmart their opponents in order to score a goal.

Soccer – Soccer players must master the skills of running, accurate kicking, manipulation of the ball, and footwork that allows the student to maneuver when in motion.

The key to soccer strategy is for students to understand that the goal is to get the ball to the right person's feet – the one who has the most time and space (facing the least pressure) and is in the most advantageous position to score (or make a goal-scoring pass). Broadly, offensive strategy will spread the team out, to allow for coverage of more of the field. Defensive strategy will have the team compress to a compact unit that is able to cover the goal effectively.

Team Handball – Skills that students will learn in a handball class will include catching and accurately throwing the ball, taking steps while bouncing the ball (similar to basketball's dribble), and quick analysis of the playing situation to ascertain who the best target is for a pass.

Strategy in handball centers around staying one step ahead of the opposing team, keeping them guessing, and having multiple contingencies for given situations so that game play doesn't become predictable (and easier to counter). Specific tactics can include types of shots that are harder for the opponent to hit and shots that will put the ball out of play (when it is advantageous to do so).

Ultimate Frisbee – Skills that students must acquire to play ultimate Frisbee proficiently include catching the Frisbee, accurately throwing the Frisbee, and running. Instructors should also emphasize strategic thinking, as there is limited time to select a destination for and execute a throw.

The goal of offensive strategy in ultimate Frisbee is to create open lanes in the field that are free of defenders. Common offensive strategies include the 'vertical stack' and 'horizontal stack' (similar to a spread offense in football). Defensive strategy aims to gain control of the Frisbee and deflect passes made by the opposing team. A basic defensive principle is the 'force', which calls for the defense to cut off the handler's access to half of the field, thereby forcing the offensive player to throw the Frisbee to the other side of the field.
TEAM STRIKING/FIELDING SPORTS – OVERVIEW

Baseball – Skills that students studying baseball will acquire include accurate throwing and catching, and the correct way to swing and hit with a baseball bat.

Defensive strategy in baseball focuses on the actions of the pitcher, who is responsible for trying to strike out the team that is at bat. Offensive strategy in baseball centers on batting, and attempting to turn batters into runners.

Safety practices in baseball include maintaining discipline among the students, as horseplay and lack of attentiveness can lead to injury (e.g. a ball could hit a student who isn't paying attention). In addition, instructors should remind students the baseball bat is not a toy, and they should handle it with care and not swing it near other students.

Equipment required for baseball practice includes baseball bats, baseballs, baseball gloves (though for some educational situations, the gloves are not necessary), base markers of some kind, and protective padding for the catcher.

Cricket – Skills that students in cricket class will acquire include accurate throwing and catching, swinging the bat correctly, and the proper form for the execution of an effective pitch.
Unlike baseball and softball, where pitching controls the game, in cricket batting controls the game. Since in cricket the batter can hit in any direction around him, he will focus on weak spots in the opposing team's field deployment, and the defensive strategy of the opposing team will focus on minimizing weak spots for the batter to exploit.

Safety practices in cricket are similar to baseball and softball; enforcing discipline and maximizing attentiveness to prevent the chance of injury, and reminding students that they should not swing the bat when other students are in the vicinity.

Equipment required for cricket practice includes cricket bats, cricket balls, appropriate protective gear, and base markers.

Field hockey – Skills that students of field hockey will acquire include running, tactical thinking on the field, and the ability to manipulate the ball with the stick (including running with the ball and different types of shots).

Offensive strategy in field hockey focuses on maneuvering the ball between team members to prevent the opposing team from intercepting, in order to get close enough to the opposing team's net to score a goal. Defensive strategy will strive to create solid coverage of the advancing team, to enable interception of the ball.

Safety practices include emphasizing mindfulness on the part of the students to prevent accidents, and reinforcing the safety regulations of the game concerning legal use of the hockey stick.

Equipment needed for the practice of field hockey with students includes an appropriate ball, sticks for the students, and appropriate protective gear.

Softball – Skills students in softball classes will acquire include accurate throwing and catching, and the correct way to swing and hit with a softball bat.

Softball is similar in strategy to baseball. Defensive strategy focuses on the pitcher, who is responsible for trying to strike out the team that is at bat. Offensive strategy centers on batting, and attempting to turn batters into runners.

Safety practices in softball are also similar to baseball. Enforcing discipline and maintaining student attentiveness to prevent the chance of injury is of utmost importance. Instructors must also emphasize to the students that they should not swing the bat when other students are in the area.

Equipment required for softball practice includes a softball bat and softball, fielding gloves, appropriate protective gear, and base markers of some sort.

SAFETY PRACTICES AND EQUIPMENT

Combative activities

Related safety issues include stressing the potential harm that can result from the techniques being practiced (stressing specific damage potential to musculoskeletal systems), emphasizing students' responsibility for the well-being of their training partners, maintaining discipline throughout the class (ensuring students remain focused on their training activities and alert to the educator's instructions), and ensuring that students are aware and observant of the limits to force that they may apply (no-striking zones, like above the neck and below the belt; limits on striking force, like semi-contact or no-contact sparring; familiarity with the concept of a tap-out indicating submission). Students should perform warm-up, cool-down, and stretching as with any physical training program.

Net/Wall Sports

In addition to the general safety procedures discussed in the previous skill, there are several specific safety considerations for net/wall sports. First, because most of these sports involve swinging a racket or paddle and hitting a ball with a great deal of force, monitoring the area of play is very important. Instructors must ensure that students only swing rackets and hit balls at appropriate times. Second, instructors and students must keep the playing area clear of stray balls and other obstacles to prevent injuries. Finally, some of the net/wall sports, such as handball, require use of protective eyewear.

The following is a list of sport-specific equipment for net/wall sports:

- Badminton – rackets, nets, shuttlecocks
- Handball – a wall, handballs, protective eyewear
- Pickleball – wood paddle rackets, plastic balls, nets, a paved surface

- Table Tennis – paddles, balls, table, nets
- Tennis – court, nets, rackets, tennis balls
- Volleyball – nets, volleyballs

Team passing sports

Important safety considerations for team passing sports include proper maintenance of facilities and playing fields, use of protective equipment, and proper enforcement of the rules of play. Enforcement of rules is particularly important to prevent participants from injuring other participants whether intentionally or unintentionally through reckless play.

The following is a list of sport-specific equipment for team passing sports:

- Basketball – basketballs, goals, appropriate shoes
- Touch or Flag Football – footballs, flags and flag belts, cones to mark boundaries and end zones
- Lacrosse – lacrosse sticks and balls, protective pads, goals (nets)
- Soccer – soccer balls, goals, field markers, protective shin guards
- Team Handball – handballs and goals
- Ultimate Frisbee – Frisbees and an open playing field

INDIVIDUAL AND DUAL SPORT STRATEGIES

Archery strategies for correcting errors in aiming and releasing:

- Shifting position.

- Relaxing both the arms and shoulders at the moment of release.

- Reaching point of aim before releasing string.

- Pointing aim to the right or left of direct line between the archer and the target's center.

- Aiming with the left eye.

- Sighting with both eyes.

- Using the proper arrow.

Bowling for spares strategies:

- Identifying the key pin and determining where to hit it to pick up remaining pins.

- Using the three basic alignments: center position for center pins, left position for left pins, and right position for right pins.

- Rolling the spare ball in the same manner as rolled for the first ball of frame.

- Concentrating harder for the spare ball because of the reduced opportunity for pin action and margin of error.

Badminton Strategies:

Strategies for Return of Service

- Returning serves with shots that are straight ahead.

- Returning service so that opponent must move out of his/her starting position.

- Returning long serves with an overhead clear or drop shot to near corner.

- Returning short serves with underhand clear or a net drop to near corner.

Strategies for Serving

- Serving long to the backcourt near centerline.

- Serving short when opponent is standing too deep in his/her receiving court to return the serve, or using a short serve to eliminate a smash return if opponent has a powerful smash from the backcourt.

Handball or Racquetball Strategies:

- Identifying opponent's strengths and weaknesses.

- Making opponent use less dominant hand or backhand shots if they are weaker.

- Frequently alternating fastballs and lobs to change the pace (changing the pace is particularly effective for serving).

- Maintaining position near middle of court (the well) that is close enough to play low balls and corner shots.

- Placing shots that keep opponent's position at a disadvantage to return cross-court and angle shots.

- Using high lob shots that go overhead but do not hit the back wall with enough force to rebound to drive an opponent out of position when he/she persistently plays close to the front wall.

Tennis Strategies:

- Lobbing – using a high, lob shot for defense giving the player more time to get back into position.

- Identifying opponent's weaknesses, attacking them, and recognizing and protecting one's own weaknesses.

- Outrunning and out-thinking an opponent.

- Using change of pace, lobs, spins, approaching the net, and deception at the correct time.

- Hitting cross-court (from corner to corner of the court) for maximum safety and opportunity to regain position.

- Directing the ball where the opponent is not.

TEAM SPORT STRATEGIES

Basketball Strategies:

Use a Zone Defense

- To prevent drive-ins for easy lay-up shots.

- When playing area is small.

- When team is in foul trouble.

- To keep an excellent rebounder near opponent's basket.

- When opponents' outside shooting is weak.

- When opponents have an advantage in height.

- When opponents have an exceptional offensive player, or when the best defenders cannot handle one-on-one defense.

Offensive Strategies Against Zone Defense

- Using quick, sharp passing to penetrate zone forcing opposing player out of assigned position.

- Overloading and mismatching.

Offensive Strategies for One-On-One Defense

- Using the "pick-and-roll" and the "give-and-go" to screen defensive players to open up offensive players for shot attempts.

- Teams may use free-lancing (spontaneous one-one-one offense), but more commonly they use "sets" of plays.

Soccer Strategies:

- **Heading** – using the head to pass, to shoot, or to clear the ball.

- **Tackling** – objective is to take possession of the ball from an opponent. Successful play requires knowledgeable utilization of space.

Volleyball Strategies:

- Using forearm passes (bumps, digs, or passes) to play balls below the waist, to play balls that are driven hard, to pass the serve, and to contact balls distant from a player.

RULES OF INDIVIDUAL AND DUAL SPORTS

ARCHERY:

- Arrows that bounce off the target or go through the target count as 7 points.

- Arrows landing on lines between two rings receive the higher score of the two rings.

- Arrows hitting the petticoat receive no score.

BADMINTON:

- Intentionally balking opponent or making preliminary feints results in a fault (side in = loss of serve; side out = point awarded to side in).

- When a shuttlecock falls on a line, it is in play (i.e. a fair play).

- If the striking team hits shuttlecock before it crosses net it is a fault.

- Touching the net when the shuttlecock is in play is a fault.

- The same player hitting the shuttlecock twice is a fault.

- The shuttlecock going through the net is a fault.

BOWLING:

- No score for a pin knocked down by a pinsetter (human or mechanical).

- There is no score for the pins when any part of the foot, hand, or arm extends or crosses over the foul line (even after ball leaves the hand) or if any part of the body contacts division boards, walls, or uprights that are beyond the foul line.

- There is no count for pins displaced or knocked down by a ball leaving the lane before it reaches the pins.

- There is no count when balls rebound from the rear cushion.

RACQUETBALL/HANDBALL:

- A server stepping outside service area when serving faults.

- The server is out (relinquishes serve) if he/she steps outside of serving zone twice in succession while serving.

- Server is out if he/she fails to hit the ball rebounding off the floor during the serve.

- The opponent must have a chance to take a position or the referee must call for play before the server can serve the ball.

- The server re-serves the ball if the receiver is not behind the short line at the time of the serve.

- A served ball that hits the front line and does not land back of the short line is "short"; therefore, it is a fault. The ball is also short when it hits the front wall and two sidewalls before it lands on the floor back of the short line.

- A serve is a fault when the ball touches the ceiling from rebounding off the front wall.

- A fault occurs when any part of the foot steps over the outer edges of the service or the short line while serving.

- A hinder (dead ball) is called when a returned ball hits an opponent on its way to the front wall - even if the ball continues to the front wall.

- A hinder is any intentional or unintentional interference of an opponent's opportunity to return the ball.

TENNIS:

A player loses a point when:

- The ball bounces twice on her side of the net.

- The player returns the ball to any place outside of designated areas.

- The player stops or touches the ball in the air before it lands out-of-bounds.

- The player intentionally strikes the ball twice with the racket.

- The ball strikes any part of a player or racket after initial attempt to hit the ball.

- A player reaches over the net to hit the ball.

- A player throws his racket at the ball.

- The ball strikes any permanent fixture that is out-of-bounds (other than the net).

  - a ball touching the net and landing inside the boundary lines is in play (except on the serve, where a ball contacting the net results in a "let" – replay of the point)

- A player fails, on two consecutive attempts, to serve the ball into the designated area (i.e. double fault).

RULES OF TEAM SPORTS

BASKETBALL:

- A player touching the floor on or outside the boundary line is out-of-bounds.

- The ball is out of bounds if it touches anything (a player, the floor, an object, or any person) that is on or outside the boundary line.

- An offensive player remaining in the three-second zone of the free-throw lane for more than three seconds is a violation.

- A ball firmly held by two opposing players results in a jump ball.

- A throw-in is awarded to the opposing team of the last player touching a ball that goes out-of-bounds.

SOCCER:

The following are direct free-kick offenses:

- Hand or arm contact with the ball

- Using hands to hold an opponent

- Pushing an opponent

- Striking/kicking/tripping or attempting to strike/kick/trip an opponent

- Goalie using the ball to strike an opponent

- Jumping at or charging an opponent

- Kneeing an opponent

- Any contact fouls

The following are indirect free-kick offenses:

- Same player playing the ball twice at the kickoff, on a throw-in, on a goal kick, on a free kick, or on a corner kick.

- The goalie delaying the game by holding the ball or carrying the ball more than four steps.

- Failure to notify the referee of substitutions/re-substitutions and that player then handling the ball in the penalty area.

- Any person, who is not a player, entering playing field without a referee's permission.

- Unsportsmanlike actions or words in reference to a referee's decision.

- Dangerously lowering the head or raising the foot too high to make a play.

- A player resuming play after being ordered off the field.

- Offsides – an offensive player must have two defenders between him and the goal when a teammate passes the ball to him or else he is offsides.

- Attempting to kick the ball when the goalkeeper has possession or interference with the goalkeeper to hinder him/her from releasing the ball.

- Illegal charging.

- Leaving the playing field without referee's permission while the ball is in play.

SOFTBALL:

- Each team plays nine players in the field (sometimes 10 for slow pitch).

- Field positions are one pitcher, one catcher, four infielders, and three outfielders (four outfielders in ten player formats).

- The four bases are 60 feet apart.

- Any ball hit outside of the first or third base line is a foul ball (i.e. runners cannot advance and the pitch counts as a strike against the batter)

- If a batter receives three strikes (i.e. failed attempts at hitting the ball) in a single at bat he/she strikes out.

- The pitcher must start with both feet on the pitcher's rubber and can only take one step forward when delivering the underhand pitch.

- A base runner is out if:

  - The opposition tags him with the ball before he reaches a base.
  - The ball reaches first base before he does.
  - He runs outside of the base path to avoid a tag.
  - A batted ball strikes him in fair territory.

- A team must maintain the same batting order throughout the game.

- Runners cannot lead off and base stealing is illegal.

- Runners may overrun first base, but can be tagged out if off any other base.

VOLLEYBALL:

The following infractions by the receiving team result in a point awarded to the serving side and an infraction by serving team results in side-out:

- Illegal serves or serving out of turn.

- Illegal returns or catching or holding the ball.

- Dribbling or a player touching the ball twice in succession.
-
Contact with the net (two opposing players making contact with the net at the same time results in a replay of the point).

- Touching the ball after it has been played three times without passing over the net.

- A player's foot completely touching the floor over the centerline.

- Reaching under the net and touching a player or the ball while the ball is in play.

- The players changing positions prior to the serve.

SAMPLE OFFICIATING SITUATIONS

NOTE: Since rules change yearly, acquiring new rulebooks every year is necessary for proper officiating.

Basketball situation: Actions of the spectators interfere with the progression of the game.

Ruling: An official may call a foul on the team whose supporters are interfering with the game.

Basketball situation: A1 is attempting a field goal and B1 fouls him. A1 continues with the field goal attempt and, before releasing the ball, crashes into B2 who has a legal position on the floor. A1 successfully completes the field goal.

Ruling: The ball was immediately dead when A1 fouled B2; therefore, field goal does not count. However, since B1 fouled A1 while attempting the field goal, A1 receives two free throws.

Basketball situation: The official in the frontcourt runs into a pass thrown from the backcourt by A1 and goes out-of-bounds.

Ruling: B receives a throw-in. The official is part of the court.

Basketball Situation: A1 catches the ball in mid-air and lands with the right foot first and then the left foot. A1 pivots on the left foot.

Ruling: A violation has occurred because A1 can only pivot on the foot that first lands on the floor, which was the right foot.

Soccer situation: The ball is alive when a substitute enters the playing field.

Ruling: A non-player foul. Referee can either penalize at location of the next dead ball or at the place of entry (usually when the team offended is at an advantage).

Soccer situation: B1 charges A1's goalie in A1's penalty area.

Ruling: Team A receives a direct free kick at the spot of foul. A flagrant charge awards Team A a penalty-kick at the other end of the field, and B1 is disqualified.

Soccer situation: The goalie is out of position when a back on team B heads the ball out and falls into the net. A2 gets the ball, passes it to A1, and has only the goalie to beat.

Ruling: A1 is not offside because team B's back left the field during legal play.

Volleyball situation: Team A's second volley hits an obstruction directly over the net, returns to A's playing area, and team A plays it again.

Ruling: Fair play and the next play is team A's third play.

Volleyball situation: The serving team has three front line players standing close together in front of the server at the spiking line.

Ruling: Illegal alignment is called for intentional screening.

Volleyball situation: RB and CB on the receiving team are overlapping when at the time of the serve, and the serve lands out-of-bounds.

Ruling: Serving team receives a point because of receiving team's illegal alignment.

Volleyball situation: LB on team B saves a spiked ball and it deflects off his/her shoulder.

Ruling: A legal hit.

TERMINOLOGY OF TARGET SPORTS

Archery Terminology:

- Addressing the target – standing ready to shoot with a proper shooting stance.

- Anchor point – specific location on the archer's face to which index finger comes while holding and aiming.

- Archery golf (adaptation of golf to archery) – players shoot for holes, scoring according to the number of shots required to hit the target.

- Arm guard – a piece of leather or plastic worn on the inside of the forearm, protecting the arm from the bowstring.

Arrow plate – a protective piece of hard material set into the bow where the arrow crosses it.

- Arrow rest – a small projection at the top of the bow handle where the arrow rests.

- Back – the side of the bow away from the shooter.

- Bow arm – the arm that holds the bow.

- Bow sight – a device attached to the bow through which the archer sights when aiming.

- Bow weight – designates the amount of effort needed to pull a bowstring a specific distance.

- Cant – shooting while holding the bow slightly turned or tilted.

- Cast – the distance a bow can shoot an arrow.

- Clout shooting – a type of shooting using a target 48 feet in diameter laid on the ground at a distance of 180 yards for men and 120 or 140 yards for women. Participants usually shoot 36 arrows per round.

- Cock/Index feather – the feather that is set at a right angle to the arrow nock; differently colored than the other two feathers.

- Creeping – letting the drawing hand move forward at the release.

- Crest – the archer's identifying marks located just below the fletchings.

- Draw – pulling the bowstring back into the anchor position.

- End – a specific number of arrows shot at one time or from one position before retrieval of arrows.

- Face – the part of the bow facing the shooter.

- Finger tab – a leather flap worn on the drawing hand protecting the fingers and providing a smooth release of the bowstring.

- Fletchings – the feathers of the arrow that give guidance to its flight.

- Flight shooting – shooting an arrow the farthest possible distance.

- Handle – the grip at the midsection of the bow.

Hen feathers – the two feathers that are not set at right angles to the arrow nock.

- Instinctive shooting – aiming and shooting instinctively rather than using a bow sight or point-of-aim method.

- Limbs – upper and lower parts of the bow divided by the handle.

- Nock – the groove in the arrow's end where the string is placed.

- Nocking point – the point on the string where the arrow is placed.

- Notch – the grooves of the upper and lower tips of the limbs where the bowstring is fitted.

- Over bow – using too strong a bow that is too powerful to pull a bowstring the proper distance.

- Overdraw – drawing the bow so that the pile of the arrow is inside the bow.

- Petticoat – the part of the target face outside the white ring.

- Pile/point – the arrow's pointed, metal tip.

- Plucking – jerking the drawing hand laterally away from the face on the release causing the arrow's flight to veer to the left.

- Point-blank range – the distance from the target where the point of aim is right on the bull's eye.

- Point-of-aim – a method of aiming that aligns the pile of the arrow with the target.

- Quiver – a receptacle for carrying or holding arrows.

- Recurve bow – a bow that is curved on the ends.

- Release – the act of letting the bowstring slip off the fingertips.

- Round – the term used to indicate shooting a specified number of arrows at a designated distance or distances.

- Roving – an outdoor archery game that uses natural targets (trees, bushes, stumps, etc.) for competition.

- Serving – the thread wrapped around the bowstring at the nocking point.

- Shaft – the long, body part of the arrow.

- Spine – the rigidity and flexibility characteristics of an arrow.

- Tackle – archery equipment referred to in its entirety.

- Target face – the painted front of a target.

- Trajectory – the flight path of the arrow.

- Vane – an arrow's plastic feather.

Bowling Terminology:

- Anchor – the teammate who shoots last.

- Baby split – the 1-7 or 3-10 pin railroads.

- Backup – a reverse hook rotating to the right for a right-handed bowler.

- Bed posts – the 7-10 railroad.

- Blow – an error or missing a spare that is not split.

- Box – a frame.

- Brooklyn – a crossover ball striking the 1-2 pocket.

- Bucket – the 2-4-5-8 or 3-5-6-9 leaves.

- Cherry – chopping off the front pin on a spare.

- Double – two consecutive strikes.

- Double pinochle – the 7-6 and 4-10 split.

- Crossover – same as a Brooklyn.

- Dutch 200 (Dutchman) – a score of 200 made by alternating strikes and spares for the entire game.

- Error – same as a "blow."

- Foul – touching or going beyond the foul line in delivering the ball.

- Frame – the box where scores are entered.

- Gutter ball – a ball that falls into either gutter.

- Handicap – awarding an individual or team a bonus score or score adjustment that is based on averages.

- Head pin – the number one pin.

- Hook – a ball that breaks to the left for a right-handed bowler and breaks to the right for a left-handed bowler.

- Jersey side – same as a Brooklyn.

- Kegler – synonym for a bowler.

- Lane – a bowling alley.

- Leave – pin or pins left standing after a throw.

- Light hit – hitting the head pin lightly to the right or left side.

- Line – a complete game as recorded on the score sheet.

- Mark – getting a strike or spare.

- Open frame – a frame in which no mark is made, leaving at least one pin standing after rolling both balls in a frame.

- Pocket – space between the head pin and pins on either side.

- Railroad – synonym for a split.

- Sleeper – a pin hidden from view.

- Spare – knocking all pins down with two balls.

- Split – a leave, after throwing the first ball, in which the number one pin plus a second pin are down, and when seven pins remain standing.

- Spot – a bowler's point of aim on the alley.

- Striking out – obtaining three strikes in the last frame.

- Tap – a pin that remains standing after an apparently perfect hit.

- Turkey – three consecutive strikes.

TERMINOLOGY OF NET/WALL SPORTS

Badminton Terminology:

- Alley – the area on each side of the court used for doubles that is 1.5 feet wide.

- Around-the-head stroke – an overhead stroke used to hit a forehand-like overhead stroke that is on the backhand side of the body.

- Back alley – the area between the baseline and the doubles long service line.

- Backcourt – the back third of the court.

- Backhand – a stroke made on the non-racket side of the body.

- Baseline – the back boundary line of the court.

- Bird – another name for the shuttlecock/shuttle.

- Block – a soft shot used mainly to defend a smash; intercepting opponent's smash and returning it back over the net.

- Carry/Throw – a call when the shuttle remains on the racket during a stroke. It is legal if the racket follows the intended line of flight.

- Centerline – the mid-line separating the service courts.

- Clear – a high shot that goes over the opponent's head and lands close to the baseline.

- Combination alignment – partners playing both up-and-back and side-by-side during doubles games and/or volleys.

- Crosscourt – a diagonal shot hit into the opposite court.

- Defense – the team or player hitting the shuttle upwards.

- Double hit – an illegal shot where the player contacts the shuttle twice with the racket in one swing.

- Doubles service court – the short, wide area to which the server must serve in doubles play.

- Down the line shot – a straight-ahead shot (usually down the sideline).

- Drive – a hard, driven shot traveling parallel to the floor (clears net but does not have enough height for opponent to smash).

- Drop – a shot just clearing the net and then falling close to it.

- Face – the racket's string area.

- Fault – an infraction of the rules resulting in loss of serve or a point awarded to the server.

- First serve – a term used in doubles play to indicate that the server is the "first server" during an inning.

- Foot fault – Illegal movement/position of the feet by either the server or receiver.

- Forecourt – the front area of the court (between the net and the short service line).

- Forehand – a stroke made on the racket side of the body.

- Game point – the point, if won, that allows the server to win the game.

- Hand in – a term indicating that the server retains the serve.

- Hand out – the term used in doubles to denote that one player has lost the service.

- Home base – a center court position where a player can best play any shot hit by an opponent.

- Inning – the period a player or team holds service.

- Let – stopping the point because of some type of outside interference. Players replay the point.

- Lifting the shuttle – stroking the shuttle underhanded and hitting it upward.

- Long serve – a high, deep serve landing near the long service line in doubles or the back boundary line in singles.

- Love – the term used to indicate a zero score.

- Match – a series of games. Winning two out of three games wins the match.

- Match point – the point, if won by the server, which makes that person the winner of the match.

- Midcourt – the middle-third of the court (between short service line and long service line for doubles).

- Net shot – a shot taken near the net.

- Non-racket side – the opposite side of the hand holding the racket.

- Offense – the team or player that is stroking the shuttle downward.

- Overhead – a motion used to strike the shuttle when it is above the head.

- Racket foot or leg – the foot or leg on the same side as the hand holding the racket.

- Ready position – the position a player assumes to be ready to move in any direction.

- Receiver – the player to whom the shuttle is served.

- Second serve – in doubles, the term indicates that one partner has lost the serve, and the other partner is now serving.

- Server – the player putting the shuttle into play.

- Setting – choosing the amount of additional points to play when certain tie scores occur.

- Short-serve – a serve barely clearing the net and landing just beyond the short service line.

- Shuttlecock/Shuttle – the feathered, plastic or nylon object that players volley back and forth over the net.

- Side Alley – see alley.

- Smash – an overhead stroke hit downward with great velocity and angle.

- "T" – the intersection of the centerline and the short service line.

- Underhand – an upward stroke to hit the shuttle when it has fallen below shoulder level.

- Unsight – illegal position taken by the server's partner so the receiver cannot see the shuttle.

- Up-and-back – an offensive alignment used in doubles. The "up" player is responsible for the forecourt and the "back" player is responsible for both.

Racquetball/Handball Terminology:

- Ace – a serve that completely eludes the receiver.

- Back-wall shot – a shot made from a rebound off the back wall.

- Box – see service box.

- Ceiling shot – a shot that first strikes the ceiling, then the front wall.

- Crotch – the junction of any two playing surfaces, as between the floor and any wall.

- Crotch shot – a ball that simultaneously strikes the front wall and floor (not good).

- Cut throat – a three-man game in which the server plays against the other two players. Each player keeps an individual score.

- Drive shot – a power shot against the front wall rebounding in a fast, low, and straight line.

- Fault – an illegally served ball.

- Handout – retiring the server who fails to serve legally or when the serving team fails to return a ball that is in play.

- Hinder – interference or obstruction of the flight of the ball during play.

- Kill – a ball rebounded off the front wall so close to the floor that it is impossible to return.

- Passing shot – a shot placed out of an opponent's reach on either side.

- Rally – continuous play of the ball by opponents.

- Receiving line – the broken line parallel to the short line on a racquetball court.

- Run-around shot – a ball striking one sidewall, the rear wall, and the other sidewall.

- Safety zone – a five-foot area bounded by the back edge of the short line and receiving line that is only observed during the serve in racquetball.

- Screen – a hinder due to obstruction of the opponent's vision.

- Server – person in the "hand-in" position and eligible to serve.

- Service box – the service zone bounded by the sidewall and a parallel line 18 inches away; denotes where server's partner must stand in doubles during the serve.

- Service court – the area where the ball must land when it is returned from the front wall on the serve.

- Service line – the line that is parallel to and five feet in front of the short line.

- Service zone – the area where the ball must be served.

- Short line – the line on the floor parallel to front wall and equidistant from front and back wall. The serve must go over this line when returning from the front wall.

- Shoot – attempt kill shots.

- Side out – loss of serve.

- Thong – the strap on the bottom handle of the racquetball racquet that is worn around the player's wrist.

- Volley – returning the ball to the front wall before it bounces on the floor.

- Z-ball – defensive shot that strikes the front wall, a sidewall, and then the opposite sidewall.

Tennis Terminology:

- Ace – serving a ball untouched by the opponent's racket.

- Advantage (Ad) – a scoring term. The next point won after the score is "deuce."

- Alley – the 4.5-foot strip on either side of the singles court that enlarges the court for doubles.

- Approach shot – a shot hit inside the baseline while approaching the net.

- Backcourt – the area between the service line and the baseline.

- Backhand – strokes hit on the left side of a right-handed player.

- Backspin – spin placed on a ball that causes the ball to bounce back toward the hitter.

- Back swing – the beginning of all groundstrokes and service motion requiring a back swing to gather energy for the forward swing.

- Baseline – the end line of a tennis court.

- Break – winning a game in when the opponent serves.

- Center mark – a short mark bisecting the baseline.

- Center service line – the perpendicular line to the net dividing the two service courts in halves.

- Center strap – the strap at the center of the net anchored to the court to facilitate a constant 3-foot height for the net at its center.

- Center stripe – same as the center service line.

- Chip – a short chopping motion of the racket against the back and bottom side of the ball imparting backspin.

- Chop – placing backspin on the ball with a short, high-to-low forward swing.

- Cross-court – a shot hit diagonally from one corner of the court over the net into the opposite corner of the court.

- Cut off the angle – moving forward quickly against an opponent's cross-court shot, allowing the player to hit the ball near the center of the court rather than near the sidelines.

- Deep (depth) – a shot bouncing near the baseline on groundstrokes and near the service line on serves.

- Default – a player who forfeits his/her position in a tournament by not playing a scheduled match.

- Deuce – a term used when the game score is 40-40.

- Dink – a ball hit very softly and relatively high to ensure its safe landing.

- Double fault – two consecutive out-of-bounds serves on the same point resulting in loss of the point.

- Doubles lines – the outside sidelines on a court used only for doubles.

- Down the line – a shot hit near a sideline traveling close to, and parallel to, the same line from which the shot was initially hit.

- Drive – an offensive shot hit with extra force.

- Drop shot – a groundstroke hit so that it drops just over the net with little or no forward bounce.

- Drop volley – a volley hit in such a manner that it drops just over the net with little or no forward bounce.

- Error – a mistake made by a player during competition.

- Flat shot – a ball hit so there is no rotation or spin when traveling through the air.

- Foot fault – illegal foot movement before service, penalized by losing that particular serve. Common foot faults are stepping on or ahead of the baseline before contacting the ball and running along the baseline before serving.

- Forecourt – the area between the net and the service line.

- Forehand – the stroke hit on the right side of a right-handed player.

- Frame – the rim of the racket head plus the handle of the racket.

- Game – scoring term when a player wins 4 points before an opponent while holding a minimum 2-point lead.

- Grip – the portion of the racket that the player grasps in his hand.

- Groundstroke – any ball hit after it has bounced.

- Half volley – a ball hit inches away from the court's surface after the ball has bounced.

- Hold serve – winning your own serve. If you lose your own serve, your serve has been "broken."

- Let (ball) – a point replayed because of some kind of interference.

- Let serve – a serve that touches the net tape, falls into the proper square, and is played over.

- Linesman – a match official who calls balls "in" or "out."

- Lob – a ball hit with sufficient height to pass over the out-stretched arm of a net player.

- Lob volley – a shot hit high into the air from a volleying position.

- Love – scoring term that means zero points or games.

- Match – a contest between two or four opponents.

- Match point – the point immediately before the final point of a match.

- Midcourt – the area in front of the baseline or behind the service line of the playing court.

- Net ball – a ball that hits the net, falling on the same side as the hitter.

- No man's land – a general area within the baseline and proper net position area. When caught in that area, the player must volley or hit ground strokes near his/her feet.

- Offensive lob – a ball hit just above the racket reach of an opposing net player.

- Open face racket – a racket whose face is moving under the ball. A wide-open racket face is parallel to the court surface.

- Overhead – a shot hit from a position higher than the player's head.

- Over-hitting – hitting shots with too much force; over-hitting usually results in errors.

- Pace – the speed of the ball.

- Passing shot – a shot passing beyond the reach of the net player landing inbounds.

- Poach – to cross over into your partner's territory in doubles in an attempt to intercept the ball.

- Racket face – the racket's hitting surface.

- Racket head – the top portion of the racket frame that includes the strings.

- Rally – opponents hitting balls back and forth across the net.

- Receiver – the player about to return the opponent's serve.

- Server – the player initiating play.

- Service line – the line at the end of the service courts parallel to the net.

- Set – a scoring term meaning the first player to win six games with a minimum two-game lead.

- Set point – the point, if won, which will give the player the set.

- Sidespin – a ball hit rotating on a horizontal plane.

- Signals in doubles – signaling your partner that you are going to poach at the net.

- Singles line – the sideline closest to the center mark that runs the entire length of the court.

- Slice – motion of the racket head going around the side of the ball, producing a horizontal spin on ball.

- Tape – the band of cloth or plastic running across the top of the net.

- Telegraphing the play – indicating the direction of one's intended target before hitting the ball.

- Topspin – forward rotation of the ball.

- Touch – the ability to make delicate, soft shots from several positions on the court.

- Twist – a special rotation applied to the ball during the serve causing the ball to jump to the left (of right-handed server).

- Umpire – the official that calls lines.

- Under spin – a counterclockwise spin placed on the ball (i.e. backspin).

- Volley – hitting the ball in the air before it bounces on the court.

TERMINOLOGY OF TEAM PASSING SPORTS

Basketball Terminology:

- Backcourt players (Guards) – players who set up a team's offensive pattern and bring the ball up the court.

- Backdoor – an offensive maneuver in which a player cuts toward the baseline to the basket, behind the defenders, and receives a ball for a field goal attempt.

- Baseline – the end line of the court.

- Blocking/Boxing out – a term used when a player is under the backboard to prevent an opposing player from achieving a good rebounding position.

- Charging – personal contact by a player with the ball against the body of a defensive opponent.

- Corner players (Forwards) – tall players that make up the sides of the offensive set-up who are responsible for the rebounding and shooting phases of the team's offense.

- Cut – a quick, offensive move by a player attempting to get free for a pass.

- Denial defense – aggressive individual defense to keep an offensive player from receiving a pass.

- Double foul – two opponents committing personal fouls against each other simultaneously.

- Dribble – ball movement by a player in control who throws or taps the ball in the air or onto the floor and then touches it. The dribble ends when the dribbler touches the ball with both hands concurrently, loses control, or permits it to come to rest while in contact with it.

- Drive – an aggressive move by a player with the ball toward the basket.

- Fake (Feint) – using a deceptive move with the ball pulling the defensive player out of position.

- Fast break – quickly moving the ball down court to score before the defense has a chance to set up.

- Field goal – a basket scored from the field.

- Freelance – no structure or set plays in the offense.

- Free throw – the right given a player to score one or two points by unhindered shots for a goal from within the free throw circle and behind the free throw line.

- Give-and-go – a maneuver when the offensive player passes to a teammate and then immediately cuts in toward the basket for a return pass.

- Held ball – occurs when two opponents have one or both hands firmly on the ball and neither can gain possession without undue roughness.

- Inside player (Center, Post, Pivot) – this player is usually the tallest team player who is situated near the basket, around the three-second lane area, and is responsible for rebounding and close-range shooting.

- Jump ball – a method of putting the ball into play by tossing it up between two opponents in the center circle to start the game or any overtime periods.

- Outlet pass – a term used that designates a direct pass from a rebounder to a teammate (the main objective is starting a fast break).

- Overtime period – an additional period of playing time when the score is tied at the end of the regulation game.

- Personal foul – a player foul that involves contact with an opponent while the ball is alive or after the ball is in possession of a player for a throw-in.

- Pick – a special type of screen where a player stands so the defensive player slides to make contact to free an offensive teammate for a shot or drive.

- Pivot – occurs when a player who is holding the ball steps once or more than once in any direction with the same foot while the other foot, called the pivot foot, remains at its point of contact with the floor. Also, another term for the inside player.

- Posting up – a player cutting to the three-second lane area, pausing, and anticipating a pass.

- Rebound – when the ball bounces off the backboard or basket.

- Restraining circles – three circles with a six-foot radius. One is located in the center of the court, and the others are located at each of the free-throw lines.

- Running time – not stopping the clock for fouls or violations.

- Screen – an offensive maneuver positioning a player between the defender and a teammate to free the teammate for an uncontested shot.

- Switching – defensive guards reversing their guarding assignments.

- Technical foul – a non-contact foul by a player, team, or coach for unsportsmanlike behavior or failing to abide by rules regarding submission of lineups, uniform numbering, and substitution procedures.

- Telegraphing a pass – a look or signal to indicate where the ball is going to be passed.

- Throw-in – a method of putting the ball in play from out-of-bounds.

- Traveling – illegal movement, in any direction, of a player in possession of the ball within bounds. Moving with the ball without dribbling.

- Violation – an infraction of the rules resulting in a throw-in from out-of-bounds.

Soccer Terminology:

- Center – passing from the outside of the field near the sideline into the center.

- Charge – illegal or legal body contact between opponents.

- Chip – lofting the ball into the air using the instep kick technique; contacting the ball very low causing it to loft quickly with backspin.

- Clear – attempting to move the ball out of danger by playing the ball a great distance.

- Corner kick – a direct free kick from the corner arc awarded to the attacking players when the defending team last played the ball over their own end line.

- Cross – a pass from the outside of the field near the end line to a position in front of the goal.

- Dead ball situation – the organized restarting of the game after stopping play.

- Direct free kick – a free kick whereby the kicker may score immediately from that initial contact.

- Dribble – the technique of a player self-propelling the ball with the foot in order to maintain control of the ball while moving from one spot to another.

- Drop ball – the method used to restart the game after temporary suspension of play when the ball is still in play.

- Goal area – the rectangular area in front of the goal where the ball is placed for a goal kick.

- Half volley – contacting the ball just as it hits the ground after being airborne.

- Head – playing the ball with the head.

- Indirect free kick – a free kick from which a player, other than the kicker, must contact the ball before the team can score a goal.

- Kickoff – the free kick starting play at the beginning of the game, after each period, or after a score.

- Obstruction – illegally using the body to shield an opponent from reaching the ball.

- One-touch – immediately passing or shooting a received ball without stopping it.

- Penalty area – the large rectangular area in front of the goal where the goalkeeper may use the hands to play the ball.

- Penalty kick – a direct free kick awarded in the penalty area against the defending team for a Direct Free Kick foul.

- Settle – taking a ball out of the air and settling it on the ground so that it is rolling and no longer bouncing.

- Square pass – a pass directed toward the side of a player.

- Tackle – a technique to take the ball away from the opponents.

- Through pass – a pass penetrating between and past the defenders.

- Throw-in – the technique to restart the game when the ball goes out of play over the sideline.

- Touchline – the side line of the field.

- Trap – the technique used for receiving the ball and bringing it under control.

- Two-touch- receiving – trapping and immediately re-passing the ball.

Volleyball Terminology:

- Attack – returning the ball across the net in an attempt to put the opponents at a disadvantage.

- Ball handling – executing any passing fundamental.

- Block – intercepting the ball just before or as it crosses the net.

- Bump – see forearm pass.

- Court coverage – a defensive player's court assignment.

- Dig – an emergency pass usually used to defend a hard-driven attack.

- Dink – a soft shot off the fingertips to lob the ball over a block.

- Double foul – infraction of rules by both teams during the same play.

- Drive – an attacking shot contacted in the center that attempts to hit the ball off the blocker's hands.

- Fault – any infraction of the rules.

- Forearm pass – a pass made off the forearms to play served balls, hard-driven spikes, or any low ball.

- Free ball – a ball returned by the opponent that is easily handled.

- Frontcourt – the playing area where it is legal to block or attack.

- Held ball – a ball that opponents simultaneously contact and momentarily hold above the net.

- Kill – an attack that the opposition cannot return.

- Lob – a soft attack contacted on the back bottom-quarter of the ball causing an upward trajectory.

- Overhand pass – a pass made by contacting the ball above the head with the fingers.

- Overlap – an illegal foot position when the ball is dead, with an adjacent player putting another out of position.

- Play over – replaying the rally because of a held ball or the official prematurely suspending play. The server re-serves with no point awarded.

- Point – a point is scored when the receiving team fails to return the ball to the opponents' court legally.

- Rotation – clockwise rotation of the players upon gaining the ball from the opponents.

- Serve – putting the ball in play over the net by striking it with the hand.

- Set – placing the ball near the net to facilitate attacking.

- Setter – the player assigned to set the ball.

- Side out – side is out when the serving team fails to win a point or plays the ball illegally.

- Spike – a ball hit with top spin and with a strong downward force into the opponents' court.

- Spiker – the player assigned to attack the ball.

- Spike-roll – an attack that first takes an upward trajectory using the spiking action (with or without jumping).

- Topspin (Overspin) – applying forward spin to the ball during the serve, spike, or spike roll.

SKILL 4.2   Analyze the importance of rules, etiquette, teamwork, and appropriate participant and spectator behavior in individual, dual, and team sports and activities.

Rules and etiquette are of great importance to sports and physical activities. Rules help ensure fair play, equity, and safety for all participants. Teamwork is another important aspect of sports. Team sports require individual players to come together, merge individual skill sets, and pool individual strengths and weaknesses to achieve team success.

APPROPRIATE BEHAVIOR IN PHYSICAL EDUCATION ACTIVITIES

Appropriate Student Etiquette/Behaviors include: following the rules and accepting the consequences of unfair action, good sportsmanship, respecting the rights of other students, reporting own accidents and mishaps, not engaging in inappropriate behavior under peer pressure encouragement, cooperation, paying attention to instructions and demonstrations, moving to assigned places and remaining in own space, complying with directions, practicing as instructed to do so, properly using equipment, and not interfering with the practice of others.

Appropriate Content Etiquette/Behaviors include the teacher describing the performance of tasks and students engaging in the task, the teacher assisting students with task performance, and the teacher modifying and developing tasks.

Appropriate Management Etiquette/Behaviors include the teacher directing the management of equipment, students, and space prior to practicing tasks; students getting equipment and partners; the teacher requesting that students stop "fooling around."

SKILL 4.3   Know key elements of successful performance in individual, dual, and team sports and activities and strategies for improving students' performance, teamwork, and skill combinations.

Skills necessary for successful participation in sports and fitness activities include proprioception, spatial orientation, hand-eye coordination, and movement skills.

Proprioception – Proprioception is the sense of the relative position of neighboring parts of the body. Unlike the six external senses (sight, taste, smell, touch, hearing, and balance), proprioception is an internal sense that provides feedback solely on the status of the body internally. It is the sense that indicates whether the body is moving with required effort, as well as where the various parts of the body are located in relation to each other. We can improve proprioception by training.

Spatial orientation – Spatial orientation refers to the process of aligning or positioning oneself with respect to a specific direction or reference system. Specifically, it is the relationship established between the body's self-oriented coordinate system and an external reference frame. This happens through the integration of sensory signals from the visual, vestibular, tactile, and proprioceptive systems.

Hand eye coordination – Hand eye coordination is the ability of the visual perception system to coordinate the information received through the eyes to control, guide, and direct the hands in the accomplishment of a given task (examples include handwriting or catching a ball). Hand eye coordination uses the eyes to direct attention and the hands to execute a task.

Movement skills – Movement skills center on the integration of balance and proprioceptive skills to produce movement that effectively manages the weight distribution of the body.

In addition to these generic skills, successful performance in individual, dual, and team sports requires many specific physical and social skills, which we will now discuss.

KEY PERFORMANCE ELEMENTS

Key elements of successful performance in individual, dual, and team sports and activities include discipline and dedication, athletic ability, technical skills, and communication. These elements are all interconnected. Without discipline and dedication, the proper levels of athletic ability and technical skills will not develop (natural talent will only carry one so far). Without communication, the athlete will not be able to coordinate their efforts with their partners or teammates (in dual or team sports, respectively), nor will they be able to effectively interact with their coaches and instructors to improve their own performance abilities.

Students can improve performance in sports and physical activities by engaging in regular, varied, and knowledge-based training on both athletic aspects and technical skills. Training must be regular and frequent (but varied so as not to result in over-training and injury). In addition, training must also be knowledge-based to ensure that it produces the maximum benefits to the athlete, both in terms of physical athletic development, and development of technical skills and reflexes.

Instructors can promote improvement of students' teamwork in sports and physical activities by creating varied training situations in which entire teams practice together (as opposed to individual training activities that promote the development of technical and athletic skills of individual team members). Effective teamwork stems from two sources. The first is the ability of all the team members to communicate and cooperate with each other (instructors can develop this by teamwork and communication training). The second source is the closer ties that develop between team members that train together for an extended period. An example is the ability to anticipate their teammates' next move.

Students can improve their skill combinations in sports and physical activities by engaging in training activities that focus on the practice and refinement of specific skill aspects individually, without removing them from a realistic training setting or context. In other words, students should practice skills individually, but not in isolation, as they must remain in the context of the game or sport.

SKILL 4.4   Apply knowledge of principles and techniques for selecting, adapting, and modifying sports activities to improve performance, promote the use of combinations of motor skills, and provide practice in specific sports skills in gamelike situations.

It is sometimes important for a physical educator to select, adapt and/or modify sports activities with the express aim of improving students' performance in the activity. This can include promoting the use of combinations of motor skills or providing practice in specific sports skills in gamelike situations. There are several factors that instructors should consider when modifying activities. Activities should emphasize discrete elements of the sports skill without detaching the movement from the rest of the activity. Properly educating students about the activities they are performing is important. Also, of course, the activities themselves should be rewarding and fun.

Emphasizing discrete elements of the sports skill means that if a student needs to improve in a specific aspect of the activity (e.g., they specifically need to improve their throwing ability in baseball), they should practice that specific element (throwing) rather than the entire sport skill (playing baseball).

Additionally, students should perform techniques within the context of the activity, and as part of a kinetic chain. For this reason, it is important that students practice the skill in situations that are as close to the main activity as possible. For instance, let us continue with the baseball example. Rather than having two students toss a tennis ball back and forth to improve throwing, they should practice with a baseball and glove.

Cognitive education should always accompany the physical practice of the activity. Students should understand the correct and incorrect process of technique execution as well as why the correct way is biomechanically correct and why the incorrect way is biomechanically incorrect. This will make it possible for the students to focus on their weaknesses and to self-monitor their progress.

Finally, students should understand the connection between their current training activity and the sports skills they are developing. Also of great importance is that the activities are fun. A more fun and rewarding training experience increases student motivation, which leads to better training results.

COMPETENCY 5.0   PRINCIPLES, TECHNIQUES, SKILLS, AND SAFETY PRACTICES FOR DANCE, PERSONAL PERFORMANCE ACTIVITIES, COOPERATIVE AND NONTRADITIONAL GAMES, RECREATIONAL ACTIVITIES, AND OUTDOOR PURSUITS

Skill 5.1   **Demonstrate knowledge of techniques, sequences, skills, steps, conditioning programs, safety practices, and types and uses of equipment for creative movement, dance, and personal performance activities.**

DANCE CONCEPTS, FORMS, AND BASIC VOCABULARY – JAZZ AND BALLET

There are several forms of dance including modern, ballet, jazz, country, ballroom, and hip-hop. Though essentially very different from each other, they all have similarities. A sense of musicality is the one constant required for each of the dance forms. Along with that, we can add timing, coordination, flexibility, and, needless to say, an interest in the concept of dance itself. We all know that we will probably experience greater success when we engage in activities that we are interested in and enjoy. Understanding of most dance forms requires knowledge of basic vocabulary. For example, in jazz, turns or kick ball turns; in tap dance, the shuffle or the flap, etc. Ballet has more specialized vocabulary than any other dance form. For example, plie, to bend; tendu, to stretch; degage, to disengage; fouette, to whip; fondu, to melt; ronde jambe, circle of the leg; pirouette, to turn on one leg; port de bras, movement of the arms; and assemble, to assemble.

Integral to dance and particularly ballet are the concepts of balance and counterbalance, pull-up and turnout, weight distribution and alignment, including shoulders down, hips square, legs turned out, and chest lifted.

In ballet, there are many different dance forms and techniques that a dancer can follow. Three of the larger ones are the Cecchetti, Russian Vaganova, and Royal Academy of Dance, (RAD), programmes. They all have levels for all dancers from beginner to advanced and they all have their advantages and disadvantages. The Cecchetti Society developed the Cecchetti technique from the teachings of the great ballet master Enrico Cecchetti. It is a full syllabus designed to train dancers for professional work. One notable emphasis in the Cecchetti syllabus is that the arms flow and blend from position to position more than any other technique. The Cecchetti technique has formed the core of the program at the National Ballet School of Canada. The Russian Vaganova technique derives and takes its name from the teachings of Agrippina Vaganova, who was the artistic director of the Kirov Ballet for many years. In the Vaganova method, the dancers bring attention to their hands. The hands do not flow invisibly from one position to the next, as in the Cecchetti method, rather they are left behind and turn at the last moment. This is where the "flapping" look comes from that many dancers make with their hands. Unlike the RAD method, the Vaganova method does not have formally established exercises for each level. Each teacher choreographs his own class according to specialized guidelines and the students dance that class in their examinations. The Vaganova method forms the core of the program at the Royal Winnipeg Ballet School. The RAD syllabus is very common. It is well suited to dance classes in community dance schools where the students usually do no more than an average of one class per day. If you go to the ballet school in your community, there is a good chance they will use the RAD method. The American School of Ballet teaches the Balanchine method. Created by George Balanchine in the American School of Ballet, the Balanchine method allows dancers to dance Balanchine's choreography much more easily than other dancers can. In the Balanchine method the hands are held differently again from any of the other systems.

DANCE CONCEPTS, FORMS, AND BASIC VOCABULARY – FOLK AND TAP

Folk dance is a term used to describe a large number of dances that originated in Europe and share several common characteristics. Most folk dances practiced today were created before the 20th century, and were practiced by people with little or no training. For this reason, folk dances are usually characterized by a spontaneous style, adaptable movements, and culturally distinctive steps representative of the dance's country of origin. Types of folk dancing include the contra dance, English country-dance, and Maypole dance.

Contra dance is a term used to describe folk dances in which couples dance in two facing lines. A pair of such lines is a set, and these sets generally run the length of a long hall. The head of a set is the end of the line closest to the band and caller. At contra dance events where dancers perform several different folk dances, the caller or dance leader teaches the movements of an individual dance to the dancers during the "walk through," a short period before the next type of dance begins. During the walk through, all dancers mark the movements following the caller's instructions. At contra dance events in North America, contra dancers traditionally change partners for every dance. On the other hand, in the United Kingdom, dancers remain with the same partner for the entire evening.

Square dance refers to a type of folk dance in which four couples begin and end each sequence in a square formation. When four couples align themselves in such a manner, the formation is "sets-in-order," and we call dances that use such formations "quadrilles." Similar to folk dance, American square dance steps are based on traditional European dances. At every square dance event, the dance caller prompts participants through a sequence of steps to the beat throughout the entirety of each dance, but does not usually participate in the dancing. Steps common to many square dances include allemande left and allemande right, where couples face, take hands, and circle around one another; promenade, where partners cross hands and walk to a counter-clockwise position; and circle right and circle left, where all dancers grasp hands and move round in a circle. Traditionally, the caller explains the steps to each individual square dance at the beginning of a session.

Tap is a form of dance born in the United States during the 19th century in which the dancer sounds out the rhythm by clicking taps on the toes and heels of his shoes. This form of percussive music and dance evolved from a fusion of Irish and African Shuffle in New York City during the 1830s. One common characteristic of modern tap dance is "syncopation," where choreographies generally begin on the eighth music beat. Learning to tap dance is a cumulative process in which new information builds on previously learned steps and terms. To teach tap dance successfully, instructors must first teach simple steps that make up the foundation of tap before introducing complex movements. The most basic steps of tap include the walk, step, heel, step-heel, stamp, ball-change, brush, toe tap, shuffle, side shuffle, back shuffle, and cramp roll. Dance instructors can combine these steps to form simple routines for beginners. Once students have mastered these steps, dancers can move on to attempt movements such as the buffalo, Maxi Ford, Cincinnati, pullback, wings, toe clips, and riffs.

AEROBIC DANCE

Dance aerobics is any type of cardiovascular exercise that is put to music, ranging from country line dancing to hip-hop. Aerobic dance can be performed on three different levels, high-impact aerobics, in which movements such as jumping cause both feet to lose contact with the ground simultaneously; low-impact aerobics, in which one foot remains in contact with the ground at all times; and step aerobics, in which dancers move on and around a slightly raised platform. A beneficial aerobics session is composed of three stages. During the warm-up, which usually lasts for 5-10 minutes, slow movements such as walking in place and stretching will prepare participants for more vigorous activity. The high-impact stage of dance aerobics follows the warm-up. High impact should last 20-30 minutes, and include anything from a dance routine to a step class. Moves common to many dance aerobic classes include the grapevine combined with kicks and lunges, high kicks, jumping jacks, and forward and back double kicks. Step routines are generally composed of movements on and off a platform, and also include kicks, swats, and lunges. In between movements of the high-impact period, dancers should always maintain constant movement, walking or marching in place to keep up their heart rate and burn more calories. The last 5-10 minutes of a dance aerobics session should be a cool down period, during which participants again stretch all muscles and slowly lower their heart rate.

Skill 5.2   **Demonstrate knowledge of strategies, techniques, skills progressions, conditioning programs, and types and uses of equipment for recreational activities and outdoor pursuits.**

RECREATIONAL ACTIVITIES AND OUTDOOR PURSUITS

Hiking – Instructors can take students on walking/hiking trips through nature reserves and national parks. Such trips can incorporate team-building activities and nature education.

Sail Training – Students taught to sail should display competence in the maintenance and piloting of a boat, including cooperative activities necessary to a successful sailing endeavor (e.g. working together to get the boat into and out of the water, paddling in rhythm, turning the boat, etc.). Prior to the start of sail training, students should understand all safety procedures and acceptable forms of behavior on a boat (e.g. only standing when necessary, no pushing, following instructions, wearing a life jacket, etc.). Students must also demonstrate swimming competence (i.e. ability to tread water, swim a distance continuously, and put on a life jacket while in the water).

Rope Challenge Courses – Good activity for team-building purposes. Challenges include personal physical challenges (climbing various structures), or group activities (e.g. requiring students to work together to coordinate the crossing of a course). Safety requirements include helmets, harnesses, spotters, trained supervisors, and strict adherence to all safety procedures and educator instructions.

Bicycling – In bicycling classes, students should learn proper bicycling form and how to gauge which gear is most appropriate for their current speed and level of inclination. Students should also become familiar with the proper way to maintain and care for their bicycles.

Bicycling strategy is similar to track events – learning to gauge the appropriate levels of energy expenditure relative to the length of the track and the fitness of the cyclist.

Safety practices while bicycling include seriousness in practice (no horseplay, which can result in injury) and attentiveness to the track so that students can avoid potentially dangerous bumps or cracks. Instructors should remind students not to race with each other, but rather to focus on their own physical activity.

Equipment required for bicycling with students includes proper gear (which includes clothing without loose appendages that can catch in bicycle gears); water for longer trips, and, of course, the bicycles themselves.

Cross-country skiing – Students in cross-country skiing classes will learn the proper form for cross-country skiing (e.g. herringbone, diagonal stride, double pole) and will greatly improve their fitness (as cross-country skiing is a very taxing activity on a very wide range of muscle groups).
Like most endurance activities, cross-country skiing strategy involves regulating the levels of energy expenditure relative to the length of the course and the fitness level of the athlete.

Safety practices in cross-country skiing include ensuring the availability of first aid and instructor attentiveness to the students (as it is easier to 'lose track' of a student who is having trouble). Instructors should also instruct students not to wander away from the group – a good solution is the implementation of a buddy system.

Equipment required for cross-country skiing trips includes appropriate dress (make sure students dress warmly), cross-country skis, and poles.

Canoeing – Students in canoeing classes will learn the various forms of paddling strokes, how to manage their weight, and how to work as a team to maneuver a canoe properly.

Strategies for effective canoeing include the clear delineation of members of a rowing team and the role that each individual serves. The 'captain' coordinates the efforts of the rowers on the canoe and should become familiar with the course and destination.

Safety practices for canoeing call for the instructor to ensure that the students are all able to swim and equipped with proper flotation equipment (e.g. lifejackets). First aid should be available and the instructor should see to it that he remains close enough to students in different canoes to be able to hear them and reach them if needed.

Equipment required for canoeing classes includes canoes, canoeing paddles, and proper flotation equipment. Instructors should advise students to have a change of clothes available in the event that they get wet.

Orienteering – Skills that students will acquire during orienteering activities include the ability to read a map, critical thinking stemming from practice identifying locations, navigation ability, and strategic thinking for selection of efficient movement patterns between several points.

Strategies for orienteering include ascertaining early the destination points and mapping an efficient course to pass through all of them.

Safety practices include ensuring the availability and accessibility of first aid, properly instructing the students in emergency procedures (e.g. blow the whistle and remain where you are), and selecting an area small enough so the instructor can hear the whistle from any position.

Equipment required for orienteering with students includes proper outdoor clothing and a whistle for use in emergency situations. Students will also need a map and possibly a compass.

Fishing – Students studying fishing will learn the correct technique for casting a line and will learn to identify spots where fish are most likely to congregate. Fishing also teaches patience to students.

Strategies for effective fishing with groups of students include deploying students in such a way that one will not interfere with another's fishing activities. Students should also learn about the habits of the fish that they are after, to allow them to tailor their approaches accordingly.

Safety practices for fishing call for instructors to remind students that their equipment does not consist of toys and they should not play with it. Students should definitely handle fishing rods and hooks carefully around other students.

Equipment required for fishing includes fishing rods, hooks, bait, gear (e.g. boots), and a bucket or other receptacle for the fish.

Inline skating – Skills that students in inline skating class will acquire include skating techniques (e.g. braking and stopping, skating backwards, skating downhill) and improved balance. Students should also learn to care for their skating equipment.

Strategies in inline skating focus on maintaining proper form during the activity.

Safety practices in inline skating include requiring students to wear appropriate protective gear and ensuring that first aid is available. Instructors should instruct students not to attempt stunts, especially without supervision.

Equipment required for inline skating includes skates and appropriate protective gear (e.g. helmets, kneepads, elbow pads).

Rock climbing – Students studying rock climbing will gain proficiency in climbing techniques (including body positioning and learning to find proper toeholds and handholds in the rock face) belaying, and managing the climbing and harness equipment.

Strategies in rock climbing require the climber to remain aware not only of the current 'next step' of the climbing process, but to also remain aware of the entire rock face, and to plan on a course that she can follow through to completion (so as to prevent climbing to a dead-end area).
Safety practices include explaining all safety practices so students understand, ensuring that students wear all safety gear (protective gear and harnesses) properly, and that all students have spotters monitoring their activities.

Equipment required for rock climbing activities includes proper attire, suitable footwear, protective equipment, and harnessing equipment.

Alpine skiing (downhill skiing) – The skills that students of alpine skiing will gain center on learning to control the direction and speed of their descent; novices will begin by learning the "snow plough" technique to turn, and will learn to point their skis inward to stop. More advanced technique will center on "carving", which allows the skis to turn without skidding or slowing down.

Alpine skiing strategy calls for awareness of the practitioner's current level of skill and avoiding over-reaching (i.e. attempting courses that are too advanced and thus dangerous). Instructors should teach students to be aware of the course ahead of them, allowing them to better plan their movements.

Safety practices in alpine skiing include proper inspection of the equipment to ensure that everything is in order and instructing the students in appropriate safety procedures. Most importantly, instructors should not allow students to attempt courses that are beyond their current skill levels.

Equipment required for alpine skiing includes appropriate dress that is adequately warm (hats, gloves, and goggles), skis, and poles.

Camping – Camping imparts a wide range of skills, from tent pitching to fire building to outdoor cooking.

Successful camping strategy focuses on planning and preparing the students (mentally, physically, and in terms of their equipment) for the camping experience.

Safety practices for camping include packing a first aid kit and emergency supplies (e.g. a map, compass, whistle), checking the weather before departure, avoiding areas of natural hazards, and putting out fires appropriately. Instructors should teach students to identify and avoid poisonous plants.

Camping equipment includes a tent, lean-to, or other shelter device, a sleeping bag and sleeping pad (or air mattress), a portable stove (where campfires are impractical or not allowed), a lantern or flashlight, a hatchet, axe or saw, ropes, and tarps.

Walking is a good, generic cardiorespiratory activity for promoting basic fitness. Instructors can incorporate it into a variety of class settings (not only physical education instructors – for example, a Biology class might include a field trip to a natural setting that would involve a great deal of walking). Walking is appropriate for practically all age groups, but can only serve as noteworthy exercise for students who lead a fairly sedentary lifestyle (athletic students who train regularly or participate in some sport will not benefit greatly from walking).

Jogging or **Running** is a classic cardiorespiratory activity in which instructors can adjust the difficulty level by modifying the running speed or the incline of the track. It is important to stress proper footwear and gradual increase of intensity to prevent overuse injuries (e.g. stress fractures or shin splints).

GENERAL SAFETY CONCERNS

Safety education related to outdoor pursuits and recreation should emphasize the importance of planning and research. Students should consider in advance what the potential dangers of an activity might be and to prepare plans accordingly (students and instructors should also examine weather forecasts). Of course, educator supervision is required. First-aid equipment and properly trained educators must be present for outdoor education activities. Students should use proper safety gear when appropriate (e.g. helmets, harnesses, etc.). Parental consent is generally required for outdoor education activities.

AQUATICS

Swimming is an excellent cardiorespiratory activity that has the added benefit of working more of the body's muscles, more evenly than most other exercises, without excessive resistance to any one part of the body that could result in an overuse injury. To use swimming as an educational cardiorespiratory activity, there must be qualified lifeguards present, and all students must pass basic tests of swimming ability.

Water safety issues include student familiarity with appropriate medical responses to life-threatening situations. Students should recognize signs that someone needs medical attention (e.g. not moving, not breathing, etc.) and have knowledge of the proper response (e.g. who to contact and where to find them). With older children, the instructor can introduce rudimentary first aid. The instructor must also ensure that students are aware and observant of safety rules (e.g. no running near the water, no chewing gum while swimming, no swimming without a lifeguard, no roughhousing near or in the water, etc.).

Swimming strokes include Butterfly, Breast Stroke, Crawl, Sidestroke, Trudgen, Freestyle, Backstroke, and Dog Paddle. When teaching children how to dive, instructors should emphasize form (arm and body alignment) and safety procedures (e.g. no diving in the shallow end, no pushing students into the water).

Water fitness activities and games should place emphasis on generating a lot of movement in the pool (gross motor activities), and may also incorporate activities that require more coordinated manipulations, like catching a ball (fine motor). Sample games include:

- **Water Tag** – Children can attempt to catch each other in the pool. When someone is caught, he becomes 'it'. Variations include freeze tag (where a caught student isn't allowed to move until someone swims between their legs to free them) and base tag (where some sections of the pool, for example the ladders or the walls, are a safe 'base' – rules must be in place limiting the time that a student can spend on the base). Water tag emphasizes gross motor activities. Safety issue: students may not hold other students or grab other students in the water.

- **Water Dodgeball** – Students divide into two teams, one on either side of the pool. They play dodgeball, throwing a ball from one side to the other. The opposing team captures a student who is hit by the ball, but if the ball is caught, the thrower is captured instead. Safety issue: students may not throw the ball at another student's head at close range.

- **Relay Races** – Students divide into teams and perform relay races (i.e. one student swims the length of the pool and back, when he returns the next one does the same, repeating until the whole team has completed the task). This can incorporate various swimming strokes; either all team members use the same stroke or each team member uses a different stroke.

Skill 5.3   Analyze the importance of rules, discipline, cooperation, etiquette, **and safety practices in personal performance and other activities.**

Rules, discipline, cooperation, etiquette, and safety practices have a vital role to play in personal performance and other movement-based activities. These activities, by their very nature, will often challenge individuals to push their physical and psychological limitations and what they might consider is behaviorally acceptable in competitive situations. Rules and discipline are critical in competitive situations where there is a strong drive to "achieve at any cost" (at least in terms of personal sacrifice and dedication). Rules and self-discipline are the lines that divide healthy athletes from those who engage in unsportsmanlike behavior and training practices that do not fit into a balanced lifestyle. Similarly, cooperation is the element that allows athletes in a hard-training situation, who are both physically and mentally exhausted, to rely on each other for support. This is a critical factor to healthy training practices. Etiquette is the formalization of these cooperative practices. In situations where individuals might try to push their personal limits beyond what they know they are capable of, safety practices are critical to prevent injuries and accidents.

Skill 5.4   **Apply knowledge of principles and procedures for selecting, adapting, and modifying activities and games based on student characteristics, instructional goals, skill levels, range of individual variation, and exceptional needs.**

SEE ALSO Skill 4.4

ADAPTING SELECTED ACTIVITIES

Physical education instructors must be able to adapt and modify activities to meet the needs of students of varying developmental levels, student characteristics and skill levels, and instructional goals. The following is a list of common motor skill activities and adaptations for different purposes.

Walking: adapt distance, distance over time, and number of steps in specified distance; provide handrails for support; change slope for incline walking; and change width of walking pathway.

Stair climbing: change pathway, pace of climbing, and number and height of steps.

Running: change distance over time, use an incline-changing slope (distance over time), and form a maze (distance over time).

Jumping: change distance and height of jump, change distance in a series and from a platform, change participants' arm positions.

Hopping: change distance for one and two hops (using preferred and non-preferred leg) and distance through obstacle course.

Galloping: change number of gallops over distance, change distance covered in number of gallops, and widen pathway.

Skipping: change number of errorless skips, change distance covered in number of skips, change number of skips in distance, and add music for skipping in rhythm.

Leaping: change distance and height of leaps.

Bouncing balls: change size of ball (larger), have participant use two hands, reduce number of dribbles, bounce ball higher, have participant stand stationary and perform bounces one at a time.

Catching: use larger balls and have participant catch balls thrown at chest level from a lower height of release, shorten catching distance, have participant stop and then catch ball (easier than moving and catching).

APPROPRIATE ACTIVITIES AND ADAPTATIONS FOR STUDENTS WITH LIMITATIONS

Appropriate activities are those activities in which handicapped students can successfully participate.

Adaptations include individualized instruction and modified rules, modified environments, and modified tasks. As needs warrant, instructors can move participants to less restrictive environments. Instructors can also initiate periodic assessments to advance a student's placement, review progress, and determine what the least restrictive environment is for each participant (including changing services to produce future optimum progress). However, the most appropriate placement depends on meeting the physical education needs, both educational and social, of the handicapped student.

FUNCTIONAL ADAPTATIONS

Instructors can provide blind students with auditory or tactile clues to help them find objects or to position their bodies in the activity area. Blind students also can learn the patterns of movement by manually mimicking the correct patterns or by verbal instructions.

Deaf students can read lips or learn signing to communicate and understand instructions.

Physically challenged students may have to use crutches to enable them to move.

Asthmatics can play goalie or similar positions requiring less cardio-respiratory demands.

Simplifying rules can accommodate a retarded participant's limited comprehension.

ADAPTING FOR PROBLEMS WITH STRENGTH, ENDURANCE, AND POWER ACTIVITIES

1. Lower basketball goals or nets; increase size of target.

2. Decrease throwing distance between partners, serving distance, and distance between bases.

3. Reduce size or weight of projectiles.

4. Shorten length and/or reduce weight of bat or other striking apparatus.

5. Play games in lying or sitting positions to lower center of gravity.

6. Select a "slow ball" (one that will not get away too fast), deflate ball in case it gets away, or attach a string to the ball for recovery.

7. Reduce playing time and lower number of points to win.

8. Use more frequent rest periods.

9. Rotate often or use frequent substitution when needed.

10. Use mobilization alternatives, such as using scooter boards one inning/period and feet for one inning/period.

ADAPTING FOR BALANCE AND AGILITY PROBLEMS

1. Verify if balance problem is due to medication (you may have to consult physician).

2. Use chairs, tables, or bars to help with stability.

3. Have participants learn to utilize eyes optimally for balance skills.

4. Teach various ways to fall and incorporate dramatics into fall activities.

5. Use carpeted surfaces.

6. Lower center of gravity.

7. Have participant extend arms or provide a lightweight pole.

8. Have participant keep as much of his/her body in contact with the surface.

9. Widen base of support (distance between feet).

10. Increase width of walking parameters.

ADAPTING FOR COORDINATION AND ACCURACY

Throwing Activities: use beanbags, yarn or nerf balls, and/or smaller-sized balls.

Catching and Striking Activities: use larger, softer, and lighter balls; throw balls to mid-line; shorten distance; and reduce speed of balls.

Striking/Kicking Activities: enlarge striking surface, choke up on bats, begin with participant successfully striking stationary objects and then progress to striking with movement, and increase target size.

EXERCISE PHYSIOLOGY ADAPTATIONS

Decrease the amount of weight, amount of reps/sets, pace, and/or distance of exercise; increase the amount of intervals; and combine together any of the previous modifications.

DOMAIN II.   **HEALTH-RELATED PHYSICAL FITNESS**

COMPETENCY 6.0   MAJOR BODY SYSTEMS, PRINCIPLES OF PHYSICAL FITNESS DEVELOPMENT AND TRAINING, AND THE BENEFITS OF A HEALTHY, ACTIVE LIFESTYLE

Skill 6.1   Demonstrate knowledge of the principles and benefits of a physically active lifestyle and ways to provide students with learning opportunities that promote participation in and enjoyment of physical activities.

Practicing healthy behaviors has many benefits. Regular physical activity and proper nutrition can help prevent diseases, illnesses, and injuries. In addition, regular exercise and a proper diet help maintain a healthy body composition, which is important physically and psychologically. Physically fit and healthy individuals are generally more productive at work. Finally, preventing disease and avoiding injury through healthy behaviors can reduce health-care costs.

Physically educated individuals are better able to care for their own health and use nutrition and exercise to prevent long-term health problems. The following is a list of benefits of a physically active lifestyle.

Physiological benefits of physical activity include:

- improved cardiorespiratory fitness

- improved muscle strength

- improved muscle endurance

- improved flexibility

- more lean muscle mass and less body fat

- quicker rate of recovery

- improved ability of the body to utilize oxygen

- lower resting heart rate

- increased cardiac output

- improved venous return and peripheral circulation

- reduced risk of musculoskeletal injuries

- lower cholesterol levels

- increased bone mass

- cardiac hypertrophy and size and strength of blood vessels

- increased number of red cells

- improved blood-sugar regulation

- improved efficiency of thyroid gland

- improved energy regulation

- increased life expectancy

Psychological benefits of physical activity include:

- relief of stress

- improved mental health via better physical health

- reduced mental tension (relieves depression, improves sleeping patterns)

- better resistance to fatigue

- better quality of life

- more enjoyment of leisure

- better capability to handle some stressors

- opportunity for successful experiences

- better self-concept

- better ability to recognize and accept limitations

- improved appearance and sense of well-being

- better ability to meet challenges

- better sense of accomplishments

Sociological benefits of physical activity include:

- the opportunity to spend time with family and friends and make new friends

- the opportunity to be part of a team

- the opportunity to participate in competitive experiences

- the opportunity to experience the thrill of victory

ROLE OF EXERCISE IN HEALTH MAINTENANCE

The health risk factors improved by physical activity include cholesterol levels, blood pressure, stress related disorders, heart diseases, weight and obesity disorders, early death, certain types of cancer, musculoskeletal problems, mental health, and susceptibility to infectious diseases.

INCORPORATING PHYSICAL ACTIVITY INTO DAILY LIFE

One of the most important tasks for physical education instructors is to introduce students to strategies to incorporate physical activity into everyday situations. For example, instructors can recommend that students walk or ride a bike to school, rather than drive or ride the bus. In addition, there are a number of everyday activities that promote fitness including yard work, sports and games, walking, and climbing stairs.

Listed below are simple ways to integrate cardiorespiratory activities into your daily life:

- Do housework. Vacuuming, dusting, and mopping all add more steps to your day. These chores also involve lifting and stretching.
- Do yard work. Rake leaves, use a push mower to mow the lawn, dig holes to plant flowers or pick up trash.
- Go for a short walk before breakfast or after dinner. Start with a 5-10 minute walk and work up to 30 minutes.
- If possible, walk or bike when doing chores rather than driving.
- Walk the dog.
- Take the stairs instead of using the elevator.
- Plan fun activities with friends that require physical activity (e.g., hiking, swimming, backpacking, etc.)

Strategies for integrating strength and endurance activities into daily life include:

- Doing yard work
- Climbing stairs
- Lifting objects (e.g. children, laundry baskets, etc.)

PROVIDING STUDENTS WITH LEARNING OPPORTUNITIES THAT PROMOTE PARTICIPATION IN AND ENJOYMENT OF PHYSICAL ACTIVITIES

Instructors can provide students with learning opportunities that promote participation in and enjoyment of physical activities by involving students in the activity selection process, by emphasizing physical activities with strong social aspects, and by providing students with self-assessment tools that allow them to track their own progress in physical activities.

Instructors can involve students in the activity selection process by explaining to them the goals of the particular activity session and asking their opinion as to the activity that they would most enjoy that would meet those goals. Giving students input into activity selection is a good way to encourage students to invest in the activity and to give them opportunities to consider the potential benefits of different activities.

Emphasizing physical activities with strong social aspects, like team and cooperative activities, is another positive way of connecting students with physical activities. Students will enjoy an activity more if they are given the opportunity to participate with their friends. Physical educators must be careful, though, to detect and address situations where such activities isolate individual students.

Finally, providing students with a deeper understanding of the physical activities in question will help them focus on improving their own performance. Also, providing students with self-assessment tools will motivate students by giving them the option of tracking their own progress.

Skill 6.2   Demonstrate knowledge of the structures, functions, components, and actions of major body systems and how various body systems produce movement, adapt to physical activity, and contribute to fitness.

Major systems of the human body consist of organs working together to perform important physiological tasks. In this section, we will discuss several major body systems including the musculoskeletal system, the cardiovascular system, the respiratory/excretory system, the nervous system, the endocrine system, the reproductive system, and the immune system. In addition, we will discuss how these systems adapt to physical activity, produce movement, and contribute to fitness.

STRUCTURES, LOCATIONS, AND FUNCTIONS OF THE THREE TYPES OF MUSCULAR TISSUE

The main function of the muscular system is movement. There are three types of muscle tissue: skeletal, cardiac, and smooth.

Skeletal muscle is voluntary. These muscles are attached to bones and are responsible for their movement. Skeletal muscle consists of long fibers and is striated due to the repeating patterns of the myofilaments (made of the proteins actin and myosin) that make up the fibers.

Cardiac muscle is found in the heart. Cardiac muscle is striated like skeletal muscle, but differs in that the plasma membrane of the cardiac muscle causes the muscle to beat even when away from the heart. The action potentials of cardiac and skeletal muscles also differ.

Smooth muscle is involuntary. It is found in organs and enables functions such as digestion and respiration. Unlike skeletal and cardiac muscle, smooth muscle is not striated. Smooth muscle has less myosin and does not generate as much tension as skeletal muscle.

MECHANISM OF SKELETAL MUSCLE CONTRACTION

A nerve impulse strikes a muscle fiber. This causes calcium ions to flood the sarcomere. Calcium ions allow ATP to expend energy. The myosin fibers creep along the actin, causing the muscle to contract. Once the nerve impulse has passed, calcium is pumped out and the contraction ends.

MOVEMENT OF BODY JOINTS

The axial skeleton consists of the bones of the skull and vertebrae. The appendicular skeleton consists of the bones of the legs, arms and tail, and shoulder girdle. Bone is a connective tissue. Parts of the bone include compact bone that gives strength, spongy bone that contains red marrow to make blood cells and yellow marrow in the center of long bones to store fat cells, and the periosteum that is the protective covering on the outside of the bone.
A joint is a place where two bones meet. Joints enable movement. Ligaments attach bone to bone. Tendons attach bone to muscle. Joints allow great flexibility in movement. There are three types of joints:

1.   Ball and socket – allows for rotational movement. An example is the joint between the shoulder and the humerus. Ball and socket joints allow humans to move their arms and legs in many different ways.

2.   Hinge – movement is restricted to a single plane. An example is the joint between the humerus and the ulna.

3.   Pivot – allows for the rotation of the forearm at the elbow and the hands at the wrist.

HUMAN NERVOUS AND ENDOCRINE SYSTEMS

The **central nervous system (CNS)** consists of the brain and spinal cord. The CNS is responsible for the body's response to environmental stimuli. The spinal cord is located inside the spine. It sends out motor commands for movement in response to stimuli. The brain is where responses to more complex stimuli occur. The meninges are the connective tissues that protect the CNS. The CNS contains fluid filled spaces called ventricles. These ventricles are filled when cerebrospinal fluid which is formed in the brain. This fluid cushions the brain and circulates nutrients, white blood cells, and hormones. The CNS's response to stimuli is a reflex. A reflex is an unconscious, automatic response.

The **peripheral nervous system (PNS)** consists of the nerves that connect the CNS to the rest of the body. The sensory division brings information to the CNS from sensory receptors and the motor division sends signals from the CNS to effector cells. The motor division consists of somatic nervous system and the autonomic nervous system. The body consciously controls the somatic nervous system in response to external stimuli. The hypothalamus in the brain unconsciously controls the autonomic nervous system to regulate the internal environment. This system is responsible for the movement of smooth muscles, cardiac muscles, and the muscles of other organ systems.

Understand the major endocrine glands and the function of their hormones

The function of the **endocrine system** is to manufacture proteins called hormones. **Hormones** circulate in the bloodstream and stimulate actions when they interact with target tissue. There are two classes of hormones, steroid and peptide. Steroid hormones come from cholesterol and include the sex hormones. Amino acids are the source of peptide hormones. Hormones are specific and fit receptors on the target tissue cell surface. The receptor activates an enzyme that converts ATP to cyclic AMP. Cyclic AMP (cAMP) is a second messenger from the cell membrane to the nucleus. The genes found in the nucleus turn on or off to cause a specific response.

Endocrine cells, which make up endocrine glands, secrete hormones. The major endocrine glands and their hormones include:

Hypothalamus – located in the lower brain; signals the pituitary gland.

Pituitary gland – located at the base of the hypothalamus; releases growth hormones and antidiuretic hormone (retention of water in kidneys).

Thyroid gland – located on the trachea; lowers blood calcium levels (calcitonin) and maintains metabolic processes (thyroxine).

Gonads – located in the testes of the male and the ovaries of the female; testes release androgens to support sperm formation and ovaries release estrogens to stimulate uterine lining growth and progesterone to promote uterine lining growth.

Pancreas – secretes insulin to lower blood glucose levels and glucagon to raise blood glucose levels.

ROLE OF NERVE IMPULSES and NEURONS

The **neuron** is the basic unit of the nervous system. It consists of an axon, which carries impulses away from the cell body to the tip of the neuron; the dendrite, which carries impulses toward the cell body; and the cell body, which contains the nucleus. Synapses are spaces between neurons. Chemicals called neurotransmitters are found close to the synapse. The myelin sheath, composed of Schwann cells, covers the neurons and provides insulation.

Nerve action depends on depolarization and an imbalance of electrical charges across the neuron. A polarized nerve has a positive charge outside the neuron. A depolarized nerve has a negative charge outside the neuron. Neurotransmitters turn off the sodium pump which results in depolarization of the membrane. This wave of depolarization (as it moves from neuron to neuron) carries an electrical impulse. This is actually a wave of opening and closing gates that allows for the flow of ions across the synapse. Nerves have an action potential. There is a threshold of the level of chemicals that must be met or exceeded in order for muscles to respond. This is the "all or nothing" response.

STRUCTURE AND FUNCTION OF THE SKIN

The skin consists of two distinct layers, the epidermis and the dermis. The epidermis is the thinner outer layer and the dermis is the thicker inner layer. Layers of tightly packed epithelial cells make up the epidermis. The tight packaging of the epithelial cells supports the skin's function as a protective barrier against infection.

The top layer of the epidermis consists of dead skin cells and contains keratin, a waterproofing protein. The dermis layer consists of connective tissue. It contains blood vessels, hair follicles, sweat glands, and sebaceous glands. The body releases an oily secretion called sebum, produced by the sebaceous gland, to the outer epidermis through the hair follicles. Sebum maintains the pH of the skin between 3 and 5, which inhibits most microorganism growth.

The skin also plays a role in thermoregulation. Increased body temperature causes skin blood vessels to dilate, which causes heat to radiate from the skin's surface. Also, increased temperature activates sweat glands, which increases evaporative cooling. Decreased body temperature causes the skin's blood vessels to constrict. This results in blood from the skin diverting to deeper tissues and reduces heat loss from the surface of the skin.

HUMAN RESPIRATORY AND EXCRETORY SYSTEMS

Surface area, volume, and function of the respiratory and excretory systems

The lungs are the respiratory surface of the human respiratory system. A dense net of capillaries contained just beneath the epithelium form the respiratory surface. The surface area of the epithelium is about $100m^2$ in humans. Based on the surface area, the volume of air inhaled and exhaled is the tidal volume. This is normally about 500mL in adults. Vital capacity is the maximum volume the lungs can inhale and exhale. This is usually around 3400mL.

The kidneys are the primary organs in the excretory system. Each human kidney is about 10cm long. Despite their small size, they receive about 20% of the blood pumped with each heartbeat. The function of the excretory system is to rid the body of nitrogenous wastes in the form of urea. .

Knowledge of process of breathing and gas exchange

The respiratory system functions in the gas exchange of oxygen and carbon dioxide waste. It delivers oxygen to the bloodstream and picks up carbon dioxide for release from the body. Air enters the mouth and nose, where it is warmed, moistened and filtered of dust and particles. Cilia in the trachea trap and expel unwanted material in mucus. The trachea splits into two bronchial tubes and the bronchial tubes divide into smaller and smaller bronchioles in the lungs. The internal surface of the lung is composed of alveoli, which are thin walled air sacs. These allow for a large surface area for gas exchange. Capillaries line the alveoli. Oxygen diffuses into the bloodstream and carbon dioxide diffuses out of the capillaries and is exhaled from the lungs due to partial pressure. Hemoglobin, a protein containing iron, carries the oxygenated blood to the heart and all parts of the body.

The thoracic cavity holds the lungs. The diaphragm muscle below the lungs is an adaptation that makes inhalation possible. As the volume of the thoracic cavity increases, the diaphragm muscle flattens out and inhalation occurs. When the diaphragm relaxes, exhalation occurs.

HUMAN CIRCULATORY AND IMMUNE SYSTEMS

Structure, function, and regulation of the heart

The function of the closed circulatory system (**cardiovascular system**) is to carry oxygenated blood and nutrients to all cells of the body and return carbon dioxide waste to the lungs for expulsion. The heart, blood vessels, and blood make up the cardiovascular system. The following figure shows the structure of the heart:

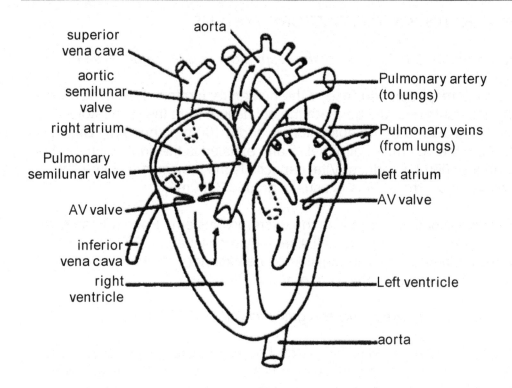

The atria are the chambers that receive blood returning to the heart. The ventricles are the chambers that pump blood out of the heart. There are four valves, which include two atrioventricular (AV) valves and two semilunar valves. The AV valves are located between each atrium and ventricle. The contraction of the ventricles closes the AV valve to keep blood from flowing back into the atria. The semilunar valves are located where the aorta leaves the left ventricle and the pulmonary artery leaves the right ventricle. Ventricular contraction opens the semilunar valves, pumping blood out into the arteries, and ventricular relaxation closes the valves.

The cardiac output is the volume of blood per minute that the left ventricle pumps. This output depends on the heart rate and stroke volume. The **heart rate** is the number of times the heart beats per minute. Furthermore, the **stroke volume** is the amount of blood pumped by the left ventricle each time it contracts. Humans have an average cardiac output of about 5.25 L/min. Heavy exercise can increase cardiac output up to five times. Also, epinephrine and increased body temperature increase heart rate and the cardiac output.

Structure, function, and regulation of the immune system

The immune system is responsible for defending the body against foreign invaders. There are two defense mechanisms: non-specific and specific.

The **non-specific** immune mechanism has two lines of defense. The first line of defense is the physical barrier of the body. These include the skin and mucous membranes. The skin prevents the penetration of bacteria and viruses as long as there are no abrasions on the skin. Mucous membranes form a protective barrier around the digestive, respiratory, and genitourinary tracts. In addition, the pH of the skin and mucous membranes inhibit the growth of many microbes. Mucous secretions (tears and saliva) wash away many microbes and contain lysozyme that kills microbes.

The second line of defense includes white blood cells and the inflammatory response. **Phagocytosis** is the ingestion of foreign particles. Neutrophils make up about seventy percent of all white blood cells. Monocytes mature to become macrophages, which are the largest phagocytic cells. Eosinophils are also phagocytic. Natural killer cells destroy the body's own infected cells instead of the invading the microbe directly.

The other second line of defense is the inflammatory response. The blood supply to the injured area increases, causing redness and heat. Typically, swelling occurs with inflammation. Basophils and mast cells release histamine in response to cell injury. This triggers the inflammatory response.

The **specific** immune mechanism recognizes specific foreign material and responds by destroying the invader. These mechanisms are specific and diverse. They are able to recognize individual pathogens. An **antigen** is any foreign particle that elicits an immune response. The body manufactures **antibodies** that recognize and latch onto antigens, hopefully destroying them. They also discriminate between foreign materials versus self material. Memory of the invaders provides immunity upon further exposure.

Immunity is the body's ability to recognize and destroy an antigen before it causes harm. Active immunity develops after recovery from an infectious disease (e.g. chicken pox) or after a vaccination (e.g. mumps, measles, rubella). Passive immunity may be passed from one individual to another and is not permanent. A good example is the immunities passed from mother to nursing child. A baby's immune system is not well developed and the passive immunity they receive through nursing keeps them healthier.

There are two main responses made by the body after exposure to an antigen:

1. **Humoral response** - Free antigens activate this response and **B** cells (lymphocytes from bone marrow) give rise to plasma cells that secrete antibodies and memory cells that will recognize future exposures to the same antigen. The antibodies defend against extracellular pathogens by binding to the antigen and making them an easy target for phagocytes to engulf and destroy. Antibodies are in a class of proteins called immunoglobulins. There are five major classes of immunoglobulins (Ig) involved in the humoral response: IgM, IgG, IgA, IgD, and IgE.

2. **Cell mediated response** – Infected cells activate T cells (lymphocytes from the thymus). These activated T cells defend against pathogens in the cells or cancer cells by binding to the infected cell and destroying them along with the antigen. T cell receptors on the T helper cells recognize antigens bound to the body's own cells. T helper cells release IL-2, which stimulates other lymphocytes (cytotoxic T cells and B cells). Cytotoxic T cells kill infected host cells by recognizing specific antigens.

Vaccines are antigens given in very small amounts. They stimulate both humoral and cell mediated responses. After vaccination, memory cells recognize future exposure to the antigen so the body can produce antibodies much faster.

HUMAN DIGESTIVE SYSTEM

Roles of basic nutrients found in foods

The function of the digestive system is to break food down into nutrients, absorb them into the blood stream, and deliver them to all cells of the body for use in cellular respiration.

Essential nutrients are those nutrients that the body needs but cannot make. There are four groups of essential nutrients: essential amino acids, essential fatty acids, vitamins, and minerals.

The human body requires approximately eight to ten essential amino acids. A lack of these amino acids results in protein deficiency. There are only a few essential fatty acids.

Vitamins are organic molecules essential for a nutritionally adequate diet. Scientists have identified thirteen vitamins essential to humans. There are two groups of vitamins: water-soluble (includes the vitamin B complex and vitamin C) and water insoluble (vitamins A, D and K). Vitamin deficiencies can cause severe problems.

Unlike vitamins, minerals are inorganic molecules. Calcium is important in bone construction and maintenance. Iron is important in cellular respiration and is a major component of hemoglobin.

Carbohydrates, fats, and proteins are fuel for the generation of ATP. Water is necessary to keep the body hydrated. We discussed the importance of water in previous sections.

Essential Amino Acids	Essential Vitamins
• Arginine	• Vitamin A
• Histidine	• Vitamin B complex (8 vitamins)
• Isoleucine	• Vitamin C
• Leucine	• Vitamin D
• Lysine	• Vitamin E
• Methionine	• Vitamin K
• Phenylalanine	
• Threonine	
• Tryptophan	
• Valine	

Mechanical and chemical digestion

The teeth and saliva begin digestion by breaking food down into smaller pieces and lubricating it to allow swallowing. The lips, cheeks, and tongue form a bolus or ball of food. The process of peristalsis (wave-like contractions) carries the food down the pharynx where it enters the stomach through the sphincter, which closes to keep food from going back up. In the stomach, pepsinogen and hydrochloric acid form pepsin, the enzyme that hydrolyzes proteins. This chemical action breaks the food down further and churns into a semifluid mass called acid chyme. The pyloric sphincter muscle opens to allow the food to enter the small intestine. Most nutrient absorption occurs in the small intestine. Its large surface area, resulting from its length and protrusions called villi and microvilli, allow for a great absorptive surface into the bloodstream. Neutralization of the chyme after arrival from the acidic stomach allows the local enzymes to function. Accessory organs function in the production of necessary enzymes and bile. The pancreas makes many enzymes to break down food in the small intestine. The liver makes bile, which breaks down and emulsifies fatty acids. Any food left after the trip through the small intestine enters the large intestine. The large intestine functions to reabsorb water and produce vitamin K. The feces, or remaining waste, pass out through the anus.

HUMAN REPRODUCTIVE SYSTEM

Hormone control and development and function of male and female reproductive systems

Hormones regulate sexual maturation in humans. Humans cannot reproduce until puberty, about the age of 8-14 depending on the individual. The hypothalamus begins secreting hormones that help mature the reproductive system and develop the secondary sex characteristics. Reproductive maturity in girls occurs with their first menstruation and occurs in boys with the first ejaculation of viable sperm.

Hormones also regulate reproduction. . In males, the primary sex hormones are the androgens, with testosterone being the most important. The testes produce androgens that dictate the primary and secondary sex characteristics of the male. Female hormone patterns are cyclic and complex. Most women have a reproductive cycle length of about 28 days. The menstrual cycle is specific to the changes in the uterus. The ovarian cycle results in ovulation and occurs in parallel with the menstrual cycle. Hormones regulate this parallelism. Five hormones participate in this regulation, most notably estrogen and progesterone. Estrogen and progesterone play an important role in signaling to the uterus and the development and maintenance of the endometrium. Estrogens also dictate the secondary sex characteristics of females.

Gametogenesis, fertilization, and birth control

Gametogenesis is the production of the sperm and egg cells.

Spermatogenesis begins at puberty in the male. One spermatogonia, the diploid precursor of sperm, produces four sperm. The sperm mature in the seminiferous tubules located in the testes. **Oogenesis**, the production of egg cells (ova), is usually complete by the birth of a female. Females do not release egg cells until menstruation begins at puberty. Meiosis forms one ovum with all the cytoplasm and three polar bodies that the body reabsorbs. The ovaries store the ovum and release them each month from puberty to menopause.

Seminiferous tubules in the testes house sperm, where they mature. The epididymis, located on top of the testes, contains mature sperm. After ejaculation, the sperm travel up the **vas deferens** where they mix with semen made in the prostate and seminal vesicles and travel out the urethra.

Ovulation releases the egg into the fallopian tubes where cilia move the egg along the length of the tubes. Fertilization of the egg by the sperm normally occurs in the fallopian tube. If pregnancy does not occur, the egg passes through the uterus and is expelled through the vagina during menstruation. Levels of progesterone and estrogen stimulate menstruation. Implantation of a fertilized egg regulates the levels, stopping menstruation.

There are many methods of contraception (birth control) that affect different stages of fertilization. Chemical contraception (birth control pills) prevents ovulation by synthetic estrogen and progesterone. Several barrier methods of contraception are available. Male and female condoms block semen from contacting the egg. Sterilization is another method of birth control. Tubal ligation in women prevents eggs from entering the uterus. A vasectomy in men involves the cutting of the vas deferens. This prevents the sperm from entering the urethra. The most effective method of birth control is abstinence. Programs exist worldwide that promote abstinence, especially amongst teenagers.

PHYSICAL ACTIVITY AND FITNESS ADAPTATIONS

The structure and function of the human body adapts greatly to physical activity and exertion. When challenged with any physical task, the human body responds through a series of integrated changes in function that involve most, if not all, of its physiological systems. Movement requires activation and control of the musculoskeletal system. The cardiovascular and respiratory systems provide the ability to sustain this movement over extended periods. When the body engages in exercise training several times, each of these physiological systems undergoes specific adaptations that increase the body's efficiency and capacity.

When the body works, it makes great demand on every muscle of the body. Either the muscles have to 'shut down' or they have to do work. The heart beats faster during strenuous exercise so that it can pump more blood to the muscles, and the stomach shuts down during strenuous exercise so that it does not waste energy that the muscles need. Exercising makes the muscles work like a motor that uses up energy in order to generate force.. Muscles, also known as 'biochemical motors', use the chemical adenosine triphosphate (ATP) as an energy source.

Different types of systems, such as the glycogen-lactic acid system, help muscles perform. Such systems help in producing ATP, which is extremely vital to working muscles. Aerobic respiration, which also helps in releasing ATP, uses the fatty acids from fat reserves in muscle and helps produce ATP for a much longer period of time.

The following points summarize the process of bodily adaptation to exercise:

• Muscle cells use the ATP they have floating around in about 3 seconds.

• The phosphagen system kicks in and supplies energy for 8 to 10 seconds.

• If exercise continues longer, the glycogen-lactic acid system kicks in.

• Finally, if exercise continues, aerobic respiration takes over. This would occur in endurance events such as an 800-meter dash, marathon run, rowing, cross-country skiing, or distance skating.

Physical activity affects the cardiovascular and musculoskeletal systems the most. However, it also helps in proper functioning of metabolic, endocrine, and immune systems.

Skill 6.3   Analyze the physiological effects of moderate and vigorous physical activity during and after exercise and knows the risks associated with inactivity and the health benefits of regular participation in physical activity.

Physical activity and inactivity greatly affects many aspects of a person's life, including physical fitness abilities, general health, physical resilience, physical self-confidence, psychological well-being, and cognitive function. Regular physical activity can improve or increase these elements, while inactivity can damage or decrease these elements.

The most obvious and direct benefit of physical activity is the physical dimension, which includes fitness and general health. Regular physical activity leads to improved physical fitness, improved strength and endurance of the muscular and cardiorespiratory systems and improved function of the circulatory system. Improved function of all these systems means that the body expends far less energy is on day-to-day activities, significantly increasing overall energy levels. Conversely, a lifestyle of physical inactivity will gradually lead to a deterioration of the muscular, cardiorespiratory, and circulatory systems, which leads to decreased energy levels.

Regular physical activity also contributes to increased physical resilience. Regular physical activity coupled with sufficient rest and a healthy diet strengthens the musculoskeletal system, which makes the individual less susceptible to injury. Physical activity also tends to improve reflexes and balance, which also reduces the likelihood of injury. Conversely, and as previously mentioned, a lifestyle of physical inactivity leads to a deterioration of the same physical systems that regular exercise strengthens and also contributes to a gradual "de-sharpening" of the reflexes and balance. In sum, these changes increase the likelihood and susceptibility of the individual to injury.

The bridge between physical and psychological benefits is the physical self-confidence derived from regular physical activity. The individual's increased ability to perform physical tasks leads to growth of their sense of ability to perform any physical activity (for example, you don't have to actually climb ten flights of stairs to know that you could if you wanted to – this is very liberating, as it creates options). Conversely, a lifestyle of physical inactivity, which implies a decreased fitness level, will eat away at the individual's physical self-confidence.

Regarding psychological well-being, physical activity causes the brain to release endorphins, which function to reduce stress levels (prolonged physical endurance activities can produce levels of endorphins that induce a pleasant and healthy "runner's high"). Most physical activities also mix a degree of repetitive motion and action that requires directed attention. In combination, this can function as a sort of meditative activity. For all of these reasons, regular physical activity contributes to psychological balance and well-being and reduced stress levels. Conversely, a lifestyle of physical inactivity allows physical confidence to deteriorate and removes alternatives of stress-relief, which can contribute negatively to the individual's psychological well-being.

Finally, regular physical activity benefits the circulatory system, which improves blood flow to the brain. This, in turn, leads to increased cognitive function and mental acuity. Those who are physically inactive do not experience these benefits.

Skill 6.4   Apply knowledge of the basic components of health-related fitness and their significance in relation to physical activity, health, and fitness.

There are five health-related components of physical fitness: **cardio-respiratory or cardiovascular endurance, muscle strength, muscle endurance, flexibility, and body composition.**

Cardiovascular endurance – is the body's ability to sustain aerobic activities (activities requiring oxygen utilization) for extended periods.

Muscle strength – is the muscle groups' ability to contract and support a given amount of weight.

Muscle endurance – is the muscle groups' ability to contract continually over a period of time and support a given amount of weight.

Flexibility – is the muscle groups' ability to stretch and bend.

Body composition – is an essential measure of health and fitness. The most important aspects of body composition are body fat percentage and ratio of body fat to muscle.

Physical activity improves each of the components of physical fitness. Aerobic training improves cardiovascular endurance. Weight training, body support activities, and calisthenics increase muscular strength and endurance. Stretching improves flexibility. Finally, all types of physical activity improve body composition by increasing muscle and decreasing body fat.

Skill 6.5   Demonstrate an understanding of basic principles of physical fitness training, and know principles and benefits of warm-up and cool-down exercise procedures.

BASIC TRAINING PRINCIPLES

The **Overload Principle** is exercising at an above normal level to improve physical or physiological capacity (a higher than normal workload).

The **Specificity Principle** is overloading a particular fitness component. In order to improve a component of fitness, you must isolate and specifically work on a single component. Metabolic and physiological adaptations depend on the type of overload; hence, specific exercise produces specific adaptations, creating specific training effects.

The **Progression Principle** states that once the body adapts to the original load/stress, no further improvement of a component of fitness will occur without the addition of an additional load.

There is also a **Reversibility-of-Training Principle** in which all gains in fitness are lost with the discontinuance of a training program.

MODIFICATIONS OF OVERLOAD

We can modify overload by varying **frequency, intensity, and time**. Frequency is the number of times we implement a training program in a given period (e.g. three days per week). Intensity is the amount of effort put forth or the amount of stress placed on the body. Time is the duration of each training session.

PRINCIPLES OF OVERLOAD, PROGRESSION, AND SPECIFICITY APPLIED TO IMPROVEMENT OF HEALTH-RELATED COMPONENTS OF FITNESS

1. Cardio-respiratory Fitness:

Overloading for cardio-respiratory fitness:

- **Frequency** = minimum of 3 days/week

- **Intensity** = exercising in target heart-rate zone

- **Time** = minimum of 15 minutes

Progression for cardiovascular fitness:

- begin at a frequency of 3 days/week and work up to no more than 6 days/week

- begin at an intensity near THR threshold and work up to 80% of THR begin at 15 minutes and work up to 60 minutes

Specificity for cardiovascular fitness:

- To develop cardiovascular fitness, you must perform aerobic (with oxygen) activities for at least fifteen minutes without developing an oxygen debt. Aerobic activities include, but are not limited to brisk walking, jogging, bicycling, and swimming.

2. Muscle Strength:

Overloading for muscle strength:

- **Frequency** = every other day

- **Intensity** = 60% to 90% of assessed muscle strength

- **Time** = 3 sets of 3 - 8 repetitions (reps) (high resistance with a low number of repetitions)

Progression for muscle strength:

- begin 3 days/week and work up to every other day

- begin near 60% of determined muscle strength and work up to no more than 90% of muscle strength

- begin with 1 set with 3 reps and work up to 3 sets with 8 reps

Specificity for muscle strength:

- to increase muscle strength for a specific part(s) of the body, you must target the specific part(s) of the body

3. Muscle endurance:

Overloading for muscle endurance:

- **Frequency** = every other day

- **Intensity** = 30% to 60% of assessed muscle strength

- **Time** = 3 sets of 12 - 20 reps (low resistance with a high number of repetitions)

Progression for muscle endurance:

- begin 3 days/week and work up to every other day
- begin at 20% to 30% of muscle strength and work up to no more than 60% of muscle strength

- begin with 1 set with 12 reps and work up to 3 sets with 20 reps

Specificity for muscle endurance:

- same as muscle strength

4. Flexibility:

Overloading for flexibility:

- **Frequency**: 3 to 7 days/week

- **Intensity**: stretch muscle beyond its normal length

- **Time**: 3 sets of 3 reps holding stretch 15 to 60 seconds

Progression for flexibility:

- begin 3 days/week and work up to every day

- begin stretching with slow movement as far as possible without pain, holding at the end of the range of motion (ROM) and work up to stretching no more than 10% beyond the normal ROM

- begin with 1 set with 1 rep, holding stretches 15 seconds, and work up to 3 sets with 3 reps, holding stretches for 60 seconds

Specificity for flexibility:

- ROM is joint specific

5. Body composition:

Overloading to improve body composition:

- **Frequency**: daily aerobic exercise

- **Intensity**: low

- **Time**: approximately one hour

Progression to improve body composition:

- begin daily

- begin a low aerobic intensity and work up to a longer duration (see cardio-respiratory progression)

- begin low-intensity aerobic exercise for 30 minutes and work up to 60 minutes

Specificity to improve body composition:

- increase aerobic exercise and decrease caloric intake

TECHNIQUES AND BENEFITS OF WARMING UP AND COOLING DOWN

A warm-up should consist of 5 to 10 minutes of aerobic activity in which the participant uses the muscles needed in the activity to follow (similar movements at a lower activity). Warm-ups also include stretching of major muscle groups after the gradual warm-up.

The benefits of warming up are:

- preparing the body for physical activity

- reducing the risk of musculoskeletal injuries

- releasing oxygen from myoglobin

- warming the body's inner core

- increasing the reaction of muscles

- bringing the heart rate to an aerobic conditioning level

Cooling down is a moderate to light tapering off of a vigorous activity at the end of an exercise session.

The benefits of cooling down are:

- redistributing circulation of the blood throughout the body to prevent pooling of blood

- preventing dizziness

- facilitating the removal of lactic acid

Skill 6.6   Analyze individual variation in levels of health and fitness and know principles and techniques for designing, implementing, and maintaining individualized health and fitness plans.

Naturally, variations in levels of health and fitness exist. There is no two individual exactly alike. These variations are apparent in all areas of physical fitness including body composition, cardiovascular endurance, muscular strength and endurance, and flexibility.

Body composition describes the physical make-up of the body. The two components of body composition are fat tissue and lean tissue (i.e., muscle, bone, etc.). We can measure body mass by circumference and skinfold measurements. A more practical method of measuring body composition is the Body Mass Index (BMI). We use the BMI to assess body weight relative to height. BMI equals weight in kilograms divided by height in meters, squared (kg/m^2). Although this method does not distinguish between fat mass and muscle mass, a BMI of 25 and higher increases many health risks such as high blood pressure, high cholesterol, type 2 diabetes, heart attack and stroke. Normal values fall between 18.5 and 24.9.

Cardiovascular fitness relates to the ability to perform moderate to high intensity exercise for a prolonged period. Peak levels of cardiovascular fitness usually occur around age 20-25 and decrease by approximately 10% each decade thereafter (one percent per year). Low levels of fitness increases the risk of premature death from cardiovascular disease. High levels of fitness reduce the risk of premature death from many causes and provide many health benefits. Men often have higher levels of cardiovascular fitness than women do. Everyone should engage in cardiovascular exercise three to five days per week, for 20-60 minutes, at an intensity of 55-90% of maximum heart rate (220 – age). The mode of exercise should engage large muscle groups in a continuous, rhythmic motion. In addition, everyone should choose a mode they enjoy to increase adherence to an exercise routine.

Muscular fitness relates to how much force a muscle group can generate (strength) and how effectively the muscle group can sustain that force over a period of time (endurance). Gains in strength, muscle mass, and endurance require different training methods. Lifting heavy weights 4 to 8 repetitions per exercise encourages strength development. Lifting moderate weight 8 to 12 repetitions per exercise leads to an increase in muscle size (hypertrophy). Lifting light weights 12 to 15 repetitions per exercise develops muscular endurance. A minimum weight training regimen consists of one set of eight to twelve repetitions using ten of the primary muscle groups (four lower body, six upper body) on two non-consecutive days of the week. Generally, men show greater muscular fitness levels than women, but with age, the margin becomes smaller. Peak levels of muscular fitness occur in the second decade of life.

Flexibility is the ability of a joint to move through its range of motion (ROM). Measurements of flexibility are joint specific, so it is difficult to establish overall flexibility by just one test. Like cardiovascular and muscular fitness, flexibility decreases with age. Minimal requirements to improve flexibility include stretching each major joint to tightness, holding for 15-30 seconds, repeating each stretch 2 to 4 times per session, and engaging in flexibility training 2 to 4 days per week.

Improvement in each of these categories leads to a decreased risk of injury and disease and allows performance of normal, everyday activities with greater ease.

Strategies for enhancing adherence to these fitness programs include appropriately maintained facilities/equipment, emphasizing short-term goals, minimizing injuries, encouraging group participation, emphasizing variety and enjoyment, and recruiting support and motivation from family and friends.

GOAL SETTING

Goal setting is an effective way of achieving progress. In order to preserve and/or increase self-confidence, you and your students must set goals that are frequently reachable. One such way of achieving this is to set several small, short-term goals to attain one long-term goal. Be realistic in goal setting to increase fitness levels gradually. As students reach their goals, set more in order to continue performance improvement. Keep in mind that maintaining a current fitness level is an adequate goal provided the individual is in a healthy state. Reward your students when they reach goals. Rewards serve as motivation to reach the next goal. Also, be sure to prepare for lapses. Try to get back on track as soon as possible.

Skill 6.7   Know how to promote students' ability to assess their own fitness levels, interests, and skill levels in order to encourage participation in lifelong physical activity.

Physical education instructors can foster critical-thinking and evaluative skills in the context of physical education and health-related activities by making children active partners in the entire learning and training process. If instructors provide students with an understanding of the mechanisms (e.g. cardiorespiratory, muscular, circulatory) underlying their training (in addition to the knowledge they are given about specific training exercises), students can get more involved and think more critically about their training routines and how they could adapt them to better suit their needs.

Instructors should encourage students to employ self-assessment and self-monitoring techniques and skills. For example, they could keep a journal tracking their personal achievements – cardiorespiratory (measured in resting heart rate, active heart rate, intensity, and duration of exercise), muscular development (measured by their ability to perform callisthenic exercises). In addition, the instructor should ask children to consider questions like, "Where am I now? Where am I trying to go? What am I trying to achieve? How can I get from here to there?" This type of questioning involves the child more deeply in the learning process.

Instructors should also encourage students to explore and increase their understanding (with educator assistance) of the way that the underlying bodily systems work in relation to other disciplines. For example, students can learn about the chemistry involved in the gas and energy exchanges happening between the cardiorespiratory and circulatory system, they can learn about the biology of the digestive system and the effects of different types of nutrition on the body, and they can learn about the physics involved in energy expenditure by the muscular system.

COMPETENCY 7.0   PRINCIPLES AND ACTIVITIES FOR DEVELOPING AND MAINTAINING CARDIOVASCULAR ENDURANCE

Skill 7.1   Demonstrate knowledge of principles, skills, exercises, and **physiological processes involved in aerobic conditioning.**

PRINCIPLES AND ACTIVITIES FOR DEVELOPING AEROBIC ENDURANCE

The term aerobic refers to conditioning or exercise that requires the use of oxygen to derive energy. Aerobic conditioning is essential for fat loss, energy production, and effective functioning of the cardiovascular system. Aerobic exercise is difficult to perform for many people and participants must follow certain principles and activities in order to develop aerobic endurance.

Slow twitch muscle tissue, fueled by oxygen, powers aerobic activities. For the body to sustain aerobic activity for an extended period, the heart must pump oxygen-rich blood to the muscles of the body. When the heart tires due to insufficient cardiorespiratory fitness, the quantities of oxygen delivered to the muscles decreases to levels that cannot sustain the activity.

Other physiological processes involved in aerobic endurance include the respiratory system (which must take sufficient air into the body and efficiently supply oxygen to the blood), the blood itself (which must efficiently carry oxygen), the circulatory system (that takes blood to the muscles and then returns it to the heart), and the muscles themselves (which must efficiently extract oxygen from the blood).

Tips that aid in developing and building aerobic endurance include working out for extended periods at the target heart rate, slowly increasing aerobic exercises, exercising for three or four times per week, and taking adequate rest to help the body recover.

Exercising in the target heart rate zone for 30-45 minute periods is the most important principle in the development of aerobic endurance. Submaximal intensity activities, such as walking and slow jogging, are effective aerobic activities that improve aerobic endurance without unnecessary strain on the body.

The following is an example of a **cardiorespiratory fitness** program design:

- **mode:** aerobic activities (e.g. walking, jogging, swimming, cycling, rowing)

- **frequency:** 3 to 5 days/week

- **intensity:** 60% to 90% of maximum oxygen uptake or 60% to 80% THR

- **time:** 20 to 60 minutes of continuous or interval (non-continuous) activity (time depends on intensity level)

- **progression:** instructor adjusts prescription according to an individual's fitness level and conditioning effects.

Skill 7.2   Evaluate and select appropriate cardiovascular endurance activities for various developmental levels and purposes.

Aerobics are a fundamental component of every physical education or training program. Aerobic activities are necessary for all because they are central to weight reduction, cardiovascular fitness, muscular strength development, and performance in all sports events.

Appropriate aerobic activities for various developmental levels vary from low and moderate intensity exercises to high intensity ones. Low and moderate intensity activities include doing household work, walking, playing with children, and working on the lawn. High-intensity aerobic activities include jogging, cycling, participating in sports like ice or roller-skating, downhill skiing, and swimming. Treadmills and other equipment help create strenuous aerobic exercises.

Instructors and students must take care while undertaking such high-intensity aerobic exercises, because they can be highly strenuous and taxing on muscles, especially during the initial stages. At this beginning stage, the exercise intensity must be low. With passage of time and development towards higher stages, the student can increase the level and intensity of aerobic exercises.

Whether the goal is to develop the body's ability to undergo high levels of muscular activity or just to remain fit, there are aerobic activities suited to every developmental stage and for every person.

CARDIOVASCULAR ACTIVITIES

Walking is a good generic cardiorespiratory activity for promoting basic fitness. Instructors can incorporate it into a variety of class settings (not only physical education instructors – for example, a Biology class might include a field trip to a natural setting that would involve a great deal of walking). Walking is appropriate for practically all age groups, but can only serve as noteworthy exercise for students who lead a fairly sedentary lifestyle (athletic students who train regularly or participate in some sport will not benefit greatly from walking).

Jogging or **Running** is a classic cardiorespiratory activity in which instructors can adjust the difficulty level by modifying the running speed or the incline of the track. It is important to stress proper footwear and gradual increase of intensity to prevent overuse injuries (e.g. stress fractures or shin splints).

Bicycling is another good cardiorespiratory activity that is appropriate for most age groups. Obviously, knowing how to ride a bicycle is a prerequisite, and it is important to follow safety procedures (e.g. ensuring that students wear helmets). An additional benefit of bicycle riding is that it places less strain on the knee joints than walking or running.

Swimming is an excellent cardiorespiratory activity that has the added benefit of working more of the body's muscles, more evenly than most other exercises, without excessive resistance to any one part of the body that could result in an overuse injury. To use swimming as an educational cardiorespiratory activity, there must be qualified lifeguards present, and all students must have passed basic tests of swimming ability.

There are many alternatives for cardiorespiratory activities, like **inline skating** and **cross-country skiing**. More importantly, instructors should modify the above exercises to match the developmental needs of the students – for example, younger students should receive most of their exercise in the form of games. An instructor could incorporate running in the form of a game of tag, soccer, or a relay race.

Skill 7.3   Demonstrate knowledge of techniques for monitoring intensity, duration, and endurance levels during aerobic activities and techniques for student self-assessment of cardiovascular health and fitness.

We can measure cardiorespiratory fitness in a number of ways. The simplest way is for the students to check their resting heart rate. To do this, the students should:

- Find their pulse in any point of the body where an artery is close to the surface (e.g., wrist [radial artery], neck [Carotid artery], or the elbow [brachial artery]).
- Count how many heartbeats they feel in one minute's time.

We usually express resting heart rate in "beats per minute" (bpm). For males, the norm is about 70 bpm. For women, the norm is about 75 bpm. This rate varies between people and the reference range is normally between 60 bpm and 100 bpm. It is important to note that resting heart rates can be significantly lower in athletes, and significantly higher in the obese.

Another way to measure cardiorespiratory fitness is by having students determine their Target Heart Rate (THR). The Target Heart Rate, or Training Heart Rate, is a desired range of heart rate reached during aerobic exercise, which allows a student's heart and lungs to receive the most benefit from a workout. Students should check their heart rates frequently during activity to ensure they train within their THR zones.

Finally, another useful technique for self-assessment, which instructors can combine with the pulse-rate monitoring mentioned above, is to instruct the students to keep a training log. The indicators tracked in the log may be very concrete (e.g. heart rate during exertion, duration of exertion, or resting heart rate and blood pressure), or more subjective (e.g. how students feel during and after their workouts). Instructors should also encourage older students to devise their own training benchmarks based on their knowledge of cardiorespiratory fitness training processes and their personal fitness goals.

TARGET HEART RATE ZONE AND HEART RATE MONITORS

The target heart rate (THR) zone is another common measure of aerobic exercise intensity. Participants find their THR and attempt to raise their heart rate to the desired level for a certain period of time. Students can use electronic heart rate monitors that constantly track heart rate during physical activity. Such monitors often alert students when they enter and leave their THR, allowing for adjustment of activity level. There are three ways to calculate the target heart rate.

1. METs (maximum oxygen uptake), which is 60% to 90% of functional capacity.

2. Karvonean Formula = [Maximum heart rate (MHR) – Resting heart rate (RHR)] x intensity + RHR.   MHR= 220 - Age
Intensity = Target Heart Range (which is 60% - 80% of MHR - RHR + RHR).

THR = (MHR - RHR) x .60 + RHR to (MHR - RHR) x .80 + RHR

3. Cooper's Formula to determine target heart range is:
THR = (220 - AGE) x .60 to (220 - AGE) x .80.

PERCEIVED EXERTION

Perceived exertion is another method of monitoring the intensity of aerobic activities. Participants describe how hard they feel they are working based on physical sensations such as muscle fatigue, sweating, heart rate, and breathing rate. The Borg Scale is a quantitative rating system of perceived exertion. The following is an example of the Borg Scale, which ranges from 6 to 20, with corresponding descriptions.

6	No exertion at all
7	Extremely light
9	Very light (e.g. walking slowly at own pace for several minutes)
11	Light
13	Somewhat hard
15	Hard (heavy)
17	Very hard (i.e. a healthy person can still continue, but with great difficulty)

| 19 | Extremely hard (i.e. most strenuous exercise most have ever experienced) |
| 20 | Maximum exertion |

Skill 7.4   Analyze potential health risks involved in cardiovascular endurance training (e.g., environmental conditions) and know risk reduction techniques.

Environmental conditions can be very dangerous and potentially life threatening. Athletes must exercise caution when exercising in extremely hot, cold, and/or humid conditions. High humidity can slow the body's release of heat from the body, increasing the chances of heat related illnesses. Hydration in hot environments is very important. Drink two cups of water two hours before exercise and hydrate regularly during exercise at the same rate of the amount of sweat that is lost. In exercise lasting a long period of time, it is possible to drink too much water, resulting in a condition known as hyponutremia, or low sodium content in the body. Water cannot replace the sodium and other electrolytes lost through sweat. Drinking sports drinks can solve this problem. Cold environments can also be a problem when exercising. The human body works more efficiently at its normal temperature. Wear many layers of clothing to prevent cold-related illnesses such as frostbite and hypothermia. In populations suffering from asthma, wearing a cloth over the mouth during exercise increases the moisture of the air breathed in and can help prevent an attack.

Skill 7.5   Apply knowledge of anatomy, kinesiology, and physiological principles to design, adapt, and modify activities that promote cardiovascular endurance.

Cardiovascular fitness relates to the ability to perform moderate to high intensity exercise for a prolonged period. Performance of this type of exercise relies on the function of the respiratory, cardiovascular, and skeletal muscle systems. The function of the respiratory system is to take oxygen into the lungs. The function of the cardiovascular system is the delivery of deoxygenated blood to the lungs and oxygenated blood out to the rest of the body. The pumping of the heart accomplishes this task. Finally, the skeletal muscle absorbs the oxygen from the blood and uses it to produce energy.

To improve cardiovascular endurance, one must perform continuous and rhythmic exercise involving large muscle groups for at least 20 minutes per day, at least three days per week, at an intensity of at least 55% of maximum heart rate. As endurance improves, the duration, frequency, and intensity of exercise must increase, as the cardiovascular system will adapt to training.

Examples of activities promoting enhancement of cardiovascular endurance include, but are not limited to, walking, running, cycling, swimming, stair climbing, dancing, skating, and skiing. Certain sports such as basketball, tennis, hockey, and racquetball also have the potential to increase cardiovascular endurance provided they are performed at a sufficient duration and intensity. Factors involved in choosing a mode of exercise include level of enjoyment and status of health/injury. Instructors should allow individuals to choose the modes of exercise they enjoy in order to increase adherence to an exercise program. Orthopedic complications such as sprains, strains, arthritis, and osteoporosis can contraindicate certain exercises like walking, running, and stair climbing. Those with orthopedic complications should participate in non-weight bearing activities, such as swimming and cycling.

An important factor to understand about cardiovascular fitness is the specificity of training principle. This principle states that performance of a certain mode of exercise will not necessarily carry over to other modes. For example, let's say a person trains by **cycling** for 30 minutes a day, five days a week, at an intensity of 75% of their maximum heart rate. The results from such training when performing a **running** program at the same duration, frequency, and intensity do not fully transfer. In other words, the cyclist will not necessarily be able to perform a running program with the same elements of frequency, intensity, and time.

COMPETENCY 8.0   PRINCIPLES AND ACTIVITIES FOR DEVELOPING AND MAINTAINING FLEXIBILITY, POSTURE, AND MUSCULAR STRENGTH AND ENDURANCE

Skill 8.1   Demonstrate knowledge of principles, skills, exercises, and proper form for promoting strength and endurance of the muscles of the abdomen, lower back, upper body, trunk, and legs.

Muscular strength is the ability of the muscles to exert force during an activity. It also helps the muscles to perform without fatigue. The activities that can help improve muscular endurance include walking, jogging, bicycling or dancing. Muscle strength is a measure of how much you can lift one time in a maximal effort situation. Larger people tend to have an edge over smaller people in terms of pounds lifted. The exercises that can help build muscular strength are push-ups (keep body straight, one leg raised), back lunges (keep tummy tight, back straight, head up), and two-point oblique (lie on back with back pushed into floor, right hand behind right ear, right knee bent with foot flat on floor).

The following is an example of a **muscle strength** program design:

- **mode:** weight training (isotonic/dynamic)

- **frequency:** minimum 3 days/week to a maximum of every other day

- **intensity:** 60% to 90% of maximum muscle strength (1-RM)

- **time:** 3 sets with 3 to 8 reps and a 60 second rest interval

- **progression:** increase workload (overload) when individual can perform 15 reps at 10 RM level

The following is an example of a **muscle endurance** program design:

- **mode:** weight training

- **frequency:** minimum 3 days/week up to every other day

- **intensity:** 30% to 60% of maximum muscle strength (1-RM)

- **time:** 3 sets with 12 to 20 reps, or until point of muscle fatigue with a 15 to 60 second rest interval

- **progression:** increase workload (overload) periodically based on number of continuous repetitions

EXERCISES THAT BENEFIT THE MAJOR MUSCLE GROUPS OF THE BODY

Some of the major muscle groups of the body important to physical fitness are trapezius, deltoid, pectoralis, latissimus dorsi (lats), obliques, abdominals (abs), biceps, quadriceps, hamstrings, adductors, triceps, biceps, and gluteals or gluteus maximus (gluts).

Dumbbell Shoulder Shrug
(Trapezius)

Seated Bent-Over Rear Deltoid Raise
(Rear Deltoids)

Lying Low-Pulley One-Arm Chest
(Lateral Pectorals)

Flat Dumbbell Press
(Pectorals)

Medium-Grip Front-to-Rear Lat Pull Down
(Lats)

Straight-Arm Close-Grip Lat Pull Down
(Lats)

Dumbbell Side Bend
(Obliques)

Seated Barbell Twist
(Obliques)

Leg Pull-In
(Lower Abdominals)

Jackknife Sit-Up
(Upper and Lower Abdominals)

Standing Alternated Dumbbell Curl
(Biceps)

Standing Medium-Grip Barbell Curl
(Biceps)

Standing Close-Grip Easy-Curl-Bar Triceps Curl
(Triceps)

Standing Bent-Over One-Arm-Dumbbell Triceps Extension
(Triceps)

Flat-Footed Medium-Stance Barbell Half-Squat
(Thighs)

Freehand Front Lunge
(Thighs and Hamstrings)

Thigh Curl on Leg Extension Machine
(Hamstrings)

One-at-a-Time Thigh Curl on Leg Extension Machine
(Hamstrings)

Hip Abduction
(Hips)

Hip Adduction
(Inner Thigh)

Standing Toe Raise on Wall Calf Machine
(Main Calf Muscles)

Standing Barbell Toe Raise
(Main Calf Muscles)

Hip Extension
(Hips and Thighs)

Hip Flexion
(Hip Flexors)

Skill 8.2   Demonstrate knowledge of principles, skills, exercises, and proper form for promoting good posture and flexibility of major joints and areas of the body.

Flexibility is the range of motion around a joint or muscle. Flexibility has two major components: static and dynamic. Static flexibility is the range of motion without a consideration for speed of movement. Dynamic flexibility is the use of the desired range of motion at a desired velocity. These movements are useful for most athletes.

Good flexibility can help prevent injuries during all stages of life and can keep an athlete safe. To improve flexibility, you can lengthen muscles through activities such as swimming, a basic stretching program, or Pilates. These activities all improve your muscles' range of motion. While joints also consist of ligaments and tendons, muscles are the main target of flexibility training. Muscles are the most elastic component of joints while ligaments and tendons are less elastic and resist elongation. Overstretching tendons and ligaments can weaken joint stability and lead to injury.

Coaches, athletes and sports medicine personnel use stretching methods as part of their training routine for athletes. They help the body to relax and to warm-up for more intense fitness activities.

The following is an example of a **flexibility** program design:

- **mode:** stretching

- **frequency:** 3 to 7 days/week

- **intensity:** just below individual's threshold of pain

- **time:** 3 sets with 3 reps holding stretches 15 to 30 seconds, with a 60 rest interval between sets

Flexibility training is perhaps the most undervalued component of conditioning. Dynamic flexibility is the ability to perform dynamic movements within the full range of motion of the specified joint. Static active flexibility refers to the ability to stretch an antagonist muscle using only the tension in the antagonist muscle. Static-passive flexibility is the ability to hold a stretch using body weight or some other external force.

Dynamic stretching is generally very safe and very effective for warming up muscle groups and moderately improving flexibility. When performing dynamic stretches, participants must be careful to avoid sudden, jerky movements.

Static stretching is also safe, if the participant warms up the muscles prior to stretching. Because cold muscles are less elastic, static stretching without adequate warm up can lead to injury. Static stretching is very effective in increasing muscle flexibility.

Isometric, PNF, and ballistic stretching are more advanced techniques that require extreme caution and supervision. Most physical trainers believe ballistic stretching, bouncing into stretches, is ineffective and dangerous. Most trainers do not recommend ballistic stretching. PNF and isometric stretching are effective in certain situations such as rehabilitation and advanced training, but require close supervision.

DEVELOPMENTAL PROGRESSIONS

When starting any exercise program, the best way to begin is by stretching or flexing muscles as a warm up. This will allow the body to adapt to exercise. Flexibility activities are necessary for any physical training or exercising program as they help prevent against injuries.

Activities that can improve flexibility include stretching, bending, doing yoga, dancing, martial arts, and even other muscle work that is gentle and not strenuous at all. The different classifications of stretching and flexibility exercises include proprioceptive neuromuscular facilitation (PNF), static, dynamic, and partner resistance.

Static and dynamic stretching are the two most traditional classifications of flexibility training. Static stretching involves holding a position. In other words, the participant stretches to the farthest point possible and holds for several seconds. Dynamic stretching, on the other hand, involves slow, steady movements through a range of motion. Examples of dynamic stretches include arm and leg swings. Both static and dynamic stretching is suitable to individuals of all developmental levels. Static stretching is effective for improving range of flexibility. A warm up is necessary prior to static stretching to reduce the risk of injury. Dynamic stretching is an excellent warm up in itself because it involves slow, gradual movements.

Proprioceptive neuromuscular facilitation (PNF) is a more advanced form of flexibility training that combines traditional stretching with muscle contraction. Particularly effective for rehabilitation, PNF can also target specific muscle groups and increase muscular strength. PNF is best suited for individuals training at higher levels of fitness. PNF is not suitable for children or any persons whose bones are still growing.

Finally, in partner resistance stretching a partner applies resistance to a specific body part to stretch the targeted muscle actively. This is a more advanced technique that is a key component of PNF. Partner resistance stretching is best suited for more advanced athletes and caution is necessary to avoid injury.

Because the partner cannot feel the stretch, he or she must communicate with the participant to prevent overextension.

Skill 8.3   Demonstrate knowledge of procedures for evaluating muscular strength and endurance and flexibility.

EVALUATING MUSCULAR STRENGTH AND ENDURANCE

The standard procedure for evaluating muscular strength and endurance is measurement of repetitions performed and/or amount of weight used for various resistance exercises. For example, the instructor may ask students to perform as many pull-ups as they can or bench press a given weight as many times as they can. Comparing individual results to age based and size based norms allows instructors to tailor fitness programs to meet the needs of each student.

Muscle strength tests – dynamometers (hand, back, and leg), cable tensiometer, the 1-RM Test (repetition maximum: bench press, standing press, arm curl, and leg press), bench-squat, sit-ups (one sit up holding a weight plate behind the neck), and lateral pull-down.

Muscle endurance tests – squat-thrust, pull-ups, sit-ups, lateral pull-down, bench-press, arm curl, push-ups, and dips.

EVALUATING FLEXIBILITY

Standard methods of evaluating flexibility include the sit and reach test and having students try to touch their hands behind their backs. Instructors can devise additional flexibility tests to evaluate the range of motion of specific joints. In these cases, the tests should reflect practical function.

Flexibility tests – sit and reach, Kraus-Webber Floor Touch Test, trunk extension, forward bend of trunk, Leighton Flexometer, shoulder rotation/flexion, and goniometer.

Skill 8.4   Apply knowledge of anatomy, kinesiology, and physiological principles to design, adapt, modify, evaluate, and select appropriate activities for improving muscular strength and endurance, flexibility, and posture.

MUSCULAR STRENGTH AND ENDURANCE ACTIVITIES

Possessing the strength and ability to overcome any resistance in one single effort or in repeated efforts over a period of time is muscular strength and endurance. It represents the ability to complete a heavy task in a single effort. Muscular strength and endurance not only helps in keeping body ailments in check, but also in enabling better performance in any sporting event.

Most fitness experts regard calisthenics as the best form of exercises in order to increase muscular development and strength. Although calisthenics are good beginning exercises, later on participants should complement them with progressive resistance training so that there will be an increase in bone mass and connective tissue strength. Such a combination would also help in minimizing any damages or injuries that are apt to occur at the beginning or initial training stages.

Besides calisthenics and progressive resistance training, aerobics can also help in maintaining muscular strength and endurance.

Muscular strength is the maximum amount of force that one can generate in an isolated movement. Muscular endurance is the ability of the muscles to perform a submaximal task repeatedly or to maintain a submaximal muscle contraction for extended periods. Body-support activities (e.g. push-ups and sit-ups) and callisthenic activities (e.g. rope jumping) are good exercises for young students or beginners of all ages. Such exercises use multiple muscle groups and have minimal risk of injury. At more advanced levels of development and for those students interested in developing higher levels of strength and muscle mass, weight lifting is the optimal activity.

To improve muscular strength and endurance a student can:

- Train with free weights
- Perform exercises that use an individual's body weight for resistance (e.g., push-ups, sit-ups, dips, etc.)
- Do strength training exercises two times per week that incorporate all major muscle groups

COMPONENTS OF FLEXIBILITY

To effectively select, adapt, and modify flexibility activities, instructors must understand the components of flexibility. The components of flexibility are muscles, joints, tendons, and ligaments. Each of these components has unique characteristics and limitations that we must consider when planning a flexibility training program.

Muscles – Muscle is the body's contractile tissue. Its function is to produce force and cause motion (movement within the internal organs and, especially for our purposes, locomotion). Muscles are generally split into Type I (slow twitch) which carries more oxygen and sustains aerobic activity, and Type II (fast twitch), which carries less oxygen and powers anaerobic activity. Muscles that are too short can limit flexibility, and failing to stretch after resistance training can cause the muscles to shorten. The stretch reflex, whereby the opposing muscle will contract in order to prevent over-expansion, can also curtail flexibility (this contraction is generally premature, and part of flexibility training is to re-train the opposing muscle not to contract as quickly).

Joints – Joints are the locations at which two bones make contact. Their construction allows movement and provides functional mechanical support. We can classify joints as fibrous (connected by collagen), cartilaginous (connected by cartilage), or synovial (capped by cartilage, supported by ligaments, enveloped by the synovial membrane, and filled with synovial fluid). The limits of its range of motion, imposed by the joint's physical structure or, more often, by lack of flexibility of the muscles, ligaments and tendons, define a joint's flexibility.

Ligaments – A ligament is a short band of tough fibrous connective tissue composed mainly of long, stringy collagen fibers. They connect bones to other bones to form a joint. Ligaments can limit the mobility of a joint or prevent certain movements altogether. Ligaments are slightly elastic and under tension, they will gradually lengthen. Ligaments that are too short may curtail flexibility by limiting a joint's range of motion.

Tendons – A tendon (or sinew) is a tough band of fibrous connective tissue (similar in structure to ligaments) that connects muscle to bone or muscle to muscle. Tendons are composed mainly of water, type-I collagen, and cells called tenocytes. Most of the strength of tendons stems from the parallel, hierarchical arrangement of densely packed collagen fibrils, which have great strength, little extensibility, and no ability to contract.

POSTURE AND BODY MECHANICS

Posture is the position of the body while standing, sitting, or lying down. Posture is extremely important as it keeps bones and the joints aligned and ensures the proper use of muscles. When this is the case, a body will use less energy and fatigue will be less likely. Good posture allows the body to use the strongest muscles for the most difficult tasks, preventing undue strain on muscles and bones. Cornerstones of good posture include proper alignment of the vertebral column, and releasing unnecessary tension in the muscles of the body (e.g. tensed shoulders).

Developing a critical image of the body is one of the first steps in assessing posture. We need a comprehensive view of the body and how it moves as a result of posture, to evaluate the body accurately.

Here are some key points to look for while assessing posture:
- Slouching leads to neck, shoulder, and backaches as well as joint stiffness.
- First, you must exercise. To help your body stand straighter and taller, you have to strengthen the abs and back muscles.
- You can look in the mirror while standing. The ears, shoulders, hips, knees, and ankles should be in a straight line.
- Keep you knees at hip level when sitting.
- Sit as far back against the back of the chair as possible.

When sleeping, always sleep on a firm mattress on your side and never on your stomach. When bending to lift and carry heavy objects, bend from the knees, not the waist, and keep the back straight. Bending from the knees places the burden on the legs and reduces strain on the lower back.

CORRECTING POOR POSTURE

An imbalance of strength between opposing muscles can cause poor posture. An important step toward rectifying poor posture is to strengthen the muscles used to hold the body in the proper way. A lack of flexibility in key muscles can also cause poor posture (whereby the student would feel strain to maintain correct posture). In this case, the student must stretch the appropriate muscles.

Proper posture is also important during exertion, for example when lifting and carrying. You should utilize the strong muscles of the legs, rather than the weaker muscles of the lower back, when carrying heavy objects. Thus, instructors should teach students that when bending to lift something, they should keep their backs straight and bend with their knees. A helpful visualization tool for students is to have them imagine the spine as an arrow, with the arrowhead at the base of the spine. Bad posture tends to point the arrow backwards, whereas good posture will point the arrow down.

Skill 8.5   Apply knowledge of principles, safety practices, and equipment for progressive-resistance exercise.

The practice of progressive resistance is an integral part of individual physical development and training programs. As with all other forms of exercise, participants should always follow certain principles and safety practices when performing progressive-resistance exercises.

As a safety precaution, instructors should formulate a health or medical questionnaire for students to complete. This can serve as a screening tool before enrolling a student into a progressive-resistance program. When beginning a weight-training program, novices should not attempt to lift too much weight.

Other principles and guidelines that participants should follow include:
- Warm-up prior to performing resistance exercises
- Gradually increase the number of repetitions for each exercise
- Exercise at least two days and receive adequate rest to achieve proper muscle development
- Perform exercises in a controlled manner
- Perform each exercise through a functional range of motion
- Work in conjunction with instructors who provide adequate feedback and guidance

Apart from the aforementioned principles, other basic principles of progressive resistance training include careful monitoring of types of lifts, intensity, volume, and variety of lifts, and taking adequate rest for recovery.

The equipment used for progressive resistance training or exercise include fit strips, dumbbells or barbells, and weight machines. Circuit training involves engaging in a variety of fitness exercises to achieve a full-body workout.

Partner-Resistance Exercises

For partner-resistance exercises, instructors should instruct students to pair-up with classmates of comparable size and strength, to ensure that the activity is productive and both training partners can apply sufficient resistance. Safety procedures for partner-resistance activities include properly demonstrating the required activity and clarifying to students that excessive competitiveness (to the extent of risking damage to another student) is not acceptable. In partner-resistance activities, the paired students serve as spotters for each other.

Weight Training

Weight training involves the use of weights (e.g. barbells or dumbbells) to create resistance to physical motion of body parts. In the case of weight training, properly demonstrating the required activity is fundamental, as the physical weights can present a heightened possibility for injuries. Instructors should instruct students to err on the side of less weight when unsure how much to use. A spotter should monitor students at all times. For students to make educated decisions about weight training (always under supervision), they must understand the risks and benefits of weight training for personal muscular strength and endurance development.

Circuit Training

Athletes use circuit training to increase the efficiency and intensity of a training routine by alternating exercises that target different muscle groups instead of alternating exercises with rest-periods. This form of workout promotes muscular endurance development, but is more taxing on the students. Only those students who already exercising regularly and have proven their ability to remain disciplined and follow directions should attempt circuit training.

Proper Technique

Instructors should stress proper exercise technique at all times, especially with beginners to prevent development of bad habits. Whether it is weightlifting, running, or stretching, participants should not force any body part beyond the normal range of motion. Pain is a good indicator of overextension. Living by the phrase, "No pain, no gain", is potentially dangerous. Participants should use slow and controlled movements. In addition, participants must engage in a proper warm-up and cool-down before and after exercise. When lifting weights, lifters should always have a partner. A spotter can help correct the lifter's technique and help lift the weight to safety if the lifter is unable to do so. A partner can also offer encouragement and motivation. Flexibility is an often overlooked, yet important, part of exercise that can play a key role in injury prevention. Participants should perform stretching exercises after each workout session.

Skill 8.6   Know how to determine appropriate intensity, duration, and frequency for training.

To achieve maximum progress and gain the full benefit of fitness training, we must train at an appropriate level and balance training with adequate sleep and rest. Sleep gives the body a break from the normal tasks of daily living. During sleep, the body performs many important cleansing and restoration tasks. The immune and excretory systems clear waste and repair cellular damage that accumulates in the body each day. Similarly, the body requires adequate rest and sleep to build and repair muscles. Without adequate rest, even the most strenuous exercise program will not produce muscular development.

There are specific guidelines that coaches and athletes should follow when implementing a training program. The following is an example of the application of the fitness principles of overload, progression, and specificity to muscular strength and endurance development program design.

Overloading for muscle strength:

- **Frequency** = every other day,

- **Intensity** = 60% to 90% of assessed muscle strength;

- **Time** = 3 sets of 3 - 8 reps (high resistance with a low number of repetitions).

Progression for muscle strength:

- begin 3/days week and work up to every other day,

- begin near 60% of determined muscle strength and work up to no more than 90% of muscle strength
- begin with 1 set with 3 reps and work up to 3 sets with 8 reps.

Specificity for muscle strength:

- to increase muscle strength for a specific part(s) of the body, we must target that/those body part(s).

MUSCLE ENDURANCE:

Overloading for muscle endurance:

- **Frequency** = every other day

- **Intensity** = 30% to 60% of assessed muscle strength

- **Time** = 3 sets of 12 - 20 reps (low resistance with a high number of repetitions)

Progression for muscle endurance:

- begin 3 days/week and work up to every other day

- begin at 20% to 30% of muscle strength and work up to no more than 60% of muscle strength

- begin with 1 set with 12 reps and work up to 3 sets with 20 reps

Specificity for muscle endurance:

- same as muscle strength

Skill 8.7   **Evaluate the safety and effectiveness of various exercises and types of training for promoting muscular strength and endurance, flexibility, and good posture, including contraindicated exercises and body positions.**

SAFETY AND EFFECTIVENESS – MUSCULAR STRENGTH AND ENDURANCE ACTIVITIES

SEE Skills 8.4 and 8.5

EFFECTIVENESS – FLEXIBILITY ACTIVITIES

SEE Skill 8.2

SAFETY – FLEXIBILITY ACTIVITIES

Safety and proper form are important considerations when engaging in flexibility exercises. The following is a list of rules that participants should follow when performing stretches:

- Always warm up before stretching. Next, perform light to moderate cardiovascular activity prior to stretching to increase muscle elasticity – stretching while "cold" can cause injury because the muscles are tight and less elastic

- Stop if you feel pain. Stretching should not cause acute pain. Also, mild discomfort or a mild pulling sensation is acceptable

- Move into each stretch slowly and steadily – do not bounce

- Avoid "locking" joints by completely straightening them during stretches – always allow a small amount of bend when stretching

- Relax the shoulders, hands, and feet while stretching

- Maintain proper posture

INDICATED AND CONTRAINDICATED EXERCISES AND BODY POSITIONS

Contraindicated exercises and body positions in physical education activities are those that could result in injury. This includes exercises that may result in injury if performed incorrectly, where it is difficult to execute the technique properly without experience and careful supervision. Exercises that participants should avoid include sit-ups and any exercise in which the knee exceeds a 90-degree angle.

Participants should avoid sit-ups because they do not work the abdominal muscles. Instead sit ups emphasize sitting up instead of pulling the sternum towards the pelvis and the hip flexors do most of the work. More significantly, sit-ups can damage the lower back because when the abdominal muscles contract, they attempt to round the lower back, whereas contraction of the hip flexors encourages an exaggerated arch. This opposite motion creates a grinding effect on the lowest vertebrae, which can eventually lead to chronic lower back pain.

The reason why exercises should never involve bending the knee in excess of a 90-degree angle is that bending it further puts the knee in a position where it can not safely bear weight, and greatly increases the chance of injury. Participants should also avoid exercises that involve twisting the knee. It is better to rotate the foot on the ball or heel than to twist the knee.

Indicated exercises and body positions (i.e. those that participants should use) in physical education activities are safe and they offer the maximum benefit to the student's physical development. These exercises are easy to perform and target major muscle groups. Good example exercises include push-ups, pull-ups, and abdominal crunches.

COMPETENCY 9.0   HEALTH AND WELLNESS CONCEPTS, INCLUDING
THOSE RELATED TO NUTRITION, WEIGHT
CONTROL, STRESS MANAGEMENT, AND WAYS IN
WHICH BEHAVIORS INFLUENCE HEALTH AND
WELLNESS

Skill 9.1   Demonstrate knowledge of basic principles of nutrition and
weight management and ways in which diet and exercise
patterns affect physical performance and personal health and
well-being.

Exercise and diet maintain proper body weight by equalizing caloric intake to
caloric output.

Nutrition and exercise are closely related concepts important to student health.
An important responsibility of physical education instructors is to teach students
about proper nutrition and exercise and how they relate to each other. The two
key components of a healthy lifestyle are consumption of a balanced diet and
regular physical activity. Nutrition can affect physical performance. Proper
nutrition produces high energy levels and allows for peak performance.
Inadequate or improper nutrition can impair physical performance and lead to
short-term and long-term health problems (e.g. depressed immune system and
heart disease, respectively). Regular exercise improves overall health. Benefits
of regular exercise include a stronger immune system, stronger muscles, bones,
and joints, reduced risk of premature death, reduced risk of heart disease,
improved psychological well-being, and weight management.

NUTRITION AND WEIGHT CONTROL

Identify the components of nutrition

The components of nutrition are **carbohydrates, proteins, fats, vitamins,
minerals, and water.**

Carbohydrates – the main source of energy (glucose) in the human diet. The
two types of carbohydrates are simple and complex. Complex carbohydrates
have greater nutritional value because they take longer to digest, contain dietary
fiber, and do not excessively elevate blood sugar levels. Common sources of
carbohydrates are fruits, vegetables, grains, dairy products, and legumes.

Proteins – are necessary for growth, development, and cellular function. The
body breaks down consumed protein into component amino acids for future use.
Major sources of protein are meat, poultry, fish, legumes, eggs, dairy products,
grains, and legumes.

Fats – a concentrated energy source and important component of the human body. The different types of fats are saturated, monounsaturated, and polyunsaturated. Polyunsaturated fatty acids contain multiple carbon-carbon double bonds. Thus, there is room for two or more hydrogens. Polyunsaturated fats are healthier than saturated fats. Common sources of saturated fats include dairy products, meat, coconut oil, and palm oil. Common sources of unsaturated fats include nuts, most vegetable oils, and fish.

Vitamins and minerals – Vitamins and minerals are organic substances that the body requires in small quantities for proper functioning. People acquire vitamins and minerals in their diets and in supplements. Important vitamins include A, B, C, D, E, and K. Important minerals include calcium, phosphorus, magnesium, potassium, sodium, chlorine, and sulfur.

Water – makes up 55 – 75% of the human body Water is essential for most bodily functions. Also, water is attained through foods and liquids.

Nutritional requirements *vary from person-to-person.* General guidelines for meeting adequate nutritional needs are: *no more than 30% total caloric intake from fats* (preferably 10% from saturated fats, 10% from monounsaturated fats, 10% from polyunsaturated fats), *no more than 15% total caloric intake from protein* (complete), *and* at least *55% of caloric intake from carbohydrates* (mainly complex carbohydrates).

Exercise and diet help maintain proper body weight by equalizing caloric intake and caloric output.

BODY COMPOSITION MANAGEMENT

It is vital to analyze procedures, activities, resources, and benefits involved in developing and maintaining healthy levels of body composition. Maintaining a healthy body composition allows an individual to move freely and to obtain a certain pattern that is necessary for a specific activity. Furthermore, maintaining a healthy body composition is positively related with long-term health and resistance to disease and sickness.

The total weight of an individual is a combination of bones, ligaments, tendons, organs, fluids, muscles and fat. Because muscle weighs three times more than fat per unit of volume, a person who exercises often gains muscle. This could cause an individual to be smaller physically, but weigh more than he/she appears to weigh.

The only proven method for maintaining a healthy body composition is following a healthy diet and engaging in regular exercise. A healthy diet emphasizes fruits, vegetables, whole grains, unsaturated fats, and lean protein, and minimizes saturated fat and sugar consumption. Such a program of nutrition and exercise helps balance caloric intake and output, thus preventing excessive body fat production.

Skill 9.2   Know principles and techniques for evaluating body composition and identify appropriate activities and strategies for developing and maintaining a healthy body composition.

Body composition includes the relative amount of fat, bone, and other vital parts of the body. The measurement of body composition allows for the estimation of body tissues, organs, and their distribution in a living person without inflicting harm. It is important to recognize that there is no measurement method that is error-free. Rather, the principle is to make every individual aware of body composition evaluation techniques and the fact that monitoring body composition is an exemplary method for maintaining a maximum level of physical fitness. The different methods of evaluating body composition include skinfold tests, electronic impedance, and body mass index.

Skinfold tests estimate body fat percentage by measuring the thickness of skinfolds at specific sights on the body with calipers. While skinfold tests are not a valid measurement of body fat percentage, they are useful in monitoring progress in body fat reduction.

Electronic impedance is a technique that estimates body fat percentage by measuring the conductive potential of the body. A bioimpedance meter sends a small electrical current through the body and measures conductive potential. Lean tissue (i.e. muscle, bone, ligaments) are more conductive than fat tissue because of the higher water content.

Body mass index (BMI) is a measure of body fat based on height and weight. BMI is a generic measurement that is not specific to the individual. BMI labels individuals as underweight, normal, overweight, or obese. While BMI is a useful tool in estimating body fat and determining a target weight, it can overestimate fatness in muscular or athletic people.

BODY COMPOSITION DEVELOPMENT AND MAINTENANCE

Development and maintenance of a healthy body composition involves consumption of a balanced diet and regular physical activity. Both strength training and aerobic exercise are important for body composition maintenance.

The following is an example of a **body composition** program design:

- **mode:** combining aerobic exercise and weight training and a moderate reduction of caloric intake

- **frequency:** minimum of 3 days/week; however, daily is best

- **intensity:** low intensity, long duration

- **time:** 45 to 60 minutes of aerobic activity; 3 sets with a minimum of 6 reps for weights every other day

- **progression:** periodically increase as individual improves

Skill 9.3 **Analyze the effects of various factors on physical performance and on health and demonstrate knowledge of techniques and principles for evaluating personal health risk factors.**

The effect of factors such as gender, age, environment, nutrition, heredity and substance abuse is crucial in understanding adolescent fitness performance. Girls mature earlier than boys do, but boys quickly catch up and grow larger and stronger. Age, combined with maturity level, influences a child's physical strength, flexibility, and coordination. Good nutrition positively influences the quality of a child's physical activity level, while poor nutrition has the opposite effect. Sleep gives the body a break from the normal tasks of daily living. During sleep, the body performs many important cleansing and restoration tasks. The immune and excretory systems clear waste and repair cellular damage that accumulates in the body each day. Lack of rest and sleep leaves the body vulnerable to infection and disease. Adverse environmental conditions such as high heat or poor air quality strongly affect activity level. Students that inherit favorable physical characteristics will perform better and with more ease than those who aren't so fortunate. Substance abuse of any sort – alcohol, tobacco, or drugs – is a detriment to physical performance.

Dealing with factors that are out of the teacher's control requires both structure and flexibility. When necessary, make adjustments amongst the students and/or the activity. For example, when teaching how to throw a softball, don't hesitate to pair girls with boys if their maturity and strength levels are similar. If the distance is too far for some pairs, move them closer. If some pairs are more advanced, challenge them by increasing the partner's distance while continuing to work on accuracy and speed. Add a personal challenge to see how many times they can toss without dropping the ball. Finally, having more advanced students teach their peers that aren't as competent will benefit all students.

CRITICAL HEALTH RISK FACTORS

The Centers for Disease Control (CDC) has identified six critical health behaviors among youths and an additional six important health topics. The six critical health behaviors include Alcohol and Drug Use, Injury and Violence (including suicide), Tobacco Use, Nutrition, Physical Activity, and Sexual Risk Behaviors. Generally, people establish these behaviors during childhood, the behaviors are inter-related, and they are preventable. Besides causing serious health problems, they also contribute to educational and social problems, including failure to graduate from high school, unemployment, and criminal behavior.

Alcohol and Drug Use - Alcohol abuse is the third leading preventable cause of death in the United States (4% of the total deaths in 2000), and is a factor in approximately 41% of all deaths from motor vehicle crashes.

Injury and Violence - Injury and violence is the leading cause of death among youth aged 10-24 years: motor vehicle crashes (37% of all deaths), all other unintentional injuries (16%), homicide (18%), and suicide (13%).

Tobacco Use - Every day about 4,000 American youth aged 12–17 years try their first cigarette. The CDC estimates that smoking causes 435,000 deaths each year in the United States.

Nutrition - Almost 80% of young people do not eat the recommended servings of fruits and vegetables. Nearly 9 million youth in the United States aged 6–19 years are overweight.

Physical Activity - Participation in physical activity declines as children get older. Overall, in 2005, 36% of 9-12 graders had participated in at least 60 minutes per day of physical activity. Nearly 37% of 9th graders, but only 33% of 12th graders, participated in 60 minutes of physical activity on a regular basis.

Sexual Risk Behaviors - Each year, there are approximately 19 million new STD infections in the United States, and almost half of them are among youth aged 15 to 24. 34% of young women become pregnant at least once before they reach the age of 20.

The six additional important health topics identified by the CDC are Asthma, Crisis Preparedness & Response, Food Safety, Mental Health, Childhood Obesity, and Skin Cancer.

Asthma - On average, in a classroom of 30 children, about three are likely to have asthma. Five million school-aged children and youth currently have asthma, and asthma is one of the leading causes of school absenteeism.

Crisis Preparedness & Response - Preparation is the responsibility of every school, community, and state. Should an event or threat occur, every staff member should know how to respond based on protocols or community-based plans established in advance in collaboration with public health and first responder agencies.

Food Safety - Educating students, families, and school staff on simple but effective food safety measures can help prevent the approximately 76 million cases of food borne illness that occur in the United States annually, resulting in an average of 325,000 hospitalizations and 5,000 deaths. Food safety is especially important in schools, because each day more than 27 million children get their lunch through the National School Lunch Program. Furthermore, educating students in school about food safety can help them build good food safety habits that last a lifetime.

Mental Health - Mental health is an under-recognized serious health problem. An estimated 21% of young people in the United States between the ages 9 and 17 have diagnosable emotional or behavioral health disorders, but less than a third get help for these problems.

Childhood Obesity - The prevalence of obesity among children ages 6 to 11 has more than doubled in the past 20 years, going from 7% in 1980 to 19% in 2004. Several chronic disease risk factors arise from childhood obesity, including high blood pressure and high cholesterol. Additionally, overweight young people have a great likelihood of becoming overweight adults and developing diseases associated with adulthood obesity, such as type 2 diabetes and heart disease.

Skin Cancer - The most common form of cancer in the United States is skin cancer. Skin cancer is a preventable disease, as exposure to the sun's ultraviolet rays appears to be the most important environmental factor. Schools are in a good position to encourage children to develop sun protection habits.

[*Source: CDC website*]

Skill 9.4 Apply knowledge of positive health behaviors and strategies for promoting students' understanding of relationships between behavior choices and personal health.

Basic healthy behaviors reduce the risk of injuries, illness, disease, and other health problems.

Injuries are usually a result of unforeseen accidents. Falls are the leading cause of death among home accidents. Falls occur most frequently for the elderly and young children. The most common location of falls is in bathtubs and showers. Examples of precautions that can help decrease the risk of falls include using rubber mats in bathtubs and showers, using safety gates to block young children from stairs, wearing appropriate safety equipment during physical activity, and promptly removing ice and snow from steps and sidewalks.

Positive health behaviors can help decrease the risk of illness and disease. Good nutrition and regular exercise can help prevent everyday illnesses such as colds and flu, and chronic diseases such as heart disease and cancer. Exercise and a healthy diet helps maintain a healthy body composition, reduces cholesterol levels, strengthens the heart, lungs, and musculoskeletal system, and strengthens the body's immune system.

STRATEGIES FOR POSITIVE BEHAVIOR CHANGE

Strategies for positive behavior change in students will relate the teaching of new behaviors to the students' perceptions and frames of reference, and will focus on a series of small, incremental changes. Instructors should actively involve students in the process of change and instructors should positively reinforce steps in the right direction.

It is important that when teaching the processes of behavioral change to the student (via discussion, classroom-type teaching, counseling, etc.) that the instructor present information in a way that corresponds with the student's perceptions, and works within the student's frame of reference.

It is better to encourage small, incremental changes, which the student can achieve on a regular basis and the instructor can reward, as opposed to larger, more major changes that are less likely to have a lasting impact because of the impracticality of application. Instructors should link new behaviors to existing behaviors, with the goal being to gradually modify the behavioral patterns and introduce new behaviors. Simply suppressing behaviors is a difficult process, and will often fail to work.

Instructors should actively involve students in the process of behavioral change (the behavioral change should be the student's goal, not the teacher's goal for them). In this way, the process of change becomes intrinsically motivated, making it far more likely the student will seriously commit to the process. Obviously, the instructor should reinforce positive behaviors via reward, but not excessively – behavioral change should be (for the most part) intrinsically motivated.

SUPPORTING POSITIVE CHANGE

Proper health and fitness education is a necessary prerequisite for positive health choices. Obviously, without an understanding of the various choices available, and the ramifications of each choice, it is difficult to make a wise decision regarding personal and family health choices and behavior. This education should include an introduction to research skills, so that the individual has the freedom to inform themselves of pertinent information when new situations arise that call for them to make health decisions. Good venues for these personal research habits include the Internet, local libraries, and fitness and health-care professionals in the community.

Positive health choices and behavior will also require a layer of economic support, as healthy lifestyle choices will sometimes be more expensive than the less healthy alternative. It is also important for the environment to be conducive to positive choices and behavior regarding health. For example, the availability of resources (both educational and practical) and facilities (medical and fitness) in proximity to the individual can positively impact the decision-making process.

ASSESSING BEHAVIORAL RISK FACTORS

There are various resources available to assess the behavioral health risk factors of a community. The Centers for Disease Control and Prevention (CDC) annually publishes the Youth Risk Behavior Survey (YRBS). This survey explains national and state adolescent health risks. This information is available directly from the CDC. State education agencies compile and maintain statistics on youth health risks. Individual schools or school districts provide data regarding the types of problems seen in the school health room. Individual schools or school districts can also supply information regarding the number of referrals for pregnancy and substance abuse and data on absenteeism, dropouts, and disciplinary actions.

Other sources of information regarding community behavioral health risk factors include the state office of vital statistics, the state and local departments of health, and the medical examiners' office. The state police department can provide highway safety data. The poison control centers and local police departments can provide information regarding injuries, disease, and death. Additionally, emergency room and emergency medical services records and hospital discharge records can expose potential abuse.

Another source of information is social service agencies, as they have data on poverty, unemployment, and child abuse. Lastly, one could choose to assess the community's health behavior risk factors personally. When personally assessing a community's behavioral risk factors, utilize surveys, conduct health risk appraisals, and review healthcare utilization and cost data.

Skill 9.5   Know the effects of stress on the body, techniques for managing stress, and the physiological and psychological benefits of stress management.

Stress has many negative effects. It is important that instructors and students recognize the significance of stress to long-term health. To successfully manage stress, instructors and students must understand the sources of stress and signs and symptoms of stress.

SOURCES OF STRESS

The following are common stressors that many people experience: death of a spouse, death of a close family member or a close personal friend, divorce or separation from a significant other, divorce of parents, addition of a new family member, personal injury/illness, unintentional pregnancy, getting married, jail term, dysfunctional family and social ties, financial problems, fired from a job, moving, poor time management, overcrowding, expectations of others, workaholic personality, lack of self-control, lack of self confidence, lack of self-efficacy, low self-esteem, lack of social support, general insecurity, change, heat/cold extremes, poor living conditions, unsafe work environment, one's occupation, retirement, academic/business readjustment, taking out a major loan, discrimination, being a victim of a crime, exposure to water borne or air borne chemicals, and noise.

SIGNS AND SYMPTOMS OF STRESS

The following are lists of the signs and symptoms of stress:

Emotional signs of stress include: depression, lethargy, aggressiveness, irritability, anxiety, edginess, fearfulness, impulsiveness, chronic fatigue hyper excitability, inability to concentrate, frequent feelings of boredom, feeling overwhelmed, apathy, impatience, pessimism, sarcasm, humorlessness, confusion, helplessness, melancholy, alienation, isolation, numbness, purposelessness, isolation, numbness, self-consciousness; inability to maintain an intimate relationship.

Behavioral signs of stress include: elevated use of substances (alcohol, drugs; tobacco), crying, yelling, insomnia or excessive sleep, excessive TV watching, school/job burnout, panic attacks, poor problems solving capability, avoidance of people, aberrant behavior, procrastination, accident proneness, restlessness, loss of memory, indecisiveness, aggressiveness, inflexibility, phobic responses, tardiness, disorganization; sexual problems.

Physical signs of stress: pounding heart, stuttering, trembling/nervous tics, excessive perspiration, teeth grinding, gastrointestinal problems (constipation, indigestion, diarrhea, queasy stomach), dry mouth, aching lower back, migraine/tension headaches, stiff neck, asthma attacks, allergy attacks, skin problems, frequent colds or low grade fevers, muscle tension, hyperventilation, high blood pressure, amenorrhea, nightmares; cold intolerance.

STRESS MANAGEMENT

General stress management principles of interest to physical education instructors include regular physical activity, exercise, physical play, and proper nutrition. Proper nutrition refers to the consumption of a balanced diet, consisting of adequate amounts of lean protein, complex carbohydrates, fruits, vegetables, and unsaturated fats.

Stress management and good nutrition are among the cornerstones of healthy living. Physical education instructors can introduce students to these important concepts through development of individualized fitness and wellness plans. Fitness and wellness plans should include a concrete exercise plan and a detailed nutritional plan.

Skill 9.6 **Demonstrate knowledge of common student misconceptions and faulty practices related to physical activity, health, exercise, and diet and know how to educate students about these misconceptions and faulty practices.**

Students and the general public often have commonly held misconceptions about exercise and diet. To promote better understanding of health concepts and eliminate misconceptions and faulty practices, physical education instructors must teach the fundamentals of exercise and diet. Instructors must also encourage students to rely on their own knowledge and learning in evaluating health claims, rather than relying on advertising or the media. We will consider common misconceptions related to two important areas of health, diet plans and exercise.

FALLACIES AND DANGERS UNDERLYING SELECTED DIET PLANS

High Carbohydrate diets (i.e. Pritikin, Bloomingdale's) can produce rapid or gradual weight loss, depending on caloric intake. Usually requires vitamin and mineral supplements because protein intake is low. These diets may or may not recommend exercising or permanent lifestyle changes, which are necessary to maintain one's weight.

High-Protein Diets promote the same myths, fallacies, and results as high carbohydrate diets. High-protein diets also require vitamin and mineral supplements. In addition, these diets are usually high in saturated fats and cholesterol because of the emphasis on meat products.

Liquid Formulas that are physician/hospital run (i.e. Medifast, Optifast) provide 800 or fewer calories a day consumed in liquid form. Dieters forgo food intake for 12 to 16 weeks in lieu of the protein supplement. Liquid diets require vitamin and mineral supplements and close medical supervision. Dieters should gradually reintroduce food after the initial fast. These diets can result in severe and/or dangerous metabolic problems in addition to an irregular heartbeat, kidney infections and failure, hair loss, and sensations of feeling cold and/or cold intolerance. These diets are very expensive and have a high rate of failure.

Over-The-Counter Liquid Diets (i.e. Slimfast) are liquid/food bar supplements taken in place of one or more meals per day. Such diets advocate an intake of 1,000 calories daily. Carbohydrate, protein, vitamin, and mineral intake may be so low that the diet can be as dangerous as the medically supervised liquid diets when relied on for the only source of nutrition. Because of the lack of medical supervision, the side effects can be even more dangerous.

Over-The-Counter Diet Pills/Aids and Prescription Diet Pills (appetite suppressants) have as their main ingredient phenyl propanolamine hydrochloride [PPA]. Keeping weight off by the use of these products is difficult. Dizziness, sleeplessness, high blood pressure, palpitation, headaches, and tachycardia are potential side effects of these products. Moreover, prescription diet pills can be addictive.

Low Calorie Diets (caloric restricted) are the most misunderstood method of weight loss. However, restricting the intake of calories is the way most people choose to lose weight. All the focus is on food, creating anxiety over the restriction of food - especially favorite foods. These diets are also difficult to maintain and have a high failure rate. Like the other diets, once the diet is over, dieters regain weight quickly because they fail to make permanent behavioral changes. Side effects of caloric restriction include diarrhea, constipation, Ketosis, a lower basal metabolic rate, blood-sugar imbalances, loss of lean body tissue, fatigue, weakness, and emotional problems. Low calorie diets require dietary supplements. Those who choose **fasting** (complete caloric restriction) to lose weight can deplete enough of the body's energy stores to cause death.

IDENTIFY EXERCISE MYTHS AND GIMMICKS

Exercise myths and gimmicks include:

- drinking beer/alcoholic beverages is a good way to replenish loss of body fluids after exercising,

- women should not exercise while menstruating or pregnant,

- physically fit people will not die from heart disease,

- you cannot be too flexible,

- spot reduction is effective,

- children are naturally active and do not need to exercise,

- muscle will turn into fat with the cessation of exercising,

- fat can turn into muscle,

- women will develop large muscles by weight training, you should exercise while sick regardless how ill you are,

- cardiac hypertrophy developed by exercising is harmful to health,

- exercise increases the appetite,

- exercise gets rid of sagging skin and wrinkles,

- yoga is a good way to develop fitness;

- losing cellulite requires special treatment, body wraps are a good way to lose weight.

Skill 9.7   Know how to evaluate information related to health and fitness products, programs, facilities, and services.

CONSUMER EDUCATION

We can find information relating to physical activity at local public and university libraries and online. Educators should regularly inform themselves about updates in the field, and should periodically search for resources that they can use with their students. Instructors should encourage students should to make use of free resources such as libraries and the Internet, to expand their knowledge and understanding of the subject matter.

We can find products relating to physical activity at sporting goods stores, gym boutiques, nutritional supplement stores, and wholesalers. Local community centers may also sell or rent equipment, and prices may be more favorable.

We can find services for promoting consumer awareness skills in relation to physical activity, recreation, fitness, and wellness online and at local community centers. Many community centers have outreach programs to increase public participation in physical activities. Health food stores may also offer seminars on fitness and wellness. Physical education professionals can work to build ties between these publicly offered services and their own curriculums.

There is generally a wide array of information available related to health, fitness and recreational activities, products, facilities, and services. It can be difficult for the untrained consumer to sort through it all to find information that is pertinent and accurate.

When evaluating information relating to fitness and sports equipment, consumers (for example, parents of students who are seeking to equip their home with training facilities for themselves and their children) should ask the sales staff about the differences between their choices; not just in terms of prices, but also in terms of potential fitness benefits and especially safety (Is the equipment in question safe to use? Is it safe for all ages? Is a spotter required for its use?).

When evaluating weight control products and programs, consumers should ask sales staff to explain the mechanism by which the program functions (e.g. does it limit caloric intake, maximize caloric expenditure, or function by means of some other process?). The word of the sales staff is not sufficient, however, and consumers should investigate further using the tools at their disposal, which include public and university libraries, the internet, and physical education professionals at their children's schools.

When evaluating fitness-training facilities, consumers should consider several factors. These factors are quality and availability of training equipment, hygiene of the facility, and overall atmosphere. You can determine the general quality of the equipment by its age and you can glean further information from a discussion with the training staff on-site. You can investigate the availability of the equipment by visiting the facility at peak training times (which vary depending on the demographics of the facility – again, you should ask the training staff for the appropriate times). If it takes too long for equipment to become available and lines seem to form, this may not be the best facility for your needs (unless you're not interested in visiting the facility during those hours). Most important, though, is the atmosphere at the facility. The best way to get a feel for this is to have some short conversations with some customers about their experiences there.

TRENDS IN ADVERTISING AND MARKETING

Current trends in media advertising and marketing practices related to fitness, recreational, and sports products and programs will typically display happy and fit individuals participating in the activity or making use of the advertised product. This trend has positive and negative ramifications for the work of physical educators.

On the positive side, the media advertising and marketing trend paints physical activity in a very positive light (as it should). The exposure that students have to the media today makes this a very helpful reinforcement of the messages that physical education professionals work to promote in the classroom and school gymnasium. On the negative side, these trends ignore the reality that the current national level of fitness is poor, and obesity and heart disease are on the rise.

DOMAIN III.   THE PHYSICAL EDUCATION PROGRAM

COMPETENCY 10.0   EFFECTIVE, DEVELOPMENTALLY APPROPRIATE INSTRUCTION AND ASSESSMENT

Skill 10.1   **Demonstrate knowledge of how students differ in their approaches to learning and physical performance and use this knowledge to provide equitable and appropriate instruction that draws upon student strengths as a basis for growth.**

Students display a range of approaches to learning. The major learning styles are visual, auditory, and kinesthetic. Students can be comfortable with more than one style of learning, though they will tend to prefer one to the others. It is best to blend teaching techniques to accommodate multiple learning styles, so different students can process information in the way that they are most comfortable, and so that students can process information in multiple ways, thereby helping them grasp the subject matter faster.

Visual – Students who are primarily visual learners are comfortable and processing information visually. In order to best accommodate and communicate with these students, instructors should convey information should with illustrations, diagrams, and demonstrations.

Auditory – Students who are primarily auditory learners are comfortable and more effective processing auditory information. In order to best accommodate and communicate with these students, instructors should convey information orally, with clear sequential descriptions of tasks.

Kinesthetic – Students who are primarily kinesthetic learners are comfortable and more effective processing kinesthetically presented information. In order to best accommodate and communicate with these students, instructors should convey information using tools and aides that the students can touch and feel, and instructors should assist the students in trying out the tasks that they will perform, so they can get a "feel" for them.

The types of intelligence stemming from the Gardner's theory of multiple intelligence that we need to discuss for instructional purposes include linguistic, logical-mathematical, spatial-visual interpersonal, intrapersonal, and bodily-kinesthetic. As with the learning styles described above, instructors should blend teaching techniques to accommodate the abilities of more students in the class.

Linguistic – Children whose abilities center around linguistic intelligence will best process information presented to them verbally – descriptions should be rich and detailed.

Logical-mathematical – Children whose abilities center on logical-mathematical intelligence best process information presented as procedures and sequences. Instructors should present information in compartmentalized tasks, with emphasis placed on cause-and-effect relationships.

Spatial-visual – Children whose abilities center on spatial-visual intelligence best process information presented visually with illustrations, diagrams, and demonstrations.

Interpersonal – Children whose abilities center on interpersonal intelligence will tend to focus on the social aspect of educational activities. In order to capture and maintain their interest and attention, activities should involve group work and teamwork.

Intrapersonal – Children whose abilities center on intrapersonal intelligence will tend to be more introspective, assigning value to learned material by relating the material to their own personal experiences. In order to communicate information to such children effectively, the instructor should "personalize" the subject matter and give examples to help children connect with ways that the material is relevant to their own lives.

Bodily-kinesthetic – Children whose abilities center on bodily-kinesthetic intelligence will be better at grasping information related to physical activities and body movements. Instructors should present information kinesthetically (i.e. use of tools and aides that students can touch and feel). To communicate with such children, the instructor should give students the opportunity to experience what they are learning physically.

APPLICATION OF LEARNING THEORIES TO INSTRUCTION

Instructors apply learning theories in a physical education setting by tailoring the educational experience to help stimulate students to make positive changes to their lifestyles (as related to physical activity). It is important to consider that physical education, more so than most educational disciplines covered in elementary and secondary education, involves stimulating lifestyle changes (i.e. changing "problematic" lifestyle habits). Physical educators who model healthy lifestyles and physical activity habits for their students (i.e. "do as I say and as I do") best harness the power of social learning theory. Instructors harness the health belief and transtheoretical models by helping students to see both inactive lifestyles as harmful, and make the cost-benefit decision-making process "easy" by emphasizing easy and pleasant ways to integrate physical activity into their lifestyles.

Instructors can also apply learning theories to children with special/diverse needs, to the personal experiences and circumstances of students, to their cultural background, and to their health conditions, by providing them with pertinent information that speaks to their particular situation. Instructors should also identify role models to whom they can relate (e.g. someone in the same situation or from the same cultural background). When teaching about the negative effects of a sedentary lifestyle and the benefits of an active lifestyle, instructors should show students how they can make an active lifestyle pleasant and easily accessible.

STUDENT APPROACHES TO PHYSICAL PERFORMANCE AND ACTIVITY

In evaluating students' approaches to physical performance, let us look at some statistics.

-Nearly half of students between the ages of 12 and 21 do not exercise on a regular basis, with a significant decline occurring during adolescence.

-About 14% report no recent physical activity, and this statistic is more prevalent among females.

-About 25% take part in light to moderate physical activity (walk or bicycle) nearly every day.

-Participation in all types of physical activity declines significantly as age and grade in school increase.

-More males participate in vigorous physical activity and strengthening activities than females.

-Daily attendance in school physical education programs declined from 42% in early 1990 to less than 25% in 1999.

Source: Exercise Physiology: Energy, Nutrition, and Human Performance, William McArdle et al, pg. 873.

The main goal of physical education is to get students to incorporate some type of physical activity into their daily schedule in any way possible, provided it is safe and the benefits of the activity outweigh the risks. Children should reduce the amount of time spent on sedentary activities such as watching TV, excessive reading, and computer use, and increase participation in physical activities. Routine physical activities need not be organized fitness programs. They can include walking or biking to school, pushing the lawn mower, and using stairs instead of elevators. Development of these habits early increases the likelihood of continuation into adulthood.

Children should participate in organized aerobic or recreational exercises at least three times a week. Students can choose their favorite activity from a variety of choices. Boys usually prefer higher intensity activities such as competitive sports. Girls tend to favor dance, skating, and aerobics.

Skill 10.2   Know how to design and implement instruction that is based on the Texas Essential Knowledge and Skills (TEKS) for physical education and that is safe, achieves goals, and ensures student progress, motivation, and safety.

The Texas Essential Knowledge and Skills (TEKS) for Physical Education emphasizes core physical education content that instructors must impart to students. Instructors must observe educational "best practices" to educate students in a way that is safe, achieves goals, and ensures students' continued progress and motivation. For example, instructors must tailor the lessons to a variety of learning styles, implement knowledge-based assessment systems to track students' progress over the course of a semester, advance consideration of potential safety hazards in chosen activities, implement compensatory safety procedures, and create a pleasant, fun educational environment that encourages student involvement.

Tailoring the lessons to a variety of learning styles ensures that the instructor's message will get through. This means that students are more likely to understand both the content material and the related safety procedures.

Implementing knowledge based assessment systems to track student progress is a critical step toward ensuring student progress. Ideally, this tracking should happen on a variety of levels relative to the range of student skills. This way, the educator will have a clear picture of where students are progressing well, and where they are struggling.

Advance consideration of potential safety hazards in chosen activities will allow the physical educator to consider how to avoid these hazards, and how to educate the students to make the activity as safe as possible. In some cases, it will be necessary to omit the activity from the curriculum, though a creative physical education professional will usually be able to make an activity work within appropriate safety guidelines.

Finally, physical educators must remember that the creation of a pleasant, fun educational environment is always the best way to involve and motivate students, and is the best way to foster effort and encourage student progress in the curriculum.

Skill 10.3   Know how to use a variety of instructional models, strategies materials, technologies, to address specific purposes, objectives, learning needs, and program goals.

INSTRUCTIONAL METHODS FOR VARIOUS OBJECTIVES, SITUATIONS, AND DEVELOPMENTAL LEVELS

When selecting instructional methods, it is essential that the physical educator understands that the use of well-planned, sequential unit and lesson plans will maximize the value of the instruction. Additionally, the unit and lesson plans should not only build upon the students' prior physical education experience, but should also accommodate the various ability levels of the students and maximize the practice time for all students. When selecting an instructional format, the physical educator may choose to utilize more than one configuration in any given lesson. The physical educator can select from five basic instructional formats: cognitive structuring, large-group skill instruction, small-group skill instruction, individual skill instruction, and testing.

When utilizing cognitive structuring, the teacher addresses the whole class through lecture, demonstration, or questioning. This method is particularly effective for imparting basic knowledge in a short amount of time. Large-group skill instruction involves all of the students in the class in the related activities. In small-group skill instruction (also called stations); the instructor divides students into groups, each of which works on a different skill or activity. A significant advantage of this instructional format is the ability to maximize instruction in situations where equipment is limited. In addition, small-group activities increase the amount of practice time for each student. In the individual skill instruction format, the instructor asks each student to select a skill on which to work. The students independently decide when they are ready to progress to the next skill. When ready to progress, the students simply put away their equipment, gather equipment for the next selected skill, and work at their own pace on the next skill. This self-paced arrangement allows for greatest chance of skill mastery. The final instructional format is testing. During testing, the instructor assesses the students utilizing a written or skills test.

Finally, the physical educator may choose to supplement his or her teaching with the use of instructional devices. Examples of instructional devices include basic physical education equipment such as cones or targets, but may also include other types of technology such as pedometers, DVDs, computer programs, or interactive white boards.

INSTRUCTIONAL STRATEGIES

No educational program can succeed without teachers with well-developed teaching skills. Many physical education teachers attempt to instruct their classes by employing the methods used to teach academic subjects. This ineffective teaching style can cause confusion and prevent students from fully appreciating the value of physical education. There are two recognized phases of physical education, cognitive and psychomotor, and studies show that the academic method of teaching is ineffective in both phases.

Subjects covered in the cognitive phase include the history of sports and physical education, terminology, playing rules, safety, and kinesiology as applied to movement skills. Traditional methods of teaching can be effective in the cognitive phase but not in the psychomotor phase. Instructors can use lecture as an effective method of teaching of special topics that require a degree of authoritativeness. However, experts in the field consider this a poor approach, as children easily get bored and lose interest.

Some effective methods of teaching are question and answer forums, group discussions, demonstrations, projects, problem-solving exercises, and homework assignments. Instructors should use these methods appropriately, meaning the teacher should keep particular student limitations in mind.

One approach to teaching motor skills is the whole-part method, which follows Gestalt's theory of learning. This theory states that when students gain an insight into a whole activity, it enables them to identify specific learning objectives. By carefully analyzing the parts that make up the whole, students begin to achieve permanency of learning. This method is effective in teaching special skills in sports, dance, gymnastics, and basic game skills.

Another approach for teaching motor skills is the part-whole method, which relies on the Thorndike stimulus-response theory. This theory states that the parts are more important than the whole since the parts make up the whole.

There are other specific teaching suggestions and procedures for the development of skills. These methods require the instructor to teach basic knowledge to the class. Instructors should clearly delineate the expected standards of performance by having the skill demonstrated in class. The class should then evaluate the elements of correct form displayed by the demonstrator.

TECHNOLOGY

The best sources of current technological resources for accessing information on physical activity and health are the Internet and computers.

Internet resources form an important part of current technology, which helps in accessing information on physical activity and health. There are internet sources, which also enable educators, students, performers, parents, and athletes to stay aware of up-to-date information and programs about physical activity and health.

Numerous websites also exist that allow educators as well as performers to know about the developments in the physical education training systems. Use of technological resources also helps students to grasp more knowledge about physical activity and health-related issues.

Some organizations such as the NASPE also provide information on physical fitness and health. For example, NASPE invites school districts nationwide to post their school wellness policy on the NASPE Forum.

Research also shows there are different types of devices that athletes can use to monitor physical activity and health. Such devices include virtual bicycles, rowing machines, and tread mills. Such technology helps plan and implement workouts and view workout results.

Technology is the application of science to commercial, educational, health-related, military, or industrial objectives. Technology includes the use of computers, calculators, communication devices (telephone, videoconference devices), or other entities and methodologies to achieve those objectives.

Successful physical education instructors integrate technology into the instructional process. Technology is not simply a practice tool or device without purpose. The use of a particular technological device or product of technology should be appropriate to the lesson content.

Instructors can use technology in a variety of ways to help students and athletes improve or learn. Some ways in which instructors can use technology include:

1. Actual use of technology – the teacher and the students use the technology in a "hands-on" setting. For example, students use a video or digital camera in physical education to analyze their skills.

2. Use of products of technology – the use of products of technology in instruction and learning. May include gathering information or resources from the Internet, imaging results for analyzing a motor skill, etc. In such a situation, the teacher can use the technology, or the products of technology, to present information, to provide examples and illustrations, and as the medium or object of intrusion.

Some of the offered examples currently available in technology-mediated instruction include audio technologies such as radio, telephone, voice mail, and audiocassettes; video technologies such as television, teleconferencing, compressed video, and prerecorded videocassettes; and information technologies such as stand-alone workstations, CD ROM prepackaged multimedia, e-mail, chat rooms, bulletin boards, and the World Wide Web.

Skill 10.4 **Know how to create, modify, and adapt physical education activities, games, rules, equipment, and settings to ensure that all students have an equal opportunity to participate, learn, are successful, and enjoy physical activity.**

ACTIVITIES FOR VARIOUS OBJECTIVES, SITUATIONS, AND DEVELOPMENTAL LEVELS

The following is a list of physical activities that may reduce specific health risks, improve overall health, and develop skill-related components of physical activity. Some of these activities, such as walking and calisthenics, are more suitable to students at beginning developmental levels, while other, such as circuit training and rowing are best suited for students at more advanced levels of development.

1. **Aerobic Dance:**
Health-related components of fitness = *cardio-respiratory, body composition.*
Skill-related components of fitness = *agility, coordination.*

2. **Bicycling:**
Health-related components of fitness = *cardio-respiratory, muscle strength, muscle endurance, body composition.*
Skill-related components of fitness = *balance.*

3. **Calisthenics:**
Health-related components of fitness = *cardio-respiratory, muscle strength, muscle endurance, flexibility, body composition.*
Skill-related components of fitness = *agility.*

4. **Circuit Training:**
Health-related components of fitness = *cardio-respiratory, muscle strength, muscle endurance, body composition.*
Skill-related components of fitness = *power.*

5. **Cross Country Skiing:**
Health-related component of fitness = *cardio-respiratory, muscle strength, muscle endurance, body composition.*
Skill-related components of fitness = *agility, coordination; power.*

6. **Jogging/Running:**
Health-related components of fitness = *cardio-respiratory, body composition.*

7. **Rope Jumping:**
Health-related components of fitness = *cardio-respiratory, body composition.*
Skill-related components of fitness = *agility, coordination, reaction time, speed.*

8. Rowing:
Health-related components of fitness = *cardio-respiratory, muscle strength, muscle endurance, body composition.*
Skill-related components of fitness = *agility, coordination, power.*

9. Skating:
Health-related components of fitness = *cardio-respiratory, body composition.*
Skill-related components of fitness = *agility, balance, coordination, speed.*

10. Swimming/Water Exercises:
Health-related components of fitness = *cardio-respiratory, muscle strength, muscle endurance, flexibility, body composition.*
Skill related components of fitness = *agility, coordination.*

11. Walking (brisk):
Health-related components of fitness = *cardio-respiratory, body composition.*

In general, teachers may need to modify instructional methods to accommodate students with disabilities participating in physical education class. The physical educator should ensure that students with disabilities understand the purpose of the lesson before the activity begins. The teacher should design lesson plans that include alternate activities in the event that the originally planned activity does not work well for the student(s) with disabilities. Teachers should not place students with disabilities in activities where they have no chance of success. Thus, teachers should avoid elimination games. The physical educator should praise even minor displays of progress and achievement. The teacher should work with the student(s) with disabilities to set achievable goals, as goal attainment is a wonderful motivator.

Physical educators must have a strong, working knowledge of specific disabilities and how they affect a student's ability to learn. When working with students mentally retarded students, instructors should emphasize progressive gross motor movement. Teacher instruction should focus on demonstration rather than oral explanation. Instructors should reward effort displayed by students. Additionally, the practice periods for students with mental retardation should be short to alleviate boredom and aggravation. Instructors should also make modifications for the visually impaired student. Lesson planning for the visually impaired student should focus on individual movement activities. The physical educator should use a whistle or loud verbal cues in class. If the visually impaired student has some residual eyesight, the teacher might have the student utilize a brightly colored ball against a contrasting backdrop. When working with a student with a hearing impairment, the physical education teacher should use visual cues. The instructor or other students must read all written instructions aloud. During all stages of instruction, the hearing-impaired student should be close to the teacher. If a student with an orthopedic disability is present in class, lesson plans should focus on individual and dual sports to maximize the student's chance of success. Instructors may need to make modifications for students with emotional disabilities. Students with emotional disabilities can succeed in a stable, organized setting. The teacher should praise individual accomplishments. In order to avoid or minimize behavior disruptions, the instructor should clearly identify and consistently enforce rules and expectations. Finally, when working with a student with any given disability, it is crucial that the physical education teacher follows the physician instructions exactly.

Instructors may also need to modify instructional methods to accommodate students from diverse cultural and linguistic backgrounds. When working with students from diverse cultural backgrounds, the physical educator should self-educate regarding the cultural values and norms of the culture from which the students originate. When delivering instruction, the teacher should highlight information regarding participation in the activity in the student's home country. Often English is not the primary language for students from diverse cultural backgrounds. When working with students who utilize English as their second language, teachers should repeat instructions a number of times. The teacher should have knowledge of basic words relating to physical education in the language of the students present in class. The teacher should use precise English and avoid slang. During skill practice, the teacher could pair the student with others that might help them in their skill development. Finally, it is important that the teacher knows how to pronounce all students' names properly, especially the names of students from a diverse cultural background.

Skill 10.5   Know how to provide appropriate verbal and nonverbal teaching cues and positive feedback to students in physical education settings and how to communicate to students the importance of physical activity, health, and fitness.

SEE Skills 1.2 and 1.5

Skill 10.6   Demonstrate an understanding of the characteristics, advantages, limitations, and applications of assessment methods used in physical education and know how to select, construct, adapt, and implement, assessments for various purposes.

Evaluations determine the value of a particular activity. Instructors should integrate the continuous process of evaluation into the teaching-learning experience. The goal of an evaluation should not be limited to the school setting and the students' experiences. Rather, we should also think of it in terms of a community's progress. Measurements for evaluation provide other valuable services that instructors can use to classify students, determine students' status for grading, and aid in the diagnosis of students' weaknesses in relation to fitness skill development.

A renowned guide for educators includes the following three principles:

- Students should accept evaluations as an integral part of the teaching process.
- Instructors should use evaluations to assist students in achieving terminal competencies (psychomotor, cognitive, and affective).
- Instructors should base evaluations on the status of the individual student.

The Office of Instructional Services enumerates achievement standards for children in elementary school. An individualized, well-executed physical education program should enable a student to:

- Walk 500 yards without stopping.
- Run 30 yards dash in six seconds or less.
- Jump a standing broad jump a distance of approximately their height plus three inches.
- Bounce a ball to 2/4 or 4/4 music count.

Portfolio assessments are evaluations of the learning that happens in a natural setting. They can capitalize on student work, enhance both teacher and student involvement in evaluation, and satisfy the accountability needed to prompt school reform. Portfolio assessment includes active diaries, attitude inventories, entry-level skill test, and teacher/peer rating forms.

Interactive health CD-ROMs allow students and instructors to enter personal fitness data and evaluation results and receive immediate feedback and suggestions for improvement.

SELECTING, CONSTRUCTING, ADAPTING, AND IMPLEMENTING ASSESSMENTS

Physical educators should construct assessments that evaluate all three domains of physical education: psychomotor, cognitive, and affective. Teachers should divide assessments in the psychomotor domain into two groups: skill-related fitness and sport-specific skills. The physical education teacher can objectively measure skill-related fitness utilizing assessments specifically designed to evaluate each component. Speed, agility, coordination, balance, and reaction time are the components of skill-related fitness. Teachers may choose to use standardized tests developed to assess each of these components. Most of these tests also include normative data. Similarly, many standardized tests are also available as an objective assessment of sport-specific skills. Many of these tests also include normative data.

Teachers should thoroughly evaluate an assessment before choosing to utilize it, as some of the existing tests are quite complicated and burdensome to implement. If a teacher chooses not to use an existing assessment, adaptation of an existing assessment is always an option. To adapt an existing assessment, the physical educator can evaluate the assessment and determine which components of the assessment are reasonable to implement and provide a valid assessment of the specified skill. The teacher would delete the remaining components from the assessment prior to implementation. In addition to the option of deleting segments of the existing assessment, the teacher might choose to make general modifications to the overall assessment. The physical educator can measure both skill-related fitness and sport-specific skills subjectively through informal assessments. Examples of informal assessments include student interviews, student self-evaluation, and checklists.

In addition to psychomotor skills, the physical educator also assesses development of the cognitive domain. Evaluation of the cognitive domain includes formal written assessments. When constructing a written assessment, the physical educator should design the assessment at an age appropriate level, include all written instructions on the test, and arrange similarly formatted questions together. Sample types of written test questions include matching, multiple choice, true-false, fill-in-the-blank, short answer, and essay. When possible, the physical educator should administer written assessments in a classroom setting, rather than on the gymnasium floor. Assessment of both the psychomotor and cognitive domains will occur at the end of each unit of instruction.

Finally, the physical educator should assess development in the affective domain. Informal assessment of the affective domain might include checklists similar to the informal checklists utilized to assess development in the psychomotor domain. Utilizing these affective checklists clarifies behavioral expectations. Additionally, standardized attitude scales are also available to physical educators. Instructors should measure development in the affective domain at various intervals throughout the school year.

METHODS OF ASSESSMENT

There are many methods of assessment available to the physical education instructor. Standardized tests are traditional assessment tools that have limited effectiveness in physical education. Because students differ greatly in natural ability and fitness, measurement against personal standards is more useful than measurement against generic standards. Some of the tools for personal assessment include observational checklists, portfolios, journals, peer assessments, and rating scales.

ASSESSMENT IN THE COGNITIVE DOMAIN

1. **Standardized Tests** – scientifically constructed test with established validity and reliability.

2. **Teacher-made Tests** – developed personally by the teacher.

3. **Essay Tests/Written Assignments** – tests the ability to organize information presented logically in written paragraphs.

4. **Objective Tests** – true/false, multiple choice, matching, diagrams, completion, or short written response.

5. **Norm-Referenced Tests** – compares individual's score to the scores of others.

6. **Criterion-Referenced Tests** – Interpreting a score by comparing it to a predetermined standard.

The trend in physical education assessment is to move increasingly away from norm- and criterion-referenced evaluations (i.e. measuring a student's achievements against the achievements of a normative group or against criteria that are arbitrarily set by either the educator or the governing educational body), and towards performance-based, or "authentic" evaluations. This creates difficulty for physical educators because it eliminates preset reference points.

The advantage of performance-based evaluations is they are equally fair to individuals with diverse backgrounds, special needs, and disabilities. In all cases, the instructor evaluates students based on their personal performance.

Portfolio construction is one way of assessing the performance of a student. The student chooses the achievements to add to the portfolio. This creates a tool that assesses current abilities and serves as a benchmark against which the instructor can measure future performance (thus evaluating progress over time, and not just a localized achievement).

TYPES OF EVALUATION

Summative evaluation strategies involve assigning the student a letter or number grade, which can reflect both the student's performance and progress. Examples include:

- Performance evaluations – the instructor assigns a letter or number grade based on the student's performance on a task or set of tasks (e.g. push-ups and sit-ups, time to run one mile, etc.).

- Progress evaluations – the instructor assigns a letter or number grade based on the student's improvement in the ability to perform a task or set of tasks.

- Effort evaluations – the instructor assigns a letter or number grade based on the student's effort in working towards training goals.

- Behavior evaluations – the instructor assigns a letter or number grade based on the student's behavior in and attitude towards training and the training environment.

Formative evaluation strategies do not provide a letter or number grade to the student, but rather focus on a textual analysis of the student's performance and progress. Examples include a written analysis of the student's performance, progress, effort, attitude, and behavior.

Skill 10.7   Know how to use available technology to analyze student progress, fitness, and performance.

Physical educators can use various technological tools to analyze student performance, fitness, and performance. Two important and interrelated technological tools are videotape and movement analysis software.

VIDEOTAPE

Videotaping students participating in skill performance and fitness activities allows students and teachers to analyze technique closely. Instructors can identify and point out errors in form to the students. This visual reinforcement enhances the learning process. In addition, periodic videotaping allows instructors to monitor progress in skill performance and fitness over time.

MOVEMENT ANALYSIS SOFTWARE

Movement analysis software helps students and instructors analyze movement patterns captured on digital video cameras in great detail. For example, movement analysis software can distill the individual characteristics of a person's gate. Such high detailed analysis allows instructors and students to study individual patterns of movement, individual movement styles, and strategies for peak performance. Movement analysis software helps identify key elements of a movement that need improvement and helps track progress in development, maturation, and error correction.

Skill 10.8   **Apply skills for interpreting student performance and fitness data and skills for using data to analyze progress, provide feedback about strengths and areas of need, and recommend prescriptive exercise.**

In this section, we will discuss methods for assessing and interpreting student fitness data and motor skill performance. First, we introduce examples of fitness and skill tests. Next, we discuss fitness prescriptions and feedback. Finally, we discuss interpretation of test results and communication of results to various audiences.

SPECIFIC PHYSICAL FITNESS APPRAISALS

The following is a list of tests that instructors can use to assess the physical fitness of students.

Cardiorespiratory fitness tests – maximal stress test, sub maximal stress test, Bruce Protocol, Balke Protocol, Astrand and Rhyming Test, PWC Test, Bench Step Test, Rockport Walking Fitness Test, and Cooper 1.5 Mile Run/Walk Fitness Test.

Body Composition determination – Hydrostatic weighing, skin fold measurements, limb/girth circumference, and body mass index.

Agility tests – Illinois Agility Run.

Balance tests – Bass Test of Dynamic Balance (lengthwise and crosswise), Johnson Modification of the Bass Test of Dynamic Balance, modified sideward leap, and balance beam walk.

Coordination tests – Stick test of Coordination.

Power tests – vertical jump.

Speed tests – 50-yard dash.

SKILL ASSESSMENT IN THE EVALUATION OF STUDENT PERFORMANCE

A. General Skills:

1. **Iowa Brace Test** – measures motor educability.

2. **AAHPERD Youth Fitness Test** – measures motor capacity.

3. **AAHPERD Health Related Physical Fitness Test** – measures physical capacity.

4. **McCloy's General Motor Ability and Capacity Test** – measures motor ability and motor efficiency.

5. **Rodgers Strength Test** – measures muscular strength.

6. **Texas PE Test** – measures motor ability.

7. **Skills tests for accuracy** – involve kicking, throwing, or striking an object toward a goal; activities include volleyball serves, basketball free throws, badminton short serves, and basketball passing (e.g. AAHPERD Basketball Passing Test for Accuracy).

8. **Skills test for total bodily movement** – requires performing a test course with movements similar to the sport (e.g. AAHPERD Basketball Control Test).

9. **Wall Volley Test** - measures the number of consecutive successful time/trials to pass, kick, throw, or strike an object at a wall in a given time (e.g. AAHPERD Basketball Passing Test).

10. **Skills Tests for Power or Distance** - involve kicks, throws, or strokes to measure the ability to kick, throw, or strike an object (e.g. Badminton Drive for Distance, Cornish Handball Power Test).

11. **Combination Tests** - composed of previous groupings to assess speed and accuracy.

B. Teacher Ratings: instructors create a numerical scale from one to five and rank performance based on specific, observable movements. An example is evaluating the use of space, use of focus, and variety of movements in a creative movement class.

C. Student Progress: score improvements (e.g. archery, badminton) and charting (e.g. basketball shots missed).

Instructors can administer skills tests for specific sports in one of two ways. First, rate individual performance based on a specified number of trials. Alternatively, evaluate skills using norm-referenced scales for a specific grade level.

Two problems with skill tests are that they take too much time to administer and the reliability is suspect.

BASIC STATISTICAL APPLICATIONS

Statistical applications for physical education assessment purposes allow us to evaluate where the score of a given assessment stands in comparison to other assessments and compare different assessments of the same student's abilities (in other fields – tracking intra-individual differences, or in the same field over time – tracking the student's progress).

Central tendency and variability determine where a range of scores cluster on the assessment scale and whether they are all highly localized around one point on the scale, or spread out over a range.

Standard scores and norms allow us to evaluate where assessment results stand in relation to the 'normal' expected achievement level.

Correlations allow us to evaluate the frequency at which two assessment trends appear in conjunction. Note that correlation does not imply causation.

FITNESS PRESCRIPTIONS

Physical fitness assessments are an important tool for physical education instructors and students. Instructors must be careful not to overemphasize fitness assessments, as students that score poorly may become discouraged and students that perform well may become complacent. When used correctly, the results of fitness assessments are valuable tools in the development of exercise prescriptions. For example, an instructor can use the results of a multi-faceted fitness assessment to determine the fitness strengths and weaknesses of each student and the areas that each student needs to improve.

Simple exercises to improve aerobic endurance include walking, jogging, and bicycling. Exercises to improve muscular strength and endurance include push-ups, pull-ups, sit-ups, and weight lifting. Exercises to improve flexibility are stretches for various parts of the body. The exercises that help improve aerobic endurance, muscular strength, and muscular endurance also help improve body composition.

APPLYING AND COMMUNICATING ASSESSMENT DATA

Instructors should compare assessment data to grade equivalency norms to determine where each child is relative to where he should be. However, the instructor should place the most emphasis on evaluating the child relative to past performance. Progress is more important than current achievement. A learning-disabled child might display below average levels of achievement despite having made a great deal of progress, while a gifted child might be above grade equivalency norms despite stagnation.

Instructors should communicate assessment data should differently to students, parents, and school board members.

- **Assessment data communicated to students** should be encouraging, and should be limited to a textual analysis of the child's progress and effort (it is not helpful or encouraging to remind a child that he is below grade level norms, especially if he has worked hard and made progress). The ultimate purpose of assessment data communicated to a child is to encourage further hard work.

- **Assessment data communicated to parents** should also be encouraging and should focus on the child's progress and effort. That being said, it is also important that a parent receive an accurate picture of the child's status relative to grade level norms, especially if the child is in need of remedial assistance.

- **Assessment data communicated to school board members** is generally more summative in nature (a letter or number grade). Since school board members will generally see evaluations of entire classes at a time without knowing the individual children, it is not important for them to receive an encouraging picture of an individual child's progress. It is more important for them to see both current achievement levels and rates of progress to properly assess curriculum design, lesson planning, and program evaluation.

COMPETENCY 11.0   **FACTORS RELEVANT TO LEARNING AND PERFORMANCE IN PHYSICAL EDUCATION AND LEARNING ENVIROMENTS AND OPPORTUNITIES THAT PROMOTE STUDENTS' DEVELOPMENT**

Skill 11.1   **Analyze ways in which developmental and other factors influence student attitudes toward and engagement in physical activity**.

Many factors influence a student's participation in a particular activity. For instance, a boy may not wish to participate in a ballet dance because he perceives ballet dancing to be something for girls only. Or his cultural or ethnic norms may dictate that boys are too "macho" for that kind of dance (or any kind of dance for that matter). Similarly, a girl may not be interested in playing football because she believes football is a sport only boys play. Or perhaps her background and culture may suggest that any participation in sports or game is inappropriate for females. She may also think that she is not strong or big enough to participate in football. She may have been told that girls should play non-contact sports like tennis or participate in a dance group. The fact that only men play organized football at the highest levels reinforces the perception that women cannot play football. Perhaps contact sports are sports that her older brother(s) play and, even if she (or a boy) were interested, she (or he) is too young to participate.

In any of the above cases, the emphasis should be impartiality in terms of requirements for participation regardless of age, gender, ethnicity, and disability. We should also note that everyone is good at something and that nobody is good at everything. Those who are disabled may believe that they cannot play anything at all because of their disability. For those disabled students, many games and sports are strictly prohibited. However, instructors can modify many others to a point where the disabled student may participate and gain satisfaction.

Self-concept and motor performance are two important factors that affect student attitudes toward and engagement in physical activity. Students with more developed motor skills and healthier self-concepts are more likely to pursue participation in physical activities. We will now discuss several of the environmental and cultural factors that affect the development of self-concept and motor skills.

BIOLOGICAL AND ENVIRONMENTAL INFLUENCES ON GENDER DIFFERENCES IN MOTOR PERFORMANCES

The differences between males and females in motor performance result from certain biological and environmental influences. Generally, people perceive the males as stronger, faster, and more active than females. This higher activity level can stem from childhood behaviors influenced by certain environmental factors and superior motor performance results largely from the biological make up of males versus females.

In most cases, the male body contains less fat mass and more muscle mass than the female body. In addition, the type of muscle differs between males and females. Males have more fast-twitch muscle fibers allowing for more short duration, high intensity movements such as jumping and sprinting. In addition, males generally, but not always, display better coordination. Females have proved their superiority at certain activities, such as skipping, and tend to display better fine movements, such as neater handwriting.

Certain environmental factors also contribute to the gender differences in motor performance. As children, boys tend to be more physically active. Society expects boys to participate in sports and play games that involve running around, such as tag and foot races. On the other hand, society expects girls to be more social and less active. They participate in activities such as playing with dolls. In addition, parents rarely ask girls to perform tasks involving manual labor.

While these sedentary tasks have value, it is important for both males and females to participate in an adequate amount of physical activity each day. If children develop this type of active lifestyle early in life, they are more likely to maintain it throughout adulthood.

BODY IMAGE

Expectations relating to body image influence the development of self-concept by creating a benchmark of assumed correlations between body image and other traits. For example, a slight and skinny (ectomorphic) student may see himself as nonathletic, even though students with ectomorphic body types often excel at endurance sports. Students are also likely to generalize from body image to perceived ability to master new physical skills (for example, an athletic child might expect to be better at a new sport than less athletic children, even if the sport is new to both of them).

PHYSICAL APPEARANCE

Expectations relating to physical appearance influence the development of self-concept by virtue of assumptions correlating physical appearance with likeability. In fact, the relationship is reciprocal, and stronger in the opposite direction (students that are popular will tend to develop a more positive self-concept about their physical appearance).

SKILL LEVEL

Expectations relating to skill level influence the development of self-concept by setting the baseline for the performance that students will expect to deliver, both when attempting tasks that they are familiar with and new tasks (students with a high skill level will expect to do well, and students who are good at several things will expect to be good at other, new things).

MEDIA

Media-based expectations influence the development of self-concept by setting media-based role models as the benchmarks against which students will measure their traits. Self-concept is a set of statements describing the child's own cognitive, physical, emotional, and social self-assessment. These statements will usually tend to be fairly objective ("good at baseball" or "has red hair"), media-based expectations can change the statements to be measurements against role models ("athletic like this actor" or "tall like that pop star").

CULTURAL NORMS

Cultural norms have a significant and sometimes overlooked influence on decision relating to health behaviors, especially in the case of students belonging to minority groups. Students may not feel motivated to participate in certain physical activities, either because they are not associated with the student's sense of identity or because the student's culture discourages these activities. For example, students from cultures with strict dress codes may not be comfortable with swimming activities. On the same note, students (especially older children) may be uncomfortable with physical activities in inter-gender situations. Educators must keep such cultural considerations in mind when planning physical education curricula and educating students about physical activity.

PEER PRESSURE

Peer pressure can cause children to make decisions, both positive and negative. For example, a child that interacts with other children that practice poor health behaviors such as drug use are more likely to mimic such behaviors. On the other hand, interacting with children that are committed to exercise may encourage a previously inactive child to become physically active.

PSYCHOLOGICAL FACTORS

Certain psychological aspects may hinder participation in certain physical activities. These factors can depend on the individual, the group the individual will participate with, and the activity itself.

An individual's personality type and interests can determine their level of participation. Outgoing, energetic, and aggressive personality types usually exhibit increased levels of participation. Reserved or lazy personality types are sometimes difficult to work with and motivate. Shy individuals are usually compliant, but may not feel completely comfortable in participation, especially activities involving larger groups.

Physical education instructors often overlook the importance of activity groups to the psychological well-being of students. Instructors must construct groups with certain factors in mind. Children may feel intimidated by participating in activities with older individuals. In addition, girls may not feel comfortable participating with boys, and vise versa. Grouping students by age, gender, and skill level helps maintain self-confidence.

The type of activity can also affect participation. Everyone has different interests and instructors should not force students to participate in activities they do not enjoy. Such action can lead to a diminished physical activity level throughout life. Instructors should introduce alternate activities to increase levels of participation for all individuals.

Skill 11.2 **Demonstrate knowledge of strategies for motivating and encouraging students to participate in lifelong physical activity and for helping students become self-motivated.**

INTRINSIC MOTIVATION

Intrinsic motivation refers to the motivation to engage in an activity without any compelling external reason. It is when performing the activity is "its own reward". An understanding of the factors related to intrinsic motivation combines elements of attribution theory, self-efficacy, and research related to goal orientation. Some specific factors include:

- Attribution of educational results to internal factors that are under the control of the student (for example, the amount of effort that they put in, as opposed to their skill level, which students see as a fixed quantity).

- Belief that they are able to perform the desired tasks effectively because of their effort and skill-set (i.e. that positive results of their actions are not the result of luck).

- A connection with the subject matter – the student will enjoy the activity for the sake of the activity or enjoy the personal feeling of gaining skill in performing the activity (as opposed to rote-learning situations or receiving rewards for performance, such as good grades).

MOTIVATIONAL METHODS

Physical education instructors should give students homework just as academic teachers do. For example, when teaching the overhand throw, the instructor may ask his students to practice throwing with a friend during recess or a parent at home. Instructors should also be familiar with local sports leagues and other opportunities for physical activity in the community. The instructor can inform students of such opportunities and promote participation in physical activities throughout the year.

MOTIVATIONAL STRATEGIES

Motivation is essential to student learning physical education and all academic disciplines. Physical education instructors should recognize and understand the important elements of student motivation. Important theories and concepts in student motivation include attribution theory, social learning theory, learned helplessness, and self-efficacy.

Attribution theory describes how people make causal explanations and how they answer questions beginning with 'Why?' The theory deals with the information people use in making causal inferences and with how they utilize this information to answer causal questions. For instance, a student's aggressively competitive behavior may reflect her personality, or it may be a response to situational pressures. Attribution theory describes the processes of explaining events and the behavioral and emotional consequences of those explanations. Attribution theory also claims that students' perceptions of their educational experience affects their motivation more than the experience itself.

Social learning theory focuses on the learning that occurs within a social context. It emphasizes that people learn from one another and includes such concepts as observational learning, imitation, and modeling. Social learning theory asserts that people can learn by observing the behavior of others and the outcomes of those behaviors. It further states that learning can occur without a permanent change in behavior. Physical education instructors should also be note that cognition plays an important role in learning. Awareness and expectations of future rewards or punishments can have a major effect on the behaviors that people exhibit. Thus, socialization and reward/punishment can motivate students to learn.

Learned helplessness occurs in situations where continued failure may inhibit somebody from trying again and can also lead to many forms of depression. Thus, it is very important how physical education instructors respond to children's failures and successes. If a student feels as though he cannot control his environment, this lack of control will impair learning in certain situations. That is, learned helplessness often occurs in environments where people experience events in which they have, or feel as though they have, no control over what happens to them.

Self-efficacy describes a person's belief about his/her capability to produce designated levels of performance that exercise influence over events that affect their lives. Self-efficacy beliefs determine how people feel, think, motivate themselves, and behave. Such beliefs produce these diverse effects through cognitive, motivational, affective, and selection processes. A strong sense of efficacy enhances human accomplishment and personal well-being in many ways. People with high assurance in their capabilities view difficult tasks as challenges rather than threats. A student with high self-efficacy will be highly motivated to participate in sports and game related activities. To build efficacy, the instructor must not only raise the student's belief in his/her capabilities, but also structure situations that breed success and limit repeated failure. Students with high self-efficacy measure success in terms of self-improvement rather than by triumphs over others.

SELF-MOTIVATION

Finding intrinsic motivation for study is the main factor promoting the development of self-motivated learners. Helping learners become self-motivated is a process that revolves around connecting them personally with the material that they are studying, and instilling a belief in the their ability to control the outcome of their studies (if they believe they are not capable of mastering the material, they cannot become self-motivated learners).

This process begins with the cultivation of a positive attitude about the study of the subject matter in question. Instructors should emphasize to students that they are capable of mastering the material. Instructors can reinforce this belief by setting small, incremental milestones in the educational plan that shows the students the progress they are making.

Having convinced the students of their ability to learn the subject matter and master their goals, instructors should teach the students to become increasingly goal-oriented. This begins with students setting their own short-term goals and, after they begin developing a pattern of meeting their goals, longer-term goals. As students set goals, instructors should teach students to accept and assume responsibility for their decisions, actions, and outcomes.

Skill 11.3   Identify principles, benefits, and limitations of various classroom management approaches in physical activity settings and know techniques for organizing, allocating, scheduling, and managing resources in the physical education environment to provide active and equitable learning experiences.

The management of facilities, supplies, and other resources is an important part of the physical educator's job. Instructors must plan the availability, use, and safety of facilities. In addition, instructors must develop procedures for transporting, distributing, and collecting equipment. Finally, instructors must develop lesson plans that maximize the use of time and keep students active.

Facility management is the first task physical educators must consider. Instructors must ensure, through communication with other school personnel, that the required facilities are available when needed. In addition, instructors must inspect facilities prior to use to ensure the safety of the students. Instructors should carefully note uneven surfaces, holes, obstructions, and obstacles. Instructors may also have to modify rules or game procedures as the facility dimensions dictate.

Equipment management is another important responsibility of physical educators. Instructors must develop procedures for transporting equipment to and from the playing field or gymnasium. One way to simplify equipment transportation is to use a shopping cart, which many grocery stores will donate, to carry equipment. Instructors can also designate students as equipment managers to help carry and distribute equipment. Equipment distribution and collection is another important concern for physical educators. Spreading equipment throughout the playing area can speed the distribution process. Instructors should also establish a protocol for equipment return and set up areas for collection. Finally, instructors should develop signals, either verbal or visual, that direct students to stop the activity and either hold or put down the equipment.

One final physical educators' concern is class time management. One effective strategy for maximizing participation and the use of class time and equipment is to use stations. Stations allow students to rotate through a series of different activities in small groups. Instructors should use stations only for activities that the students are familiar with and are able to complete without constant supervision.

CLASSROOM MANAGEMENT

Proper organization of classroom procedures and information presentation is essential to classroom management and the fostering of a positive learning environment.

Instructors should establish and clearly communicate procedures and rules to maintain an orderly classroom. Organizational strategies that enhance classroom management include grouping of students, pre-planning of classroom activities, and rotation of students through various activities.

Organizational strategies that enhance information presentation include balancing instructional delivery methods, planning a variety of activities to appeal to students with different learning profiles, and planning a proper progression of information delivery to promote continual learning. Clustering, prioritizing, and categorizing are three common approaches to the organization of information.

Adequate supervision and behavioral management in the classroom is essential to student learning. Instructors must establish and communicate procedures, rules, and consequences of misbehavior to promote order in the classroom. Physical education instructors face unique behavioral management challenges because activities often take place in large, disperse environments. Techniques to consider when planning supervision and behavioral management include grouping students to achieve maximum compatibility, removing misbehaving students from activities, and establishing an orderly system to handle class procedures (e.g., activity time, instruction time, rotations, clean up, and dismissal).

Skill 11.4   Demonstrate knowledge of strategies for creating a positive climate for individual and group activities and for organizing and managing heterogeneous physical education classes in ways that promote positive interactions and active engagement in learning by all students.

Historically, there is a commonly held belief that physical education teachers and instructors do not have to face the problems of maintaining discipline. However, physical education, just like all other disciplines, requires proper management and discipline practices. The problem of management is inherent in the discipline of physical education. The central question remains whether various management and discipline practices will be beneficial or harmful to students.

Many students treat physical education classes as chance for rest and enjoyment, which makes maintaining disciplinary practices difficult. A common disciplinary goal is to create classroom rules and stick to them as well as to construct a creative environment by preparing activities for students.

Management and discipline practices are always valuable to physical education instructors. However, instructors must remember to deal with each student as an individual, taking into account their capabilities. Although implementing strict management practices might benefit the majority of the class and help in bringing decorum to the discipline, it might have negative effects too.

Curriculum design, group participation, cooperative work, fitness activities, and learning practices work well and instill exciting learning experiences for most, but there who are left out and need special care.

Professional management and disciplinary practices infuse professionalism, strictness, and decorum to any physical education setting. However, too many management practices may make the physical education setting boring and even unproductive for students.

TECHNIQUES TO MAXIMIZE PARTICIPATION

There are three options for maximizing participation: activity modification, multi-activity designs, and homogeneous or heterogeneous grouping.

Activity modification is the first option to achieve maximum participation by simply modifying the type of equipment used or the activity rules. However, keep activity as close to the original as possible (i.e. substitute a yarn ball for a birdie for badminton).

Multi-activity designs permit greater diversification of equipment and more efficient use of available facilities (keeps all students involved).

Homogeneous and heterogeneous grouping for the purpose of individualized instruction, enhancing self-concepts, equalizing competition, and promoting cooperation among classmates.

Furthermore, instructors should plan activities that encourage the greatest amount of participation by utilizing all available facilities and equipment, involving students in planning class work/activities, and being flexible. Instructors can also use tangible rewards and praise.

Skill 11.5   Analyze how participation in physical education activities can promote students' development of positive personal traits and abilities.

For most people, the development of social roles and appropriate social behaviors occurs during childhood. Physical play between parents and children, as well as between siblings and peers, serves as a strong regulator in the developmental process. Chasing games, roughhousing, wrestling, or practicing sport skills such as jumping, throwing, catching, and striking, are some examples of childhood play. These activities may be competitive or non-competitive and are important for promoting social and moral development of both boys and girls. Unfortunately, fathers will often engage in this sort of activity more with their sons than their daughters. Regardless of the sex of the child, both boys and girls enjoy these types of activities.

Physical play during infancy and early childhood is central to the development of social and emotional competence. Research shows that children who engage in play that is more physical with their parents, particularly with parents who are sensitive and responsive to the child, exhibited greater enjoyment during the play sessions and were more popular with their peers. Likewise, these early interactions with parents, siblings, and peers are important in helping children become more aware of their emotions and to learn to monitor and regulate their own emotional responses. Children learn quickly through watching the responses of their parents which behaviors make their parents smile and laugh and which behaviors cause their parents to frown and disengage from the activity.

If children want the fun to continue, they engage in the behaviors that please others. As children near adolescence, they learn through rough-and-tumble play that there are limits to how far they can go before hurting someone (physically or emotionally), which results in termination of the activity or later rejection of the child by peers. These early interactions with parents and siblings are important in helping children learn appropriate behavior in the social situations of sport and physical activity.

Children learn to assess their social competence (i.e., ability to get along with and acceptance by peers, family members, teachers and coaches) in sport through the feedback received from parents and coaches. Initially, authority figures teach children, "You can't do that because I said so." As children approach school age, parents begin the process of explaining why a behavior is right or wrong because children continuously ask, "why?"

Similarly, when children engage in sports, they learn about taking turns with their teammates, sharing playing time, and valuing rules. They understand that rules are important for everyone, and without these regulations, the game would become unfair. The learning of social competence is continuous as we expand our social arena and learn about different cultures. A constant in the learning process is the role of feedback as we assess the responses of others to our behaviors and comments.

In addition to the development of social competence, sport participation can help youth develop other forms of self-competence. Most important among these self-competencies is self-esteem. Self-esteem is how we judge our worth and indicates the extent to which an individual believes he is capable, significant, successful and worthy. Educators have suggested that one of the biggest barriers to success in the classroom today is low self-esteem.

Children develop self-esteem by evaluating abilities and by evaluating the responses of others. Children actively observe parents' and coaches' responses to their performances, looking for signs of approval or disapproval of their behavior. Children often interpret feedback and criticism as either a negative or a positive response to the behavior. In sports, research shows that the coach is a critical source of information that influences the self-esteem of children.

Little League baseball players whose coaches use a "positive approach" to coaching (e.g. more frequent encouragement, positive reinforcement for effort and corrective, instructional feedback), had significantly higher self-esteem ratings over the course of a season than children whose coaches used these techniques less frequently. The most compelling evidence supporting the importance of coaches' feedback was found for those children who started the season with the lowest self-esteem ratings and increased considerably their self-assessment and self-worth. In addition to evaluating themselves more positively, low self-esteem children evaluated their coaches more positively than did children with higher self-esteem who played for coaches who used the "positive approach." Moreover, studies show that 95 percent of children who played for coaches trained to use the positive approach signed up to play baseball the next year, compared with 75 percent of the youth who played for untrained adult coaches.

We cannot overlook the importance of enhanced self-esteem on future participation. A major part of the development of high self-esteem is the pride and joy that children experience as their physical skills improve. Children will feel good about themselves as long as their skills are improving. If children feel that their performance during a game or practice is not as good as that of others, or as good as they think mom and dad would want, they often experience shame and disappointment.

Some children will view mistakes made during a game as a failure and will look for ways to avoid participating in the task if they receive no encouragement to continue. At this point, it is critical that adults (e.g., parents and coaches) intervene to help children to interpret the mistake or "failure." We must teach children that a mistake is not synonymous with failure. Rather, a mistake shows us that we need a new strategy, more practice, and/or greater effort to succeed at the task.

Fairness is another trait that physical activities, especially rules-based sports, can foster and strengthen. Children are by nature very rules-oriented, and have a keen sense of what they believe is and isn't fair. Fair play, teamwork, and sportsmanship are all values that stem from proper practice of the spirit of physical education classes. Of course, a pleasurable physical education experience goes a long way towards promoting an understanding of the innate value of physical activity throughout the life cycle.

CONFLICT MANAGEMENT

Interpersonal conflict is a major source of stress and worry. Common sources of interpersonal conflict include problems with family relationships, competition, and disagreement over values or decisions. Teaching students to successfully manage conflict will help them reduce stress levels throughout their lives, thereby limiting the adverse health effects of stress. The following is a list of conflict resolution principles and techniques.

1. Think before reacting – In a conflict situation, it is important to resist the temptation to react immediately. You should step back, consider the situation, and plan an appropriate response. In addition, do not react to petty situations with anger.

2. Listen – Be sure to listen carefully to the opposing party. Try to understand the other person's point of view.

3. Find common ground – Try to find some common ground as soon as possible. Early compromise can help ease the tension.

4. Accept responsibility – In every conflict there is plenty of blame to go around. Admitting when you are wrong shows you are committed to resolving the conflict.

5. Attack the problem, not the person – Personal attacks are never beneficial and usually lead to greater conflict and hard feelings.

6. Focus on the future – Instead of trying to assign blame for past events, focus on what we need to do differently to avoid future conflict.

FAIRNESS, EQUITY, DIVERSITY

Physical activity and related games can introduce children to the concepts of equity and fairness. In addition, physical activity provides a venue for the interaction of diverse groups of people, allowing participants to observe and appreciate cultural differences and similarities.

- **Human Growth and Development** – Movement activities promote personal growth and development physically, by way of stimulating muscular development, and emotionally, by raising personal confidence levels among children and by allowing them to explore concepts of inter-group equity that may at first seem threatening. To the insecure child, the concept that another group may be equal to his own may seem to 'demote' his group and the child by extension.

- **Psychology** – Observation and interaction with the behavior of children from diverse backgrounds in a training environment (where the training activities tend to focus more on 'doing', which feels more genuine to children than the classroom setting of raising hands and answering questions) allows the child to see in others the same sorts of behavioral reasoning processes that he sees in himself. This humanizes others from diverse backgrounds, and promotes concepts of equity among diverse groups.
- **Aesthetics** – Human movement activities create an opportunity for individual participation in activities with intrinsic aesthetic qualities. A gymnastic technique or a perfectly executed swing of a baseball bat relies on both physical training and a level of intuitive action. This is an artistic form of expression that is readily accessible to children. Recognizing beauty in the activities and performances of others (in some cases from groups different from that of the viewing student) is a humanizing experience.

Skill 11.6 Analyze how participation in physical education activities can promote students' development of positive social behaviors and traits.

Physical education activities can promote positive social behaviors and traits in a number of different ways. Instructors can foster improved relations with adults and peers by making students active partners in the learning process and delegating responsibilities within the class environment to students. Giving students leadership positions (e.g. team captain) can give them a heightened understanding of the responsibilities and challenges facing educators.

Team-based physical activities like team sports promote collaboration and cooperation. In such activities, students learn to work together, both pooling their talents and minimizing the weaknesses of different team members, in order to achieve a common goal. The experience of functioning as a team can be very productive for development of loyalty between children, and seeing their peers in stressful situations that they can relate to can promote a more compassionate and considerate attitude among students. Similarly, the need to maximize the strengths of each student on a team (who can complement each other and compensate for weaknesses) is a powerful lesson about valuing and respecting diversity and individual differences. Varying students between leading and following positions in a team hierarchy are good ways to help students gain a comfort level being both followers and leaders.

Physical fitness activities incorporate group processes, group dynamics, and a wide range of cooperation and competition. Ranging from team sports (which are both competitive and cooperative in nature) to individual competitive sports (like racing), to cooperative team activities without a winner and loser (like a gymnastics team working together to create a human pyramid), there is a great deal of room for the development of mutual respect and support among the students, safe cooperative participation, and analytical, problem solving, teamwork, and leadership skills.

Teamwork situations are beneficial to students because they create opportunities for them to see classmates with whom they might not generally socialize, and with whom they may not even get along, in a new light. It also creates opportunities for students to develop reliance on each other and practice interdependence. Cooperation and competition can also offer opportunities for children to practice group work. These situations provide good opportunities to practice analytical thinking and problem solving in a practical setting.

The social skills and values gained from participation in physical activities include:

- The ability to make adjustments to self and others by an integration of the individual to society and the environment.

- The ability to make judgments in a group situation.

- Learning to communicate with others and be cooperative.

- The development of the social phases of personality, attitudes, and values in order to become a functioning member of society such as being considerate.

- The development of a sense of belonging and acceptance by society.

- The development of positive personality traits.

- Learning for constructive use of leisure time.

- A development of attitude that reflects good moral character.

- Respect of school rules and property.

The above list represents a sample of the socio-cultural benefits of participating in physical activity with others. Physical activity serves as a very important part of the socialization process. Physical activity during the socialization process creates an opportunity for children to define personal comfort levels with different types of physical interaction, as well as to establish guidelines for what is (and is not) acceptable physical behavior as related to their relationship with other individuals.

Participating in physical activity with others is also a step away from the trend of "playground to PlayStation", where students are less and less physically active, and spend less and less time engaging in outdoor physical activity. Physical activity on a socio-cultural level is an important aspect of the struggle against rising obesity levels in the United States, as well as related problems (like heart disease).

TRANSFERABLE SKILLS

By participating in physical activities, students develop various aspects of the self that are easily applicable to other settings (e.g., the workplace). Communication is one skill that improves enormously through participation in sports and games. Students will come to understand that skillful communication can contribute to a better all-around outcome, whether it be winning the game or successfully completing a team project. They will see that effective communication helps to develop and maintain healthy personal relationships, organize and convey information, and reduce or avoid conflict.

Physical activities also teach students how to set personal goals. At first, one can set a physical goal such as running one mile in eight minutes. After accomplishing that specific feat, the student will feel capable and will be more willing to set greater goals in various fields within his life.

Finally, physical activities teach perseverance, the importance of following directions, leadership, and teamwork. Recovering from competitive loses and withstanding personal and team setbacks help develop perseverance. All games and sports have rules that participants must follow in order to participate. Leadership and teamwork are both integral parts of team sports. In the team sport setting, participants learn how to work together and lead others to achieve a common goal. These skills are invaluable in real life and the workplace.

Skill 11.7   Apply knowledge of methods for promoting student development of self-management skills in relation to physical activity and health-related lifestyle decisions.

Physical education instructors can foster critical-thinking and evaluative skills in the context of physical education and health-related activities by making children active partners in the entire learning and training process. If instructors provide students with an understanding of the mechanisms (e.g. cardiorespiratory, muscular, circulatory) underlying their training (in addition to the knowledge they are given about specific training exercises), students can get more involved and think more critically about their training routines and how they could adapt them to better suit their needs.

Instructors should encourage students to employ self-assessment and self-monitoring techniques and skills. For example, they could keep a journal tracking their personal achievements – cardiorespiratory (measured in resting heart rate, active heart rate, intensity, and duration of exercise), muscular development (measured by their ability to perform callisthenic exercises).

Instructors should also encourage students to explore and increase their understanding (with educator assistance) of the way that the underlying bodily systems work in relation to other disciplines. For example, students can learn about the chemistry involved in the gas and energy exchanges happening between the cardiorespiratory and circulatory system, they can learn about the biology of the digestive system and the effects of different types of nutrition on the body, and they can learn about the physics involved in energy expenditure by the muscular system.

PROBLEM SOLVING

Problem solving is a higher-order cognitive process that requires the modulation and control of more routine or fundamental skills. It is the ability to solve a problem. We would have the students call upon their problem-solving skills during a game of chess. Alternatively, they could strategize during a timeout in the last few seconds of a basketball game where their team is down by two points. Development of adequate problem solving skills also provides the student with self-confidence and a sense of accomplishment.

TRUST BUILDING

Trust building activities can break down barriers and build deep feelings of trust and reliance between individuals and within small groups of students. However, the power of these activities is a double-edged sword and instructors must use caution in selecting and conducting trust-based activities. If instructors introduce trust activities too early or too fast, emotional and/or physical harm can occur, with trust broken rather than built. For example, a common trust building activity involves blindfolding a person and having another member of the group guide. It is vital to demonstrate and actively encourage a high level of care and responsibility towards people in these exercises who take the risk of trusting. It is not ok to have a blindfolded and trusting person walk into a wall or low bench. For example, we could use the circle of trust game where a group of students forms a circle around a blindfolded student or a student with her eyes closed. The blindfolded student keeps her entire body stiff and leans/falls forward or backward. The other students, keeping hands raised the entire time, keep her from falling. This is an exercise requiring both diligence and vigilance in keeping the blindfolded student safe, but the trust building rewards are worth it.

RISK TAKING

Healthy risk taking is a positive tool in an adolescent's life for discovering, developing, and consolidating his or her identity. It is important to remember that learning how to assess risks is a process that we work on throughout our lives. Children and adolescents need support, tools, and practice in order to do this. Teachers can help support students by encouraging a student to participate in something that may stretch his abilities, but not to the point where his limitations place him in a dangerous situation. For example, participation in an unfamiliar sport where the other students welcomes and supports provides a degree of satisfaction for the student. A bad example would be putting a student on a team of large football players when he is either small-framed, inexperienced, or both.

You can observe the style of risk taking by the way a student handles a new social situation. Although there are many styles, we can observe certain patterns, such as the cautious risk taker, the middle-of-the-roader, the adventurer or high-end risk taker, and the social risk taker whose boldness increases when he or she is with friends. It is also important to note that some children may be risk takers in one area – social, physical, intellectual, artistic – and not in others.

ENJOYMENT AND PERSONAL EXPRESSION

In addition to the previously discussed achievement benefits of physical activity, physical activity also provides many people with pure enjoyment and the opportunity for personal expression. Exercise promotes a sense of well-being and usually improves a person's mood. Sports also provide a venue for social interaction and enjoyment of nature. Finally, many sports and activities, especially freestyle activities like skateboarding, figure skating, dance, and surfing, allow for a high level of personal expression.

Skill 11.8   Demonstrate knowledge of principles and techniques for promoting students' goal-setting analysis, problem-solving, and decision-making skills in physical education contexts.

There are three key elements necessary for promoting students' goal-setting analysis, problem-solving, and decision-making skills in physical education contexts. First, instructors must give students a clear understanding of the goals they need to attain, problems that they need to solve, and decisions that they need to make. Second, instructors must give students the requisite information needed to attain the goals, solve the problems, and make the decisions. Third, instructors need to give students the opportunity to assume active responsibility for these matters and create opportunities for them to act on those responsibilities.

Instructors can give students a clear understanding of the goals they need to attain, problems they need to solve, and decisions they need to make, by explaining the entire scenarios to them. Instructors should leave students with a clear impression of why they need to take some action and what the desired outcome should look like.

Next, instructors should give students information to take action. This includes reasonable progression timelines, and an understanding of the physical and biomechanical principles that inform these decisions. For example, if a student is interested in building upper-body strength, the instructor should give the student an understanding of the biomechanical systems related to upper-body strength development, and what actions she can take to reach her goal.

Finally, instructors should emphasize to students that taking action is their responsibility. Whatever their personal training goals, it is the role of the physical educator to show students how to achieve their goals, but not to force them to take the requisite actions. The student must provide the motivation. This creates a reciprocal relationship between decision-making and action-taking on the part of the student. The more they get accustomed to making decisions and following through, the better equipped they will be to act similarly in future situations.

COMPETENCY 12.0 STRUCTURE, ORGANIZATION, GOALS, AND PURPOSES OF PHYSICAL EDUCATION PROGRAMS

Skill 12.1 Demonstrate knowledge of the structure, organization, goals, and purposes of physical education programs.

STRUCTURE AND ORGANIZATION

The first few weeks of the school year is the most effective time for teaching class management structure (behavioral rules, terms for compliance and violation of rules, and classroom routines).

Instructors must manage all essential procedures and routines (roll call, excuses, tardiness, changing, and showering) to productively use available class time. Good class management also insures the safety of the group through procedures and routines, provides a controlled classroom atmosphere to make instruction easier, promotes individual self-discipline and self-motivation, develops a sense of responsibility towards others, develops rapport between teacher and students that promotes learning, creates a group camaraderie where each student feels good about him/herself and feels at ease within the group, uses the instructor's time and energy productively, and organizes and coordinates classes for the most effective instruction and learning.

Long-term planning for the semester and year, as well as daily, weekly, and seasonal planning, is necessary. Instructors must effectively plan activities so that they proceed with precision, minimize "standing-around time", and allow for maximum activity time for each student. Instructors should arrange activities in advance and prepare any necessary line markings.

To determine student progress and effectiveness of teaching, instructors must plan appropriate measurement and evaluation opportunities. Instructors also must wear suitable clothing, have good knowledge of the subject, and promote desirable attitudes toward and understandings of fitness, skill learning, sportsmanship, and other physical education objectives.

The main goals and purpose of physical education is to introduce students to fitness, activity, and nutrition concepts and allow students to be physically active during the school day. Proper structure and organization allows the realization of these goals.

GOALS OF PHYSICAL EDUCATION AND CHARACTERISTICS OF VARIOUS CURRICULUM MODELS

With a history that spans centuries and roots traceable to the ancient Greeks, physical education is a technique that helps in promoting the physical fitness and well-being of a body.

The primary aim of physical education, otherwise known as physical training, is to equip students with the knowledge, skills, capabilities, values, and enthusiasm necessary to the maintenance of a healthy lifestyle into adulthood, regardless of physical ability. Activities included in the program promote physical fitness, develop motor skills, instill knowledge and understanding of rules, concepts, and strategies, and teach students to work as part of a team or as individuals in a wide variety of play-based and competitive activities.

Physical education has come to occupy a very important role in most school programs. There are various curriculum models for physical education courses. Such curricula stress the meaning of human movement, physiology of exercise, sport sociology, aesthetic appreciation of movement, and the acquisition of skills. Modern curricula include all of these competencies.

The modern physical education curriculum provides students a basic experience in the following activities: aquatics, conditioning activities, gymnastics, individual/dual sports, team sports, and rhythm and dance. All states in the United States offer physical education to students in grades K through 12, and many states require the self-contained classroom teacher to implement a physical education program.

All curriculum models have the following characteristics: physical activity, by which students will become competent in a variety of, and proficient in a few, physical activities; human movement, in which students will understand and apply principles of human movement to the learning and development of motor skills; fitness; responsible behavior, wherein students will exhibit responsible personal and social behavior in physical activity settings; respect for differences; and benefits of physical activity, by which students will identify and understand how physical activity provides personal enjoyment, challenge, self-expression, and social interaction.

Skill 12.2 Analyze philosophies, trends, and issues in physical educations and their effects on the goals, scope, and components of physical education programs.

Physical education instructors can use national and state documents, standards, benchmarks, trends and philosophies to design and develop effective curricula.

First, governmental organizations (e.g. U.S. Department of Education, individual state departments of education) regularly release documents outlining standards for physical education. Common physical education standards require that students learn skills necessary to participate in a variety of physical activities, become physically fit, participate regularly in physical activity, understand the benefits and implications of physical fitness, and value physical activity as part of a healthy lifestyle. Instructors must mold their curricula to ensure that their students meet these standards.

In addition, governmental organizations often determine benchmarks that define physical development and fitness in school-age children. For example, standards may indicate what motor skills students should possess at certain ages and the specific performance criteria that define physical fitness. Instructors can use the benchmarks and tests to evaluate student development and fitness and plan curricula for student improvement.

Finally, national trends and philosophies greatly affect physical education curricula. National trends toward greater longevity, increased obesity, and sedentary lifestyles increase the need for a renewed emphasis on fitness and activity to prevent and reduce fitness related health problems. The philosophies of life-long learning and fitness are also an important aspect of physical education. Instructors should design curricula that encourage and motivate students to become active and take a life-long interest in the physical health of their bodies. We will now discuss important trends and philosophies that affect the physical education program.

CURRENT TRENDS

National trends and philosophies greatly affect physical education curricula. National trends toward greater longevity, increased obesity, and sedentary lifestyles increase the need for a renewed emphasis on fitness and activity to prevent and reduce fitness related health problems. The philosophies of life-long learning and fitness are also an important aspect of physical education. Instructors should design curricula that encourage and motivate students to become active and take a life-long interest in the physical health of their bodies. In addition, logistical factors, such as facility availability and mainstreaming, greatly affect physical education programs.

Loss of physical education facilities

With increasingly tight public school budgets and increased emphasis on academic standards and testing, many schools are experiencing a loss of physical education facilities. In many school districts, physical education operates on a shoestring budget. The loss of facilities such as gymnasiums, playing fields, swimming pools, and related equipment limits the scope of physical education programs. Inadequate facilities prevent instructors from utilizing many types of activities. Thus, instructors must use the available facilities in the best way possible to maximize the physical education experience for all students.

Inclusion and mainstreaming

A major goal of contemporary physical education is inclusion and mainstreaming of all types of students. Instructors must modify activities to include students with disabilities and students of all ability levels. In addition, the physical education program should embrace the cultural, linguistic, and familial differences of all students. Inclusion and mainstreaming shifts the focus OF physical education from competitive, athletic activities to cooperative, skill-building activities that benefit all children and promote inclusion. Thus, the primary goal and focus of physical education is promotion of physical activity, motor-skill development, and socialization.

PAST AND PRESENT EDUCATION PHILOSOPHIES

The various philosophies of education greatly influence the goals and values of physical education. Important educational philosophies related to physical education are Idealism, Realism, Pragmatism, Naturalism, Existentialism, Humanism, and Eclecticism.

Idealism – The **mind**, developed through the acquisition of knowledge, is of highest importance. Values exist independently of individuals. Fitness and strength activities contribute to the development of one's personality. Horace Mann, Wadsworth, Kant, Plato, and Descartes were Idealists.

Realism – The physical world is **real.** A realist believes in the laws of nature, the scientific method, and mind and body harmony. Religion and philosophy co-exist. Physical fitness results in greater productivity, physical drills are important to the learning process, athletic programs lead to desired social behavior, and play and recreation help life adjustment. Aristotle was a realist.

Pragmatism – **Experience** is key to life. Dynamic experience shapes individuals' truth. Education is child-centered. Varied activities present experiences that are more meaningful. Activities are socializing. Problem solving accomplishes learning. John Dewy and Charles Pierce were pragmatists.

Naturalism – This philosophy is materialistic. Things that actually exist are found only within the physical realm of nature. Nature is valuable. The individual is more important than society. Self-activities accomplish learning and activities are more than physical in nature. Naturalists promote play and discourage high levels of competition. Physical education takes a holistic approach.

Existentialism – The chief concern is **individualism.** Existentialists do not want the individual to conform to society. They promote freedom of choice and a variety of interests. Individuals need to have their own system of values. Playing develops creativity and the discovery of the "inner self." Sartre, Soren, and Kierkegaard were Existentialists.

Humanism and **Eclecticism** – The modern philosophies of physical education that most schools follow today. The Humanistic philosophy is based on development of individual talents and total fulfillment that encourages total involvement and participation in one's environment. Humanists encourage self-actualization and self-fulfillment. Curriculums based on the Humanistic approach are more student-centered. The Eclectic approach combines beliefs from different philosophies and does not resemble any single philosophy. When blended skillfully, the Eclectic approach affords a sound philosophy for an individual.

PHILOSOPHIES OF EDUCATION APPLIED TO physical education GOALS

Physical/Organic Development Goal (Realism philosophy) – activities build physical power by strengthening the body's systems, resulting in the ability to sustain adaptive effort, shorten recovery time, and develop resistance to fatigue. The core values are individual health, greater activity, and better performance by an adequately developed and properly functioning body.

Motor/Neuromuscular Development Goal (Realism philosophy) – develops body awareness producing movement that is proficient, graceful, and aesthetic and uses as little energy as possible. Students develop as many skills as possible so their interests are wide and varied to allow more enjoyment and better adjustment to group situations. Varied motor development skills affect health by influencing how leisure time is spent. Values include reducing energy expenditure, building confidence, bringing recognition, enhancing physical and mental health, making participation safer, and contributing to aesthetic sense.

Cognitive Development Goal (Idealism philosophy) – deals with acquiring knowledge and ability to think and interpret knowledge. Scientific principles explain time, space, and flow of movement. Learning physical activities requires thinking and coordination of movement and mastering and adapting to one's environment. Individuals also should acquire knowledge of rules, techniques, and strategies of activities. Cognitive values include healthy attitudes and habits such as body awareness, personal hygiene, disease prevention, exercise, proper nutrition, and knowledge of health service providers.

Social/Emotional/Affective Development Goal (Existentialism philosophy) – deals with helping individuals make adjustments – personal, group, and societal – by positively influencing human behavior. Performance defines success, and success develops self-confidence. Wholesome attitudes throughout the various growth stages promote the development of an appropriate Self-Concept, which is very important. Values include meeting basic social needs (sense of belonging, recognition, self-respect, and love) that produce a socially, well-adjusted individual.

Skill 12.3   Demonstrate knowledge of characteristics of an effective physical education program and important state and national initiatives that influence physical education content and practices.

A comprehensive physical education curriculum emphasizes the importance of physical activity and nutrition to lifelong wellness. In addition, physical education should introduce students to various activities that promote healthy living. Finally, physical education should provide students with strategies to maintain proper nutrition and activity and design personal fitness programs.

A significant contribution to the development and maintenance of student health is the main characteristic of an effective physical education curriculum. The goal of physical education is to develop physically educated individuals who have the knowledge, skills and confidence to enjoy a lifetime of healthful activity. The following is a list of standards that students of a physical education program should be able to achieve.

- **Standard 1:** Demonstrate competency in motor skills and movement patterns needed to perform a variety of physical activities.

- **Standard 2:** Demonstrate understanding of movement concepts, principles, strategies, and tactics as they apply to the learning and performance of physical activities.

- **Standard 3:** Participate regularly in physical activity.

- **Standard 4:** Achieve and maintain a health-enhancing level of physical fitness.

- **Standard 5:** Exhibit responsible personal and social behavior that respects self and others in physical activity settings.

- **Standard 6:** Value physical activity for health, enjoyment, challenge, self-expression, and/or social interaction.

Note: This above section is adapted from:
http://www.aahperd.org/NASPE/publications-nationalstandards.html

Important state and national initiatives that influence physical education content and practices include the Texas-based "Eat Smart. Be Active" campaign, and national initiatives like the Centers for Disease Control and Prevention's (CDC) National Physical Activity Initiative, programs run by the Office of Safe and Drug-Free Schools (OSDFS) for "Health, Mental Health, Environmental Health, and Physical Education Programs", and the National Heart Lung and Blood Institute's (NHLBI) "Obesity Education Initiative" (OEI). You can find further information about these initiatives on their websites:

"Eat Smart. Be Active" - http://www.eatsmartbeactivetx.org/

CDC's National Physical Activity Initiative -
http://www.cdc.gov/nccdphp/sgr/npai.htm

Office of Safe and Drug-Free Schools (OSDFS) -
http://www.ed.gov/about/offices/list/osdfs/programs.html#health

National Heart Lung and Blood Institute -
http://www.nhlbi.nih.gov/about/oei/oei_pd.htm

Skill 12.4   Apply knowledge of principles and techniques for evaluating the effectiveness of the physical education program and for adopting and modifying practices and programs based on reflection, assessment data, observation of students, and program evaluation results.

REFLECTIVE TEACHING

The **Reflective Approach** to teaching involves continuous self-monitoring by the teacher of situations, behaviors, practices, effectiveness, and accomplishments. The instructor reflects upon and evaluates his or her own teaching and determines what changes are necessary. By evaluating and accessing one's strengths and weaknesses as a teacher, instructors can determine how they can improve their performance. For example, an instructor may choose to seek out additional coursework or resources to remedy a void in his or her teaching experience.

STUDENT AND PROGRAM EVALUATIONS IN PHYSICAL EDUCATION

The **Cheffers Adaptation of the Flanders Interaction Analysis System** (CAFAIS) and the **Academic Learning Time in Physical Education** (ALT-PE) are *Systematic Analyses* that detect continuous and discrete behaviors, actions and interactions, and teaching characteristics. Relating the goals of a systematic analysis to the data obtained during the instructional process can indicate which of the following instructional strategies need changing:

- The ability of the teacher to question and the time engaged in questioning

- The cognitive response of students

- The time spent on task instruction (rate per minute)

- The number of times task instruction takes place (rate of occurrence)

Instructors can use the following **Systematic Observational Evaluations** to identify necessary changes in events, in duration, in groups, and in self-recording:

Event Recording (rate-per-minute, rate of occurrence) – counts the number of attempts students have to try a skill and the number of positive teacher-student interactions.

- **Duration Recording** – measures amount of time teacher spends on instructions, time spent on managing student activities, and time spent managing the participation of students.

- **Group Time Sampling/Playcheck Recording** – counts the number of students participating in the activity.

- **Self-Recording** – students sign in their arrival time to class and how many completed tasks they accomplish.

Student assessments that can facilitate changes in instructional strategies include:

- **Formal assessments** such as win/loss records, written tests, skills tests, performance records, and reviewing videotaped performances.

- **Informal assessments** such as rating scales, observational performance descriptions, completion of skills checklist, and observational time utilization.

Adapting and modifying physical education programs is analogous to modifying individual fitness plans. Modification and adaptation involves identifying areas of strength and weakness from the assessment results and adjusting goals and activities to address the weaknesses. For example, if the students in a particular physical education program score poorly on cardiovascular fitness tests, the instructor should integrate more aerobic activities into the curriculum.

INDIVIDUAL FITNESS PLAN ADAPTATION

After assessing an individual's fitness level, a personal fitness trainer or instructor can prescribe a training program. Prescription of a fitness program begins with:

1. Identifying the components of fitness that need changing (via assessment)

2. Establishing short-term goals

3. Developing a plan to meet the established goals

4. Keeping records to record progress

5. Evaluating progress of goals and making changes based on success or failure

For successful programs, the instructor and student should formulate new goals and change the personal fitness program to accomplish the new goals.

For unsuccessful programs, changing the goals, particularly if the goals were too unrealistic, is an appropriate response. Adjusting goals allows individuals to make progress and succeed. In addition, analyzing positive and negative results may identify barriers preventing an individual's success in her personal fitness program. Incorporating periodic, positive rewards for advancing can provide positive reinforcement and encouragement.

Skill 12.5 Demonstrate knowledge of strategies for advocating for physical education and for identifying and publicizing opportunities and resources for physical activity in the school and community.

An important task for physical educators is to convince other educators, parents, and political decision makers of the importance of physical education. This responsibility is unique to teachers of subjects outside of the traditional academic core. Few people will question the importance of math or reading, while many will question the importance of physical education, arts, and music. One effective strategy for promoting physical education is to relate physical education to the academic curriculum. In addition, physical educators should point out the many physical, psychological, and social benefits of physical education.

An effective physical education instructor always projects a positive message about physical activity. Methods of projecting a positive message include creating an organized program with a structured schedule and delivering lessons enthusiastically. Instructors should never diminish the importance of physical education in comparison to academic subjects. Sticking to a structured schedule creates a positive environment and shows students that the instructor takes his subject seriously. The instructor's enthusiasm can inspire students to engage in physical activity outside of school.

Finally, physical education instructors should give students homework just as academic teachers do. For example, when teaching the overhand throw, the instructor may ask his students to practice throwing with a friend during recess or a parent at home. Instructors should also be familiar with local sports leagues and other opportunities for physical activity in the community. The instructor can inform students of such opportunities and promote participation in physical activities throughout the year.

COMMUNITY RESOURCES

There are many community resources available to physical education professionals that students can make use of during out-of-school hours. Private and public organizations and clubs, such as sporting teams, gyms, and community and recreation centers are all places that offer resources for physical activities. Similarly, public and private pools and skating rinks are valuable resources (participants must observe the safety regulations of the location as well as any unspecified, common-sense safety guidelines). Public parks are available for outdoor physical activities.

MAINTAINING COMMUNITY RESOURCES

In order to maintain and improve personal and community resources in relation to physical activity and fitness, educators must enhance the levels of commitment to physical activities and related resources (on both an individual and community level). Educators must also stress the value and importance of physical activity (for fitness, health and wellness, and community-building purposes).

Educators can promote this commitment by emphasizing the need to make time for family and community activities, which often have physical activity components (or can be entirely based on physical activity, like a family hiking trip). Educators can take this a step further, by instituting activities (on a family or community level) to actually maintain or improve the state of physical activity resources. For example, the educator can organize a sponsored walk or run to fund-raise for the maintenance of school exercise equipment, or a family might come together to construct a jungle-gym in their back yard for the children to play on.

Another important step in strengthening the commitment of individuals and the community to physical activities and related resources is to educate about the role of physical activity as a resource for everyone, regardless of age and ability. It is important that there are concrete examples of services and activities available that serve as opportunities for all age groups and ability/skill levels to participate in and benefit from physical activity (if physical activity is truly available to everyone, it is easier to make the case that it is a community resource that the community should be maintain and improve).

Skill 12.6 **Understand relationships between physical education and other subject areas and know strategies for integrating physical education concepts across the curriculum.**

The lines between different fields of study are growing ever more vague and blurry. Today we understand that not only is it possible to blend fields of study together, it is in the best interest of the child to do so. Increased connections between fields of knowledge in a child's mind reinforce all of the associated fields. Physical education connects to other subject areas in the following ways:

- **Life and Physical Sciences** – Giving students an understanding of the life and physical sciences that stand behind physical education can greatly reinforce the learning experience for children. For example, the physics of force and leverage can give children insight into the mechanics of gymnastic activities. The biology of carbohydrates turning into fuel for the muscles and protein used to rebuild muscle tissue, can grant insight into the study of nutrition.

- **Social Sciences** – Examination of the styles of interaction within and between groups in competitive team-based games and sports (e.g. soccer, dodge ball), interactions between children in competitive individual activities (e.g. running a race), and interactions between children engaging in personal-achievement, individual activities (e.g. gymnastics training, where no one is competing), help children understand concepts of social organization and interaction, and helps them to draw parallels with physical education experiences and other contexts.

- **Health Sciences** – Children who learn the relationship between physical activity and health – not just in a general "exercise is good for you" sort of way, but in a more detailed manner (e.g. aerobic fitness training stimulates the cardiovascular system, strengthening the heart and increasing the yield of oxygen per heartbeat) – are more likely to look to fitness training as a potential response to health problems.

- **Mathematics and Language Arts** – These two fields are more peripherally connected to physical education. The connections here are more in the use of mathematics and language arts as mediums to better quantify and communicate achievements.

- **Visual and Performing Arts** – There is a great deal of overlap between movement activities and visual and performing arts – whether it is the strenuous work of painting a large canvas, or the more obviously artistic activities of gymnastics or martial arts. Helping students to see the connections between these two disciplines can stimulate crossovers from one to the other, helping children to broaden their horizons.

COMPETENCY 13.0 LEGAL ISSUES AND RESPONSIBILITIES OF PHYSICAL EDUCATION TEACHERS IN RELATION TO SUPERVISION, PLANNING AND INSTRUCTION, SAFETY, FIRST AID, AND RISK MANAGEMENT

Skill 13.1 Apply knowledge of legal and ethical issues and responsibilities relevant to physical education.

LIABILITY CONCERNS IN PHYSICAL EDUCATION

Historically, common-law rules stated that individuals could not sue government agencies without consent of the agencies. However, federal and state courts have begun to allow individuals to sue both federal and state governments. Thus, public schools and school districts are now subject to liability lawsuits.

Compulsory elements of the school curriculum, such as physical education, prompt courts to decide based on what is in the best interests of the public.

Although school districts still have immunity in many states, teachers do not have such immunity. Whether employed by private person or a municipal corporation every employee owes a duty not to injure another by a negligent act of commission.

The following is a list of common legal terms and conditions applicable to physical education.

1. Tort – a legal wrong resulting in a direct or indirect injury; includes omissions and acts intended or unintended to cause harm.

2. Negligence – failing to fulfill a legal duty according to common reasoning; includes instruction and facility maintenance; instructors must consider sex, size, and skill of participants when planning activities and grouping students.

3. In Loco Parentis – acting in the place of the parent in relation to a child.

4. Sports Product Liability – liability of the manufacturer to the person using the manufacturer's product who sustains injury/damage from using the product.

5. Violence and legal liability (intentional injury in sports contests) – harmful, illegal contact of one person by another (referred to as battery).

6. Physical education classes held off campus and legal liability – primary concern is providing due care, which is the responsibility of management and staff members of sponsoring organization; failing to observe "due care" can result in findings of negligence.

7. Attractive Nuisance – an object that results in physical injury that the responsible party should have foreseen.

LEGAL AND ETHICAL ISSUES AND RESPONSIBILITIES

There are many issues related to the legal responsibilities of the professional physical educator. Failing to foresee potential hazardous conditions and to take practical steps to avoid these situations can result in litigation. In general, teachers must follow the standard of care expected of any physical education practitioner with a similar level of education and training. Liability refers to a legal responsibility. Often in litigious situations, the term liability refers to negligence, or breach of duty. Negligence refers to actions that do not meet the minimum standard of care. In successful litigation, the defense proves the existence of the following: duty, breach of duty, injury, and proximate cause. When determining liability, courts will determine whether the injury was foreseeable.

To avoid legal action, professional physical educators must meet their legal responsibilities in several areas: equipment and facilities, instruction, supervision, and general safety. Regular inspection of the instructional area identifies potential hazards. When physical educators find hazards, they should submit written notification to the principal immediately. Students should also receive proper instruction of equipment use prior to the first use. In an instructional setting, the physical educator protects students from unreasonable harm. Students receive appropriate training before and during activity. Supervision of all activities in a school setting is mandatory. An unsupervised student in the school at any time or on the school grounds during the school day is unacceptable. The approach to overall safety should be proactive.

Physical educators participate in safety in-service programs each year. The teacher or another school medical professional review the student's medical records prior to allowing participation in physical education. Physical education practitioners teach the safety rules for each activity at the beginning of each unit. When a student sustains an injury in physical education class, the school nurse or other medical professional evaluates the student. The physical educator completes and files an accident report the same day that the accident occurred.

An Emergency Action Plan (EAP) should be in place for the physical education department at each school. The EAP identifies the following: emergency care procedures and the individual responsible for rendering care, the individual responsible for parental notification, the individual responsible for activating the emergency medical system (EMS), the policy for transportation of injured students, and a copy of a blank student accident report. To reduce the financial consequences of litigation, each teacher should purchase and maintain personal professional liability insurance. Teachers should not rely on school district legal liability insurance for personal financial protection.

In addition to legal responsibilities, the physical educator also has ethical responsibilities. Teachers are responsible for helping each student to realize his or her abilities. Physical educators are accountable for the welfare of each student entrusted to their care. Teachers should maintain a professional relationship with their students. Teachers should maintain confidentiality. Physical educators should follow national, state, and district or school curricular standards. Teachers should establish and maintain a classroom routine that promotes student achievement. Finally, the physical education teacher is responsible for promoting healthful living within the school community.

LEGAL AND ETHICAL APPLICATIONS

There are many issues related to the ethical and legal responsibilities of the professional physical educator.

Physical educators at all levels should regularly inspect the instructional area for potential hazards. At the elementary and middle school level, the instructional areas might include the gymnasium and any outdoor areas utilized for instruction. At the high school level, the instructional area might not only include the gymnasium and outdoor field area, but might also include a weight training facility and/ or a swimming pool and surrounding deck area.

The physical education practitioner will also inspect equipment prior to student use. At the elementary and middle school level, inspected equipment might include such items as racquets, game standards, archery bows and arrows, scooters, gymnastics equipment, protection gear for high velocity sports, and golf equipment. At the high school level, inspected equipment would also include any weights and machines utilized in the weight training facility. Naturally, the physical educator provides proper instruction of equipment use prior to the first use at every grade level.

Strict enforcement of safety rules is essential. Elementary students allowed to swing a hockey stick to shoulder height might seriously injure a classmate. Supervision of all activities in a school setting is mandatory. This is especially true of the gymnasium and any other area where unsupervised students might misuse equipment. The approach to overall safety at each grade level should be proactive.

As students mature in middle school and high school, it is important to partner students for safe participation by size and ability. At the middle school level, it is especially important for teachers to be aware of potential bullying situations. Teachers should maintain a professional relationship with their students. It is particularly crucial at the middle school and high school levels for teachers to maintain a professional distance from their students. A teacher who considers students as "friends" is at risk for accusations of improper conduct. Additionally, teachers should avoid being alone with a student in a secluded or enclosed classroom at any time.

Teachers should also maintain confidentiality. At all levels, teachers should be conscious of the fact that others may overhear conversations. Sharing unnecessary student information may not only be harmful to the student's reputation, but other students or parents may overhear the unprofessional conversation. Physical educators should follow national, state, and district or school curricular standards. Teachers should establish and maintain a classroom routine that promotes student achievement. Clear definition and enforcement of classroom expectations helps to maintain an environment that promotes student achievement.

Finally, the physical education teacher is responsible for promoting healthful living within the school community. The promotion of healthful living might include such things as helping middle school and high school students make wise nutritional choices at lunch, starting a walking club for teachers and students, initiating and managing a weight loss program for faculty members, or supervising an outdoor adventure club at the high school level.

Skill 13.2   Demonstrate knowledge of state and federal laws and guidelines regarding student rights and teacher responsibilities in physical education contexts.

STATE LEGISLATION

State governments (Department of Education) are primarily responsible for education. Departments of education establish policies for course curriculum, number of class days and class time, and amount of credits required for graduation.

IMPACT OF EDUCATION REFORMS AND FEDERAL LEGISLATION

Education reforms and federal legislation caused an increase in enrollment in physical education and there was renewed administrative, parental, and student support. Additional impacts include: coeducational classes, separate teams for boys and girls and men and women (otherwise the school must create a coeducational team), equal opportunities for both sexes (for facilities, equipment and supplies, practice and games, medical and training services, academic tutoring and coaching, travel and per diem allowances, and dining and housing facilities), and equitable expenditure of funds for both sexes.

The Department of Health and Human Services recommended legislative changes - including those for education. **Title IX** prohibits sex discrimination in educational programs and **PL 94-142** requires schools to provide educational services for handicapped students. In 1990, Congress passed the **Individuals with Disabilities Education Act** (IDEA) that amended earlier laws. IDEA specifies physical education as a required educational service. In addition, IDEA defines physical education as the development of physical fitness, motor skills, and skills in-group and individual games and dance, aquatics, and lifetime sports.

Title IX takes precedence over all conflicting state and local laws and conference regulations. Federal aid (even aid not related to physical education or athletics) must comply with Title IX. Finally, Title IX prohibits discrimination in personnel standards and scholarships selection.

Finally, Congress enacted the Physical Education for Progress (PEP) Act in 2000. The PEP program provides funds that the Department of Education uses to award grants to help initiate, expand, and develop physical education programs for Kindergarten through 12th grade students.

ADAPTED PHYSICAL EDUCATION NATIONAL STANDARDS

Federal law requires that schools accommodate all students, regardless of disability or other limitations, and provide opportunities for physical education. Physical education standards adapted for disabled students include:

STANDARD 1 HUMAN DEVELOPMENT: Sets the foundation of proposed goals and activities for individuals with disabilities. Grounded in a basic understanding of human development and its applications to those with various needs.

STANDARD 2 MOTOR BEHAVIOR: Sets the standard on teaching individuals with disabilities, which requires knowledge of typical physical and motor development as well as understanding the influence of developmental delays on these processes.

STANDARD 3 EXERCISE SCIENCE: The focus of this standard is on the principles that address the physiological and biomechanical applications encountered when working with diverse populations.

STANDARD 4 MEASUREMENT AND EVALUATION: Sets the standards on the measurements in gauging motor performance that is, to a large extent, based on a good grasp of motor development and the acquisition of motor skills covered in other standards.

STANDARD 5 HISTORY AND PHILOSOPHY: This standard sets the basic knowledge base of educators on legal and philosophical factors involved in current day practices in adapted physical education (APE). This standard also covers a review of history and philosophy related to special and general education.

STANDARD 6 UNIQUE ATTRIBUTES OF LEARNERS: This standard refers to information based on the disability areas found in the Individuals with Disabilities Education Act (IDEA).

STANDARD 7 CURRICULUM THEORY AND DEVELOPMENT: Sets the standards on knowledge of certain curriculum theory and development concepts, such as selecting goals based on relevant and appropriate assessment.

STANDARD 8 ASSESSMENT: This seeks to establish the parameters and conduct of assessment, which goes beyond data gathering to include measurements for the purpose of making decisions about special services and program components for individuals with disabilities.

STANDARD 9 INSTRUCTIONAL DESIGN AND PLANNING: Administration must develop standards on instructional design and planning before an APE teacher can provide services to meet legal mandates, educational goals, and, most importantly, the unique needs of individuals with disabilities.

STANDARD 10 TEACHING: This standard integrates many of the principles addressed earlier in covering areas such as human development, motor behavior, and exercise science. This will ensure that schools meet other standards to effectively provide quality physical education to individuals with disabilities.

STANDARD 11 CONSULTATION AND STAFF DEVELOPMENT: This standard sets the key competencies that an adapted physical educator should know in relation to consultation and staff development.

STANDARD 12 STUDENT AND PROGRAM EVALUATION: Sets the standards on how to conduct program evaluation, integrating the entire range of educational services.

STANDARD 13 CONTINUING EDUCATION: This standard sets the parameters on ways teachers of APE can remain current in their field.

STANDARD 14 ETHICS: This standard ensures that teachers of APE not only understand the importance of sound ethical practices, but also adhere to and advance such practices.

STANDARD 15 COMMUNICATION: This standard includes setting the quality of information on how to communicate with families and other professionals effectively. The standard encourages a team approach to enhance service delivery to individuals with disabilities.

> **Skill 13.3** **Demonstrate an understanding of the development and use of safety rules, risk-management plans, emergency plans, and injury reports.**

EMERGENCY ACTION PLANS

The first step in establishing a safe physical education environment is creating an Emergency Action Plan (EAP). The formation of a well-planned EAP can make a significant difference in the outcome of an injury situation.

Components of an Emergency Action Plan
To ensure the safety of students during physical activity, an EAP should be easily comprehensible yet detailed enough to facilitate prompt, thorough action.

Communication
Instructors should communicate rules and expectations clearly to students. This information should include pre-participation guidelines, emergency procedures, and proper game etiquette. Instructors should collect emergency information sheets from students at the start of each school year. First-aid kits, facility maps, and incident report forms should also be readily available. Open communication between students and teachers is essential. Creating a positive environment within the classroom allows students to feel comfortable enough to approach an adult/teacher if she feels she has sustained a potential injury.

Teacher Education
At the start of each school year, every student should undergo a pre-participation physical examination. This allows a teacher to recognize the "high-risk" students before activity commences. The teacher should also take note of any student that requires any form of medication or special care. When a teacher is aware of his/her students' conditions, the learning environment is a lot safer.

Facilities and Equipment
It is the responsibility of the teacher and school district to provide a safe environment, playing area, and equipment for students. Instructors and maintenance staff should regularly inspect school facilities to confirm that the equipment and location is adequate and safe for student use.

First Aid Equipment

It is essential to have a properly stocked first aid kit in an easily reachable location. Instructors may need to include asthma inhalers and special care items to meet the specific needs of certain students. Instructors should clearly mark these special care items to avoid a potentially harmful mix-up.

Implementing the Emergency Plan

The main thing to keep in mind when implementing an EAP is to remain calm. Maintaining a sufficient level of control and activating appropriate medical assistance will facilitate the process and will leave less room for error.

STRATEGIES FOR INJURY PREVENTION

Participant screenings – evaluate injury history, anticipate and prevent potential injuries, watch for hidden injuries and reoccurrence of an injury, and maintain communication.

Standards and discipline – ensure that athletes obey rules of sportsmanship, supervision, and biomechanics.

Education and knowledge – stay current in knowledge of first aid, sports medicine, sport technique, and injury prevention through clinics, workshops, and communication with staff and trainers.

Conditioning – programs should be yearlong and participants should have access to conditioning facilities in and out of season to produce more fit and knowledgeable athletes that are less prone to injury.

Equipment – perform regular inspections; ensure proper fit and proper use.

Facilities – maintain standards and use safe equipment.

Field care – establish emergency procedures for serious injury.

Rehabilitation – use objective measures such as power output on an isokinetic dynamometer.

PREVENTION OF COMMON ATHLETIC INJURIES

Foot – start with good footwear and incorporate foot exercises.

Ankle – use high top shoes and tape support; strengthen plantar (calf), dorsiflexor (shin), and ankle eversion (ankle outward).

Shin splints – strengthen ankle dorsiflexors.

Achilles tendon – stretch dorsiflexion and strengthen plantar flexion (heel raises).

Knee – increase strength and flexibility of calf and thigh muscles.

Back – use proper body mechanics.

Tennis elbow – lateral epicondylitis caused by bent elbow, hitting late, not stepping into the ball, heavy rackets, and rackets with strings that are too tight.

Head and neck injuries – avoid dangerous techniques (i.e. grabbing facemask) and carefully supervise dangerous activities like the trampoline.

EQUIPMENT SELECTION

School officials and instructors should base **equipment selection** on quality and safety; goals of physical education and athletics; participants interests, age, sex, skills, and limitations; and trends in athletic equipment and uniforms. Knowledgeable personnel should select equipment; keeping in mind continuous service and replacement considerations (i.e. what's best in year of selection may not be best the following year). One final consideration is the possibility of reconditioning versus the purchase new equipment.

INJURY FOLLOW UP AND REPORTING

Responding to accidents and injuries is an important responsibility of physical educators. After an injury occurs, instructors must follow up with parents and school personnel. Instructors must also complete and accident report.

Instructors should contact an injured student's parents or guardians as soon as possible after the injury. Such contact makes the parents aware of the injury and allows them to make necessary arrangements.

Instructors must also complete an accident report. Accident reports describe and explain the circumstances surrounding the accident and the nature of the injury. Such reports are important for record keeping, future evaluations, and protection against lawsuits.

Finally, the physical education instructor should notify the school administration of any accidents or injuries. In addition, if the injured student requires immediate first aid, the instructor should notify the school nurse.

Skill 13.4   Demonstrate knowledge of inherent risks, physical and environmental dangers, potential safety hazards, and potential liabilities associated with participating in physical activities and techniques for informing students, families, and staff of potential risks.

There are many issues related to the legal responsibilities of the professional physical educator. Failing to foresee potential hazardous conditions and to take practical steps to avoid these situations can result in litigation. In general, teachers must follow the standard of care expected of any physical education practitioner with a similar level of education and training. Liability refers to a legal responsibility. Often in litigious situations, the term liability refers to negligence, or breach of duty. Negligence refers to actions that do not meet the minimum standard of care. In successful litigation, the defense proves the existence of the following: duty, breach of duty, injury, and proximate cause. When determining liability, courts will determine whether the injury was foreseeable.

To avoid legal action, professional physical educators must meet their legal responsibilities in several areas: equipment and facilities, instruction, supervision, and general safety. Regular inspection of the instructional area identifies potential hazards. When physical educators find hazards, they should submit written notification to the principal immediately. Students should also receive proper instruction of equipment use prior to the first use. In an instructional setting, the physical educator protects students from unreasonable harm. Students receive appropriate training before and during activity. Supervision of all activities in a school setting is mandatory. An unsupervised student in the school at any time or on the school grounds during the school day is unacceptable. The approach to overall safety should be proactive.

Physical educators participate in safety in-service programs each year. The teacher or another school medical professional review the student's medical records prior to allowing participation in physical education. Physical education practitioners teach the safety rules for each activity at the beginning of each unit. When a student sustains an injury in physical education class, the school nurse or other medical professional evaluates the student. The physical educator completes and files an accident report the same day that the accident occurred.

An Emergency Action Plan (EAP) should be in place for the physical education department at each school. The EAP identifies the following: emergency care procedures and the individual responsible for rendering care, the individual responsible for parental notification, the individual responsible for activating the emergency medical system (EMS), the policy for transportation of injured students, and a copy of a blank student accident report. To reduce the financial consequences of litigation, each teacher should purchase and maintain personal professional liability insurance. Teachers should not rely on school district legal liability insurance for personal financial protection.

In addition to legal responsibilities, the physical educator also has ethical responsibilities. Teachers are responsible for helping each student to realize his or her abilities. Physical educators are accountable for the welfare of each student entrusted to their care. Teachers should maintain a professional relationship with their students. Teachers should maintain confidentiality. Physical educators should follow national, state, and district or school curricular standards. Teachers should establish and maintain a classroom routine that promotes student achievement. Finally, the physical education teacher is responsible for promoting healthful living within the school community.

EQUIPMENT AND FACILITIES

Unsound equipment and poorly maintained facilities are the two most potentially hazardous elements of the physical education environment. Instructors must carefully inspect all equipment and facilities to ensure safety. In addition, improper student clothing and footwear is a significant hazard. Instructors should ensure that students wear rubber-soled, closed-back shoes that fasten securely to the child's foot. Backless shoes (e.g. sandals, flip-flops) are inappropriate because they can easily slip off of the child's foot. The type of activity dictates the type of clothing that is appropriate. For example, baggy pants or long dresses are inappropriate for bicycle riding because such clothing can get caught in the bicycle and cause injury.

Skill 13.5   Demonstrate an understanding of methods for minimizing risk and liability and for ensuring the safety of participants in games, sports, and other physical activities.

The management of facilities, supplies, and other resources is an important part of the physical educator's job. Instructors must plan the availability, use, and safety of facilities. In addition, instructors must develop procedures for transporting, distributing, and collecting equipment. Finally, instructors must develop lesson plans that maximize the use of time and keep students active.

Facility management is the first task physical educators must consider. Instructors must ensure, through communication with other school personnel, that the required facilities are available when needed. In addition, instructors must inspect facilities prior to use to ensure the safety of the students. Instructors should carefully note uneven surfaces, holes, obstructions, and obstacles. Instructors may also have to modify rules or game procedures as the facility dimensions dictate.

Equipment management is another important responsibility of physical educators. Instructors must develop procedures for transporting equipment to and from the playing field or gymnasium. One way to simplify equipment transportation is to use a shopping cart, which many grocery stores will donate, to carry equipment. Instructors can also designate students as equipment managers to help carry and distribute equipment. Equipment distribution and collection is another important concern for physical educators. Spreading equipment throughout the playing area can speed the distribution process. Instructors should also establish a protocol for equipment return and set up areas for collection. Finally, instructors should develop signals, either verbal or visual, that direct students to stop the activity and either hold or put down the equipment.

One final physical educators' concern is class time management. One effective strategy for maximizing participation and the use of class time and equipment is to use stations. Stations allow students to rotate through a series of different activities in small groups. Instructors should use stations only for activities that the students are familiar with and are able to complete without constant supervision.

EQUIPMENT AND FACILITY SELECTION

School officials and instructors should base **equipment selection** on the following: (a) quality and safety (b) goals of physical education and athletics (c) participants interests, age, sex, skills, and limitations (d) and (e) trends in athletic equipment and uniforms. Knowledgeable personnel should select equipment keeping in mind continuous service and replacement considerations (i.e. what's best in year of selection may not be best the following year). One final consideration is the possibility of reconditioning versus the purchase new equipment.

Additional Guidelines for Selection of Equipment

- follow purchasing policies

- relate purchasing to program, budget, and finances

- consider maintenance

- abide by legal regulations

- recognize administrative considerations (good working relationships at all personnel levels)

- determine best value for money spent

- ensure that participants have own equipment and supplies when necessary

- purchase from reputable manufacturers and distributors

- follow competitive purchasing regulations

- use school forms with clearly identified brand, trademark, and catalog specifications

Equipment Maintenance Procedures

- inspect supplies and equipment upon arrival

- label supplies and equipment with organization's identification

- have policies for issuing and returning supplies and equipment

- keep equipment in perfect operating condition

- store properly

- properly clean and care for equipment (including garments).

Facility Selection Considerations

- bond issues for construction

- availability to girls, women, minorities, and the handicapped

- energy costs and conservation

- community involvement

- convertibility (movable walls/partitions)

- environment must be safe, attractive, clean, comfortable, practical, and adaptable to individual needs

- compliance with public health codes

- effective disease control.

Facility Maintenance Procedures

- custodial staff, participants, and the physical education and athletic staffs must work together to properly maintain facility

- for pool's, water temperature, hydrogen ion concentration, and chlorine need daily monitoring

- gymnasium play areas must be free from dust and dirt

- showers and drying areas need daily cleaning and disinfecting

- participants' clothing should meet health standards to prevent odor and bacterial growth

- outdoor playing fields must be clear of rocks and free of holes and uneven surfaces

- disinfect and clean drinking fountains, sinks, urinals, and toilets daily air out and sanitize lockers frequently.

ACTIONS THAT CAN AVOID LAWSUITS

The following is a list of basic practices and actions that can prevent lawsuits related to physical education accidents.

1. Knowing the health status of each person in the program.

2. Considering the ability and skill level of participants when planning new activities.

3. Grouping students to equalize competitive levels.

4. Using safe equipment and facilities.

5. Properly organizing and supervising classes.

6. Never leaving a class.

7. Knowing first aid (Do not diagnose or prescribe).

8. Keeping accident records.

9. Giving instruction prior to dangerous activities.

10. Being sure that injured students get medical attention and examination.

11. Getting exculpatory agreements (parental consent forms).

12. Having a planned, written disposition for students who suffer injuries or become ill.

13. Providing a detailed accident report if one occurs.

Skill 13.6   Demonstrate knowledge of injury prevention techniques and of first aid, cardiopulmonary resuscitation (CPR), and emergency procedures.

CPR BASICS

Cardiopulmonary resuscitation (CPR) is a first-aid technique used to keep victims of cardiac arrest alive. It is also prevents brain damage while the individual is unconscious and more advanced medical help is on the way. CPR keeps blood flowing through the body and in and out of the lungs.

CPR Steps
- Step 1 – Call 911
- Step 2 – Tilt head, lift chin, check breathing
- Step 3 – Give two breaths
- Step 4 – Position hands in the center of chest
- Step 5 – Firmly push down two inches on the chest 15 times

Continue with two breaths and 15 pumps until help arrives. The American Heart Association and the American Red Cross both offer classes to train individuals in CPR.

INJURY TREATMENT AND FIRST AID

Immediate treatment tips

When a student endures a physical injury, the first priority is to avoid further damage. Following an injury, the teacher should look for the obvious cause of the accident (i.e., ill-fitting equipment, improper sliding technique, a missed step while running). The next step is to reduce swelling. The primary means of accomplishing this is a sequence of treatments (rest, ice, compression, elevation) known as **R.I.C.E.** It is vital to implement this procedure following an injury since swelling causes pain and a loss of motion.

Steps for the immediate treatment of an injury

1. Stop the activity immediately
2. Wrap the injured part in a compression bandage (i.e., an ACE bandage).
3. Apply ice to the injured part (crushed ice or frozen vegetables are ideal) for no more than 15 minutes at a time. You should allow the area to warm periodically.
4. Elevate the injured part.
5. For a proper diagnosis, send the injured student to the school's nurse or, for more serious injuries, to a physician.

Treating specific illnesses

Diabetes
Most children with diabetes suffer from Type 1 (insulin-dependent or juvenile) diabetes. Type 1 diabetes limits the pancreas' ability to produce insulin, a hormone vital to life. Without insulin, the body cannot use the sugar found in blood. In order to stay alive, an individual suffering from Type 1 diabetes must take one or more injections of insulin daily.

Diabetics control their disease by keeping the level of sugar (glucose) in the blood as close to normal as possible. The means to achieve diabetes control include proper nutrition, exercise, and insulin. Most children with diabetes self-monitor blood glucose levels to track their condition and respond to changes.

Some rules of thumb to keep in mind when dealing with a diabetic child are:

- Food makes the glucose level rise
- Exercise and insulin make the glucose level fall
- Hypoglycemia occurs when the blood sugar level is low
- Hyperglycemia occurs when the blood sugar level is high

Low Blood Sugar (Hypoglycemia)
This is the diabetic emergency most likely to occur. Low blood sugar may result from eating too little, engaging in too much physical activity without eating, or by injecting too much insulin.

Symptoms:
- Headache
- Sweating
- Shakiness
- Pale, moist skin
- Fatigue/Weakness
- Loss of coordination

Treatment:

Provide sugar immediately. You may give the student ½ cup of fruit juice, non-diet soda, or two to four glucose tablets. The child should feel better within the next 10 minutes. If so, the child should eat some additional food (e.g. half a peanut butter, meat, or cheese sandwich). If the child's status does not improve, treat the reaction again.

High Blood Sugar (Hyperglycemia)

Hyperglycemia can result from eating too much, engaging in too little physical activity, not injecting enough insulin, or illness. You can confirm high blood sugar levels by testing with a glucose meter.

Symptoms:

- Increased thirst
- Weakness/Fatigue
- Blurred vision
- Frequent urination
- Loss of appetite

Treatment:

If hyperglycemia occurs, the instructor should contact the student's parent or guardian immediately.

Dehydration

Dehydration occurs when a person loses more fluids than he/she takes in. The amount of water present in the body subsequently drops below the level needed for normal body functions. The two main causes of dehydration are gastrointestinal illness (vomiting, diarrhea) and sports. It is essential to replace fluids lost by sweating to prevent dehydration, especially on a hot day.

Symptoms:

- Thirst
- Dizziness
- Dry mouth
- Producing less/darker urine

Prevention/Treatment:

- Drink lots of fluids. Water is usually the best choice.
- Dress appropriately (i.e., loose-fitting clothes and a hat).
- If you begin to feel thirsty/dizzy, take a break and sit in the shade.
- Drink fluids prior to physical activity and then in 20-minute intervals after activity commences.
- Play sports or train in the early morning or late afternoon. You will avoid the hottest part of the day.

ACTIONS THAT PROMOTE SAFETY AND INJURY PREVENTION

The following is a list of practices that promote safety in all types of physical education and athletic activities.

1. Having an instructor who is properly trained and qualified.

2. Organizing the class by size, activity, and conditions of the class.

3. Inspecting buildings and other facilities regularly and immediately giving notice of any hazards.

4. Avoiding overcrowding.

5. Using adequate lighting.

6. Ensuring that students dress in appropriate clothing and shoes.

7. Presenting organized activities.

8. Inspecting all equipment regularly.

9. Adhering to building codes and fire regulations.

10. Using protective equipment.

11. Using spotters.

12. Eliminating hazards.

13. Teaching students correct ways of performing skills and activities.

14. Teaching students how to use the equipment properly and safely.

ANNOTATED LIST OF RESOURCES

This list identifies resources that may help candidates prepare to take the Physical Education examination. While not a substitute for coursework or other types of teacher preparation, these resources may enhance a candidate's knowledge of the content covered on the examination. The references listed do not represent a comprehensive listing of all potential resources. Candidates need not read all of the materials listed below, and passage of the examination will not require familiarity with these specific resources. When available, we have provided a brief summary for the reference cited. We have organized the resources alphabetically and by content domain in subtest order.

GROWTH, MOTOR DEVELOPMENT, AND MOTOR LEARNING

Colvin, A. Vonnie; Nancy J.; and Walker, Pamela. (2000). *Teaching the Nuts and Bolts of Physical Education: Building Basic Movement Skills.* Champaign, IL: Human Kinetics.

> Provides foundational content knowledge in locomotor and manipulative skills. Topics include rolling, throwing, catching, passing, dribbling, striking, kicking, and punting.

Fronske, H. (2001). *Teaching Cues for Sports Skills* (2nd edition). San Francisco, CA: Pearson/Cummings.

> Designed to provide verbal and alternate teaching cues and point out common errors in a variety of sports.

Graham, George. (1992). *Teaching Children Physical Education: Becoming a Master Teacher.* Champaign, IL: Human Kinetics.

> Includes the skills and techniques that successful teachers use to make their classes more interesting and developmentally appropriate. A reference for K-5 teachers and physical education department chairs and administrators.

Lawson, H.A. (1984). *Invitation to Physical Education.* Champaign IL: Human Kinetics.

> Shows students and practitioners how to apply basic business management principles to a variety of health promotion programs.

Pangrazi, Robert. (2004). *Dynamic Physical Education for Elementary School Children* (14th edition). San Francisco, CA: Pearson/Cummings.

> Provides step-by-step techniques for teaching physical education while navigating through today's challenging educational terrain.

Powers, S.K., and Howley, E.T. (2003). *Exercise Physiology* (5th edition). New York, NY: McGraw Hill.

> Explains theory of exercise science and physical education with application and performance models to increase understanding of classroom learning.

Schmidt, R.A., and Lee, T.D. (1999). *Motor Control Learning: A Behavioral Emphasis* (3rd Edition). Champaign: IL: Human Kinetics.

> Addresses many factors that affect the quality of movement behaviors and the ease with which students can learn them.

Sherrill, C. (1998). *Adapted Physical Activity, Recreation and Sport: Cross-disciplinary and Lifespan* (5th edition). Dubuque, IA: WCB McGraw Hill.

> Emphasizes attitude change, inclusion, and psychosocial perspectives for understanding individual differences.

Siedentop, D. (1994). *Sport Education.* Champaign, IL: Human Kinetics.

> Shows how sport can help students learn fair play, leadership skills, and self-responsibility, in addition to becoming competent players. Also shows physical educators how to implement effective sport education programs to achieve these goals.

Summers, J.J. (1992). *Approaches to the Study of Motor Control and Learning.* Amsterdam: Elsevier Science.

> Provides analysis of research with particular emphasis on the methods and paradigms employed and the future direction of their work.

Thomas, Katherine, et al. (2003). *Physical Education Methods for Elementary Teachers.* Champaign, IL: Human Kinetics.

> Takes a research approach and offers a user-friendly technique to applicable teaching modalities for physical education for grades K-12.

Winnick, J.P. (2000). *Adapted Physical Education and Sport* (3rd edition). Champaign, IL: Human Kinetics.

> Provides a thorough introduction for students preparing to work with individuals with disabilities in a variety of settings.

THE SCIENCE OF HUMAN MOVEMENT

Birrell, S., and Cole, C.L. (1994). *Women, Sport, and Culture.* Champaign, IL: Human Kinetics.

> The text is a collection of essays that examine the relationship between sport and gender.

Grantham, W.C.; Patton, R.W.; Winick, M.L.; and York, T.D. (1998). *Health Fitness Management.* Champaign, IL: Human Kinetics.

> Brings conventional business management principles and operational guidelines to the unconventional business of health and fitness.

Hall, S. (2003). *Basic Biomechanics.* Boston, MA: McGraw-Hill.

Hamill, J., and Knutzen, K. (1995). *Biomechanical Basis of Human Movement.* Hagerstown, MD: Lippincott, Williams & Wilkins.

> Integrates aspects of functional anatomy, physics, calculus, and physiology into a comprehensive discussion of human movement.

Hopper, Chris; Fisher, Bruce; and Muniz, Kathy. (1997). *Health-Related Fitness: Grades 1-2, 3-4, 5-6.* Champaign, IL: Human Kinetics.

> These three books provide a wealth of health and fitness information and are an excellent resource for classroom teachers with limited backgrounds in physical education.

Lawson, H.A. (1984). *Invitation to Physical Education.* Champaign, IL: Human Kinetics.

> Shows students and practitioners how to apply basic business management principles to a variety of health promotion programs.

Sample Test

1. **What is the proper sequential order of development for the acquisition of nonlocomotor skills?** *(Average Rigor) (Skill 1.1)*

   A. Stretch, sit, bend, turn, swing, twist, shake, rock & sway, dodge; fall.

   B. Bend, stretch, turn, twist, swing, sit, rock & sway, shake, dodge; fall.

   C. Stretch, bend, sit, shake, turn, rock & sway, swing, twist, dodge; fall.

   D. Bend, stretch, sit, turn, twist, swing, sway, rock & sway, dodge; fall.

2. **What is the proper order of sequential development for the acquisition of locomotor skills?** *(Rigorous) (Skill 1.1)*

   A. Creep, crawl, walk, jump, run, slide, gallop, hop, leap, skip; step-hop.

   B. Crawl, walk, creep, slide, walk, run, hop, leap, gallop, skip; step-hop.

   C. Creep, crawl, walk, slide, run, hop, leap, skip, gallop, jump; step-hop.

   D. Crawl, creep, walk, run, jump, hop, gallop, slide, leap, skip; step-hop.

3. **The two main categories of are knowledge of performance and information about the performance.** *(Average Rigor) (Skill 1.2)*

   A. Self assessment

   B. Intrinsic feedback

   C. Extrinsic feedback

   D. Observational learning

4. **Which movement concept involves students making decisions about an object's positional changes in space?** *(Rigorous) (Skill 1.3)*

   A. Spatial Awareness

   B. Effort Awareness

   C. Body Awareness

   D. Motion Awareness

5. **Applying the mechanical principles of balance, time, and force describes which movement concept?** *(Average Rigor) (Skill 1.3)*

   A. Spatial Awareness

   B. Effort Awareness

   C. Body Awareness

   D. Motion Awareness

6. There are two sequential phases to the development of spatial awareness. What is the order of these phases? (*Rigorous*) (*Skill 1.3*)

   A. Locating more than one object in relation to each object; the location of objects in relation to one's own body in space.

   B. The location of objects in relation to one's own body in space; locating more than one object in relation to one's own body.

   C. Locating more than one object independent of one's body; the location of objects in relation to one's own body.

   D. The location of objects in relation to one's own body in space; locating more than one object in relation to each object and independent of one's own body.

7. Process assessment does not identify which of the following errors in skill performance. (*Average Rigor*) (*Skill 1.5*)

   A. Style

   B. Form

   C. End result

   D. Mechanics

8. Which of the following principles is not a factor to assess to correct errors in performance for process assessment? (*Average Rigor*) (*Skill 1.5*)

   A. Inertia

   B. Action/Reaction

   C. Force

   D. Acceleration

9. Instructors can assess skill level achievement in bowling by: (*Easy*) (*Skill 1.5*)

   A. Calculating a student's average score.

   B. Calculating how many gutter-balls the student threw.

   C. Calculating how many strikes the student threw.

   D. Calculating how many spares

10. A subjective, observational approach to identifying errors in the form, style, or mechanics of a skill is accomplished by: (*Rigorous*) (*Skill 1.5*)

    A. Product assessment

    B. Process assessment

    C. Standardized norm-referenced tests

    D. Criterion-referenced tests

11. **What type of assessment objectively measures skill performance?** *(Rigorous) (Skill 1.5)*

    A. Process assessment

    B. Product assessment

    C. Texas PE Test

    D. Iowa Brace Test

12. **Determining poor performance of a skill using process assessment can best be accomplished by:** *(Average Rigor) (Skill 1.5)*

    A. Observing how fast a skill is performed.

    B. Observing how many skills are performed.

    C. Observing how far or how high a skill is performed.

    D. Observing several attributes comprising the entire performance of a skill.

13. **Which of the following methods measures fundamental skills using product assessment?** *(Rigorous) (Skill 1.5)*

    A. Criterion-referenced tests

    B. Standardized norm-referenced tests

    C. Both A and B

    D. Neither A nor B

14. **Product assessment measures all of the following except:** *(Rigorous) (Skill 1.5)*

    A. How the student performs the mechanics of a skill.

    B. How many times the student performs a skill.

    C. How fast the student performs a skill.

    D. How far or high the student performs a skill.

15. **Having students pretend they are playing basketball or trying to catch a bus develops which locomotor skill?** *(Easy) (Skill 2.1)*

    A. Galloping

    B. Running

    C. Leaping

    D. Skipping

16. **Having students play Fox and Hound develops:** *(Easy) (Skill 2.1)*

    A. Galloping

    B. Hopping

    C. Stepping-hopping

    D. Skipping

17. Having students take off and land with both feet together develops which locomotor skill? *(Easy) (Skill 2.1)*

A. Hopping

B. Jumping

C. Leaping

D. Skipping

18. Which nonlocomotor skill entails movement around a joint where two body parts meet? *(Easy) (Skill 2.1)*

A. Twisting

B. Swaying

C. Bending

D. Stretching

19. A sharp change of direction from one's original line of movement is which nonlocomotor skill? *(Easy) (Skill 2.1)*

A. Twisting

B. Dodging

C. Swaying

D. Swinging

20. Which manipulative skill uses the hands to stop the momentum of an object? *(Rigorous) (Skill 2.1)*

A. Trapping

B. Catching

C. Striking

D. Rolling

21. Activities such as pretending to pick fruit off a tree or reaching for a star develop which non-locomotor skill? *(Easy) (Skill 2.1)*

A. Bending

B. Stretching

C. Turning

D. Twisting

22. Picking up coins, tying shoes, and petting animals develop this nonlocomotor skill. *(Easy) (Skill 2.1)*

A. Bending

B. Stretching

C. Turning

D. Twisting

23. To enhance skill and strategy performance for striking or throwing objects, for catching or collecting objects, and for carrying and propelling objects, students must first learn techniques for: (*Rigorous*) (*Skill 2.1*)

    A. Offense

    B. Defense

    C. Controlling objects

    D. Continuous play of objects

24. Coordinated movements that project a person over an obstacle is: (*Easy*) (*Skill 2.1*)

    A. Jumping

    B. Vaulting

    C. Leaping

    D. Hopping

25. Using the same foot to take off from a surface and land is which locomotor skill? (*Easy*) (*Skill 2.1*)

    A. Jumping

    B. Vaulting

    C. Leaping

    D. Hopping

26. All of the following are parts of the sequence of an overhand throw movement except: (*Average Rigor*) (*Skill 2.2*)

    A. A stride

    B. A hip rotation

    C. A hyperextension

    D. A trunk rotation

27. Having students collapse in their own space or lower themselves as though they are a raindrop or snowflake develops this nonlocomotor skill. (*Easy*) (*Skill 2.3*)

    A. Dodging

    B. Shaking

    C. Swinging

    D. Falling

28. Which is the proper sequential order of development for the acquisition of manipulative skills? (*Rigorous*) (*Skill 2.3*)

    A. Striking, throwing, bouncing, catching, trapping, kicking, ball rolling; volleying.

    B. Striking, throwing, kicking, ball rolling, volleying, bouncing, catching; trapping.

    C. Striking, throwing, catching, trapping, kicking, ball rolling, bouncing; volleying.

    D. Striking, throwing, kicking, ball rolling, bouncing; volleying.

29. Having students hit a large balloon with both hands develops this manipulative skill. (*Average Rigor*) (*Skill 2.3*)

    A. Bouncing

    B. Striking

    C. Volleying

    D. Trapping

30. Progressively decreasing the size of a target that balls are projected at develops which manipulative skill. (*Average Rigor*) (*Skill 2.3*)

    A. Throwing

    B. Trapping

    C. Volleying

    D. Kicking

31. Hitting a stationary object while in a fixed position, then incorporating movement, develops this manipulative skill. (*Average Rigor*) (*Skill 2.3*)

    A. Bouncing

    B. Trapping

    C. Throwing

    D. Striking

32. Playing "Simon Says" and having students touch different body parts applies which movement concept? (*Average Rigor*) (*Skill 2.5*)

    A. Spatial Awareness

    B. Effort Awareness

    C. Body Awareness

    D. Motion Awareness

33. The ability to change rapidly the direction of the body is: (*Average Rigor*) (*Skill 2.5*)

    A. Coordination

    B. Reaction time

    C. Speed

    D. Agility

34. Having students move on their hands and knees, move on lines, and/or hold shapes while moving develops which quality of movement? (*Average Rigor*) (*Skill 3.1*)

    A. Balance

    B. Time

    C. Force

    D. Inertia

35. Students that paddle balls against a wall or jump over objects with various heights are demonstrating which quality of movement? (*Rigorous*) (*Skill 3.1*)

    A. Balance

    B. Time

    C. Force

    D. Inertia

36. Having students move in a specific pattern while measuring how long they take to do so develops which quality of movement? (*Average Rigor*) (*Skill 3.1*)

    A. Balance

    B. Time

    C. Force

    D. Inertia

37. Equilibrium is maintained as long as: (*Average Rigor*) (*Skill 3.1*)

    A. Body segments are moved independently.

    B. The center of gravity is over the base of support

    C. Force is applied to the base of support.

    D. The center of gravity is lowered.

38. Which of the following does not enhance equilibrium? (*Average Rigor*) *(Skill 3.1)*

    A. Shifting the center of gravity away from the direction of movement.

    B. Increasing the base of support.

    C. Lowering the base of support.

    D. Increasing the base of support and lowering the center of support.

39. All of the following affect force except: (*Easy*) *(Skill 3.1)*

    A. Magnitude

    B. Energy

    C. Motion

    D. Mass

40. For a movement to occur, applied force must overcome inertia of an object and any other resisting forces. What concept of force does this describe? (*Rigorous*) *(Skill 3.1)*

    A. Potential energy

    B. Magnitude

    C. Kinetic energy

    D. Absorption

41. The energy of an object to do work while recoiling is which type of potential energy? (*Average Rigor*) *(Skill 3.1)*

    A. Absorption

    B. Kinetic

    C. Elastic

    D. Torque

42. Gradually decelerating a moving mass by utilization of smaller forces over a long period of time is: (*Average Rigor*) *(Skill 3.1)*

    A. Stability

    B. Equilibrium

    C. Angular force

    D. Force absorption

43. The tendency of a body/object to remain in its present state of motion unless some force acts to change it is which mechanical principle of motion? (*Average Rigor*) *(Skill 3.2)*

    A. Acceleration

    B. Inertia

    C. Action/Reaction

    D. Linear motion

44. The movement response of a system depends not only on the net external force, but also on the resistance to movement change. Which mechanical principle of motion does this definition describe? (*Rigorous*) (*Skill 3.2*)

    A. Acceleration

    B. Inertia

    C. Action/Reaction

    D. Air Resistance

45. Which of the following mechanical principles of motion states that every motion has a similar, contrasting response? (*Easy*) (*Skill 3.2*)

    A. Acceleration

    B. Inertia

    C. Action/Reaction

    D. Centripetal force

46. Activities that enhance team socialization include all of the following except: (*Easy*) (*Skill 4.1*)

    A. Basketball

    B. Soccer

    C. Golf

    D. Volleyball

47. Some students practicing basketball are having difficulty with "free throws," even though the shots make it to and over the hoop. What adjustment will improve their "free throws?" (*Average Rigor*) (*Skill 4.1*)

    A. Increasing the height of release (i.e. jump shot).

    B. Increasing the vertical path of the ball.

    C. Increasing the velocity of the release.

    D. Increasing the base of support.

48. An archery student's arrow bounced off the red part of the target face. What is the correct ruling? (*Average Rigor*) (*Skill 4.1*)

    A. No score.

    B. Re-shoot arrow.

    C. 7 points awarded.

    D. Shot receives same score as highest arrow shot that did not bounce off the target.

49. A student playing badminton believed that the shuttlecock was going to land out-of-bounds. The shuttlecock landed on the line. What is the correct ruling? *(Easy) (Skill 4.1)*

A. The shuttlecock is out-of-bounds.

B. The shuttlecock is in-bounds.

C. The point is replayed.

D. That player is charged with a feint.

50. A mechanical pinsetter accidentally knocked down the only bowling pin left standing for a spare attempt after clearing all the other pins knocked down by the first ball thrown. What is the correct ruling? *(Rigorous) (Skill 4.1)*

A. Foul

B. Spare

C. Frame is replayed

D. No count for that pin

51. The ball served in racquetball hits the front line and lands in front of the short line. What is the ruling? *(Easy) (Skill 4.1)*

A. Fault

B. Reserve

C. Out-of-bounds

D. Fair ball

52. Two opposing soccer players are trying to gain control of the ball when one player "knees" the other. What is the ruling? *(Easy) (Skill 4.1)*

A. Direct free kick

B. Indirect free kick

C. Fair play

D. Ejection from the game

53. Two students are playing badminton. When receiving the shuttlecock, one student consistently stands too deep in the receiving court. What strategy should the server use to serve the shuttlecock? *(Average Rigor) (Skill 4.1)*

A. Smash serve

B. Clear serve

C. Overhead serve

D. Short serve

TEACHER CERTIFICATION STUDY GUIDE

54. A basketball team has an outstanding rebounder. In order to keep this player near the opponent's basket, which strategy should the coach implement? *(Easy) (Skill 4.1)*

A. Pick-and-Roll

B. Give-and-Go

C. Zone defense

D. Free-lancing

55. When a defensive tennis player needs more time to return to his position, what strategy should he apply? *(Rigorous) (Skill 4.1)*

A. Drop shot

B. Dink shot

C. Lob shot

D. Down-the-line shot

56. An overhead badminton stroke used to hit a fore-hand-like overhead stroke that is on the backhand side of the body is a(n): *(Rigorous) (Skill 4.1)*

A. Around-the-head-shot

B. Down-the-line shot

C. Lifting the shuttle

D. Under hand shuttle

57. A maneuver when an offensive player passes to a teammate and then immediately cuts in toward the basket for a return pass is: *(Average Rigor) (Skill 4.1)*

A. Charging

B. Pick

C. Give-and-go

D. Switching

58. A bowling pin that remains standing after an apparently perfect hit is a: *(Rigorous) (Skill 4.1)*

A. Tap

B. Turkey

C. Blow

D. Leave

59. A soccer pass from the outside of the field near the end line to a position in front of the goal is a: *(Average Rigor) (Skill 4.1)*

A. Chip

B. Settle

C. Through

D. Cross

PHYSICAL EDUCATION   216

60. Although they are still hitting the target, the score of some students practicing archery has decreased as the distance between them and the target has increased. Which of the following adjustments will improve their scores? (*Rigorous*) (*Skill 4.1*)

    A. Increasing the velocity of their arrows.

    B. Increasing the students' base of support.

    C. Increasing the weight of the arrows.

    D. Increasing the parabolic path of the arrows.

61. A volleyball that opponents simultaneously contact and momentarily hold above the net is a(n): (*Easy*) (*Skill 4.1*)

    A. Double fault

    B. Play over

    C. Overlap

    D. Held ball

62. Volleyball player LB on team A digs a spiked ball. The ball deflects off LB's shoulder. What is the ruling? (*Average Rigor*) (*Skill 4.1*)

    A. Fault

    B. Legal hit

    C. Double foul

    D. Play over

63. Instructors can evaluate skill level of achievement in archery by: (*Average Rigor*) (*Skill 4.1*)

    A. Giving students a written exam on terminology.

    B. Having students demonstrate the correct tension of arrow feathers.

    C. Totaling a student's score obtained on the target's face.

    D. Time how long a student takes to shoot all arrows.

64. Instructors can determine skill level achievement in golf by: (*Average Rigor*) (*Skill 4.1*)

A. The number of "birdies" that a student makes.

B. The number of "bogies" a student makes.

C. The score obtained after several rounds

D. The total score achieved throughout the school year.

65. Social skills and values developed by activity include all of the following except: (*Easy*) (*Skill 4.2*)

A. Winning at all costs

B. Making judgments in groups

C. Communicating and cooperating

D. Respecting rules and property

66. The sense of the relative position of neighboring parts of the body is/are called: (*Average Rigor*) (*Skill 4.3*)

A. Proprioception

B. Spatial orientation

C. Hand-eye coordination

D. Movement skills

67. _____ education should always accompany the _____practice of the activity. (*Rigorous*) (*Skill 4.4*)

A. Affective; practical

B. Cognitive; physical

C. Metacognitive; physical

D. Cognitive; practical

68. Modern, jazz, ballet, hip-hop, and ballroom are just some of the types of _____ students can physically study. (*Easy*) (*Skill 5.1*)

A. Theatre

B. Dance

C. Music

D. Art

69. Instructors can determine skill level achievement in swimming by: (*Average Rigor*) (*Skill 5.2*)

A. How long a student can float

B. How many strokes it takes a student to swim a specified distance.

C. How long a student can stay under the water without moving.

D. How many times a student can dive in five minutes.

70. An instructor notices that class participation is much lower than expected. By making changes in equipment and rules, the instructor applied which of the following concepts to enhance participation? (*Rigorous*) (*Skill 5.4*)

    A. Homogeneous grouping

    B. Heterogeneous grouping

    C. Multi-activity designs

    D. Activity modification

71. A teacher who modifies and develops tasks for a class is demonstrating knowledge of which appropriate behavior in physical education activities. (*Rigorous*) (*Skill 5.4*)

    A. Appropriate management behavior

    B. Appropriate student behavior

    C. Appropriate administration behavior

    D. Appropriate content behavior

72. Using tactile clues is a functional adaptation that can assist which type of students? (*Rigorous*) (*Skill 5.4*)

    A. Deaf students

    B. Blind students

    C. Asthmatic students

    D. Physically challenged students

73. Physiological benefits of exercise include all of the following except: (*Average Rigor*) (*Skill 6.1*)

    A. Reducing mental tension

    B. Improving muscle strength

    C. Cardiac hypertrophy

    D. Quicker recovery rate

74. Psychological benefits of exercise include all of the following except: (*Rigorous*) (*Skill 6.1*)

    A. Improved sleeping patterns

    B. Improved energy regulation

    C. Improved appearance

    D. Improved quality of life

75. The most important nutrient the body requires, without which life can only be sustained for a few days, is: (*Easy*) (*Skill 6.2*)

   A. Vitamins

   B. Minerals

   C. Water

   D. Carbohydrates

76. Which of the following conditions is not associated with a lack of physical activity? (*Average Rigor*) (*Skill 6.3*)

   A. Atherosclerosis

   B. Longer life expectancy

   C. Osteoporosis

   D. Certain cancers

77. Data from assessing _____ identifies an individual's potential of developing musculoskeletal problems and an individual's potential of performing activities of daily living. (*Rigorous*) (*Skill 6.4*)

   A. Flexibility

   B. Muscle endurance

   C. Muscle strength

   D. Motor performance

78. The ability for a muscle(s) to repeatedly contract over a period of time is: (*Average Rigor*) (*Skill 6.4*)

   A. Cardiovascular endurance

   B. Muscle endurance

   C. Muscle strength

   D. Muscle force

79. Working at a level that is above normal is which exercise training principle? (*Rigorous*) (*Skill 6.5*)

   A. Intensity

   B. Progression

   C. Specificity

   D. Overload

80. Students on a running program to improve cardio-respiratory fitness apply which exercise principle. (*Rigorous*) (*Skill 6.5*)

   A. Aerobic

   B. Progression

   C. Specificity

   D. Overload

81. **Prior to activity, students perform a 5-10 minute warm-up. Which is not recommended as part of the warm-up?** *(Easy) (Skill 6.5)*

    A. Using the muscles that will be utilized in the following activity.

    B. Using a gradual aerobic warm-up.

    C. Using a gradual anaerobic warm-up.

    D. Stretching the major muscle groups to be used in the activity.

82. **Which is not a benefit of warming up?** *(Rigorous) (Skill 6.5)*

    A. Releasing hydrogen from myoglobin.

    B. Reducing the risk of musculoskeletal injuries.

    C. Raising the body's core temperature in preparation for activity.

    D. Stretching the major muscle groups to be used in the activity.

83. **Which is not a benefit of cooling down?** *(Rigorous) (Skill 6.5)*

    A. Preventing dizziness.

    B. Redistributing circulation.

    C. Removing lactic acid.

    D. Removing myoglobin.

84. **Activities to specifically develop cardiovascular fitness must be:** *(Rigorous) (Skill 6.5)*

    A. Performed without developing an oxygen debt

    B. Performed twice daily.

    C. Performed every day.

    D. Performed for a minimum of 10 minutes.

85. **Which of following overload principles does not apply to improving body composition?** *(Average Rigor) (Skill 6.5)*

    A. Aerobic exercise three times per week.

    B. Aerobic exercise at a low intensity.

    C. Aerobic exercise for about an hour.

    D. Aerobic exercise in intervals of high intensity.

86. **Which of the following principles of progression applies to improving muscle endurance?** (*Rigorous*) (*Skill 6.5*)

    A. Lifting weights every day.

    B. Lifting weights at 20% to 30% of assessed muscle strength.

    C. Lifting weights with low resistance and low reps.

    D. Lifting weights starting at 60% of assessed muscle strength.

87. **Overloading for muscle strength includes all of the following except:** (*Rigorous*) (*Skill 6.5*)

    A. Raising heart rate to an intense level.

    B. Lifting weights every other day.

    C. Lifting with high resistance and low reps.

    D. Lifting 60% to 90% of assessed muscle strength.

88. **Adding more reps to a weightlifting set applies which exercise principle.** (*Average Rigor*) (*Skill 6.5*)

    A. Anaerobic

    B. Progression

    C. Overload

    D. Specificity

89. **Cardiovascular fitness refers to:** (*Average Rigor*) (*Skill 6.6*)

    A. the ability to perform moderate to high intensity exercise for a prolonged period.

    B. how much force a muscle group can generate and how effectively the muscle group can sustain that force over a period of time.

    C. the physical makeup of the body.

    D. ability of a joint to move through its range of motion.

90. Instructors can encourage students to self-assess their physical education progress by employing: *(Easy) (Skill 6.7)*

A. Reflection

B. Journal writing

C. Interdisciplinary study

D. All of the above

91. All of the following are elements of a quality cardiovascular fitness program except: *(Average Rigor) (Skill 7.1)*

A. Mode

B. Frequency

C. Progression

D. Endurance

92. Swimming does not improve which health or skill related component of fitness? *(Rigorous) (Skill 7.2)*

A. Cardio-respiratory function

B. Flexibility

C. Muscle strength

D. Foot Speed

93. Which of the following does not modify overload? *(Rigorous) (Skill 7.3)*

A. Frequency

B. Perceived exertion

C. Time

D. Intensity

94. Using the Karvonean Formula, compute the 60% - 80% THR for a 16-year old student with a RHR of 60. *(Rigorous) (Skill 7.3)*

A. 122-163 beats per minute

B. 130-168 beats per minute

C. 142-170 beats per minute

D. 146-175 beats per minute

95. Using Cooper's Formula, compute the THR for a 15 year old student. *(Rigorous) (Skill 7.3)*

A. 120- 153 beats per minute

B. 123-164 beats per minute

C. 135-169 beats per minute

D. 147-176 beats per minute

96. Freehand front lunges will help an individual target muscle endurance in which of the following muscle groups: (*Average Rigor*) *(Skill 8.1)*

A. Trapezoids and lateral muscles

B. Thighs and hamstrings

C. Triceps and biceps

D. Obliques and thighs

97. Students are performing trunk extensions. What component of fitness does this activity assess? (*Average Rigor*) *(Skill 8.2)*

A. Balance

B. Flexibility

C. Body Composition

D. Coordination

98. Which of the following applies the concept of progression? (*Rigorous*) *(Skill 8.2)*

A. Beginning a stretching program every day.

B. Beginning a stretching program with 3 sets of reps.

C. Beginning a stretching program with ballistic stretching.

D. Beginning a stretching program holding stretches for 15 seconds and work up to holding stretches for 60 seconds.

99. A tendon is: (*Average Rigor*) *(Skill 8.4)*

A. contractile tissue.

B. the location at which two bones make contact.

C. a touch band of fibrous connective tissue that connects muscle to bone or muscle to muscle.

D. a short band of tough fibrous connective tissue composed mainly of long, stringy collagen fibers.

100. This form of workout promotes muscular endurance development, but it more taxing than average workout programs. (*Rigorous*) (*Skill 8.5*)

A. Weight training

B. Circuit training

C. Partner-resistance exercise

D. Technique training

101. With regard to protein content, foods from animal sources are usually: (*Average Rigor*) (*Skill 9.1*)

A. Complete

B. Essential

C. Nonessential

D. Incidental

102. Fats with room for two or more hydrogen atoms per molecule-fatty acid chain are: (*Rigorous*) (*Skill 9.1*)

A. Monounsaturated

B. Polyunsaturated

C. Hydrosaturated

D. Saturated

103. An adequate diet to meet nutritional needs consists of: (*Rigorous*) (*Skill 9.1*)

A. No more than 30% caloric intake from fats, no more than 50 % caloric intake from proteins, and at least 20% caloric intake from carbohydrates.

B. No more than 30% caloric intake from fats, no more than 40% caloric intake from proteins, and at least 30% caloric intake from carbohydrates.

C. No more than 30% caloric intake from fats, no more than 15% caloric intake from proteins, and at least 55% caloric intake from carbohydrates.

D. No more than 30 % caloric intake from fats, no more than 30% caloric intake from proteins, and at least 40% caloric intake from carbohydrates.

104. Maintaining body weight is best accomplished by: (*Average Rigor*) (*Skill 9.1*)

A. Dieting

B. Aerobic exercise

C. Lifting weights

D. Equalizing caloric intake relative to output

105. **Electronic impedance, a technique that estimates body fat percentage, uses this tool to measure the conductive potential of the body.** *(Rigorous) (Skill 9.2)*

    A. Bioimpedance meter

    B. Calipers

    C. Individual's height and weight

    D. All of the above

106. **Which is not a sign of stress?** *(Rigorous) (Skill 9.5)*

    A. Irritability

    B. Assertiveness

    C. Insomnia

    D. Stomach problems

107. **Which is not a common negative stressor?** *(Rigorous) (Skill 9.5)*

    A. Loss of significant other

    B. Personal illness or injury.

    C. Moving to a new state.

    D. Landing a new job.

108. **Which of the following is a negative coping strategy for dealing with stress?** *(Average Rigor) (Skill 9.5)*

    A. Recreational diversions

    B. Active thinking

    C. Alcohol use

    D. Imagery

109. **Most high-protein diets:** *(Average Rigor) (Skill 9.6)*

    A. Are high in cholesterol

    B. Are high in saturated fats

    C. Require vitamin and mineral supplements

    D. All of the above

110. **Which one of the following statements about low-calorie diets is false?** *(Rigorous) (Skill 9.6)*

    A. Most people who "diet only" regain the weight they lose.

    B. They are the way most people try to lose weight.

    C. They make weight control easier.

    D. They lead to excess worry about weight, food, and eating.

111. The local health food store is sponsoring a "Health Watch Day" with the local high school's physical education department where students, teachers, and local citizens can come in to receive a free BMI rating and information on a balance diet. This event is a good example of: (*Average Rigor*) *(Skill 9.7)*

A. Interdisciplinary study

B. Consumer education

C. Stress management

D. Marketing diet plans

112. Through physical activities, John has developed self-discipline, fairness, respect for others, and new friends. John has experienced which of the following? (*Rigorous*) *(Skill 10.1)*

A. Positive cooperation psycho-social influences

B. Positive group psycho-social influences

C. Positive individual psycho-social influences

D. Positive accomplishment psycho-social influences

113. Which of the following psycho-social influences is not negative? (*Rigorous*) *(Skill 10.1)*

A. Avoidance of problems

B. Adherence to exercise

C. Ego-centeredness

D. Role conflict

114. Aerobic dance develops or improves each of the following skills or health components except: (*Rigorous*) *(Skill 10.1)*

A. Cardio-respiratory function

B. Body composition

C. Coordination

D. Flexibility

115. The most effective way to promote the physical education curriculum is to: (*Rigorous*) *(Skill 10.1)*

A. Relate physical education to higher thought processes

B. Relate physical education to humanitarianism

C. Relate physical education to the total educational process

D. Relate physical education to skills necessary to preserve the natural environment

116. **This method refers to instructional method when teachers address the whole class through lecture, demonstration, or questioning.** *(Average Rigor) (Skill 10.3)*

    A. Large-group skill instruction

    B. Small-group skill instruction

    C. Individual skill instruction

    D. Cognitive structuring

117. **Rowing develops which health or skill related component of fitness?** *(Rigorous) (Skill 10.4)*

    A. Muscle endurance

    B. Flexibility

    C. Balance

    D. Reaction time

118. **Calisthenics develops all of the following health and skill related components of fitness except:** *(Average Rigor) (Skill 10.4)*

    A. Muscle strength

    B. Body composition

    C. Power

    D. Agility

119. **Which health or skill related components of fitness is developed by rope jumping?** *(Average Rigor) (Skill 10.4)*

    A. Muscle Force

    B. Coordination

    C. Flexibility

    D. Muscle strength

120. **Educators can evaluate the cognitive domain by all of the following methods except:** *(Rigorous) (Skill 10.6)*

    A. Norm-Referenced Tests

    B. Criterion Referenced Tests

    C. Standardized Tests

    D. Willis Sports Inventory Tests

121. **Students are performing the vertical jump. What component of fitness does this activity assess?** *(Rigorous) (Skill 10.8)*

    A. Muscle strength

    B. Balance

    C. Power

    D. Muscle endurance

122. Which of the following body types is the most capable of motor performance involving endurance? (*Rigorous*) (*Skill 11.1*)

A. Endomorph

B. Ectomorph

C. Mesomorph

D. Metamorph

123. Movement activities promote fairness, equity, and diversity because they consider this type of individual development. (*Rigorous*) (*Skill 11.5*)

A. Psychological

B. Human growth

C. Aesthetic

D. Both A and B

124. An instructor used a similar movement from a skill learned in a different activity to teach a skill for a new activity. The technique used to facilitate cognitive learning was: (*Average Rigor*) (*Skill 11.6*)

A. Conceptual thinking

B. Transfer of learning

C. Longer instruction

D. Appropriate language

125. Long-term planning is essential for effective class management. Identify the management techniques not essential to long-term planning. (*Easy*) (*Skill 12.1*)

A. Parental observation

B. Progress evaluation

C. Precise activity planning

D. Arrangements for line markings

126. Which of the following is not a class-management technique? (*Easy*) (*Skill 12.1*)

A. Explaining procedures for roll call, excuses, and tardiness

B. Explaining routines for changing and showering

C. Explaining conditioning

D. Promoting individual self-discipline

127. The physical education philosophy based on experience is: (*Average Rigor*) (*Skill 12.2*)

A. Naturalism

B. Pragmatism

C. Idealism

D. Existentialism

128. The modern physical education philosophy that combines beliefs from different philosophies is: (Easy) (Skill 12.2)

A. Eclectic

B. Humanistic

C. Individualism

D. Realism

129. A physical education teacher emphasizes healthy attitudes and habits. She conducts her classes so that students acquire and interpret knowledge and learn to think/analyze, which is necessary for physical activities. The goals and values utilized and the philosophy applied by this instructor is: (Rigorous) (Skill 12.2)

A. Physical Development Goals and Realism Philosophy

B. Affective Development Goals and Existentialism

C. Motor Development Goals and Realism Philosophy

D. Cognitive Development Goals and Idealism Philosophy

130. The affective domain of physical education contributes to all of the following except: (Rigorous) (Skill 12.2)

A. Knowledge of exercise, health, and disease

B. Self-actualization

C. An appreciation of beauty

D. Good sportsmanship

131. An obese student's fitness assessments were poor for every component of fitness. Which would you recommend first? (Easy) (Skill 12.4)

A. A jogging program.

B. A weight lifting program.

C. A walking program.

D. A stretching program.

132. All of the following are Systematic Observational Evaluations except: (Rigorous) (Skill 12.4)

A. Reflective Recording

B. Event Recording

C. Duration Recording

D. Self Recording

133. **While studying the social science, students might:** (*Average Rigor*) (*Skill 12.6*)

A. examine the relationship between physical activity and health.

B. study the physical science that stands behind bodily movements.

C. examine the interactions between groups in competitive team-based games.

D. Both A and C.

134. **A legal wrong resulting in a direct or an indirect injury is:** (*Average Rigor*) (*Skill 13.1*)

A. Negligence

B. A Tort

C. In loco parentis

D. Legal liability

135 . **Although Mary is a paraplegic, she wants to participate in some capacity in the physical education class. What federal legislative act entitles her to do so?** (*Rigorous*) (*Skill 13.2*)

A. PE 94-142

B. Title IX

C. PL 94-142

D. Title XI

136. **A good physical education instructor anticipates and prevents potential injuries, watches for hidden injuries, and takes an injury evaluation of the entire class. Which of the following strategies to prevent injuries is the teacher demonstrating?** (*Average Rigor*) (*Skill 13.3*)

A. Maintaining hiring standards

B. Proper use of equipment

C. Proper procedures for emergencies

D. Participant screening

137. **Which of the following is not a consideration for the selection of a facility?** (*Rigorous*) (*Skill 13.5*)

A. Community involvement

B. Custodial staff

C. Availability to women, minorities, and the handicapped

D. Bond issues

138. All of the following actions help avoid lawsuits except: (*Average Rigor*) *(Skill 13.5)*

    A. Ensuring equipment and facilities are safe

    B. Getting exculpatory agreements

    C. Knowing each students' health status

    D. Grouping students with unequal competitive levels

139. Which of the following actions does not promote safety? (*Rigorous*) *(Skill 13.6)*

    A. Allowing students to wear the current style of shoes

    B. Presenting organized activities

    C. Inspecting equipment and facilities

    D. Instructing skill and activities properly

140. Which of the following sequences displays the correct order for performing CPR? (*Average Rigor*) *(Skill 13.6)*

    1. Give two breaths
    2. Firmly push down two inches on the chest 15 times
    3. Call 911
    4. Position hands in the center of the chest
    5. Tilt head, lift chin, and check breathing

    A. 1, 5, 3, 4, 2

    B. 3, 5, 1, 4, 2

    C. 5, 3, 1, 4, 2

    D. 3, 5, 4, 2, 1

Answer Key

1.	C	37.	A	73.	A	109.	D
2.	D	38.	A	74.	B	110.	C
3.	C	39.	D	75.	C	111.	B
4.	A	40.	B	76.	B	112.	B
5.	B	41.	C	77.	A	113.	B
6.	D	42.	D	78.	B	114.	D
7.	C	43.	B	79.	D	115.	C
8.	C	44.	A	80.	C	116.	D
9.	A	45.	C	81.	C	117.	A
10.	B	46.	C	82.	A	118.	C
11.	B	47.	B	83.	D	119.	B
12.	D	48.	C	84.	A	120.	D
13.	C	49.	B	85.	A	121.	C
14.	A	50.	D	86.	B	122.	B
15.	B	51.	A	87.	A	123.	D
16.	A	52.	A	88.	B	124.	B
17.	B	53.	D	89.	A	125.	A
18.	C	54.	C	90.	D	126.	C
19.	B	55.	C	91.	D	127.	B
20.	B	56.	A	92.	D	128.	A
21.	B	57.	C	93.	B	129.	D
22.	A	58.	A	94.	D	130.	A
23.	C	59.	D	95.	B	131.	C
24.	B	60.	D	96.	B	132.	A
25.	D	61.	D	97.	B	133.	C
26.	C	62.	B	98.	D	134.	B
27.	D	63.	C	99.	C	135.	C
28.	B	64.	C	100.	B	136.	D
29.	C	65.	A	101.	A	137.	A
30.	A	66.	A	102.	B	138.	D
31.	D	67.	B	103.	C	139.	A
32.	C	68.	B	104.	D	140.	B
33.	D	69.	B	105.	A		
34.	A	70.	D	106.	B		
35.	C	71.	D	107.	D		
36.	B	72.	B	108.	C		

Rigor Table

	Easy %20	Average Rigor %40	Rigorous %40
Question #	9, 15, 16, 17, 18, 19, 21, 22, 24, 25, 27, 39, 45, 46, 49, 51, 52, 54, 61, 65, 68, 75, 81, 90, 125, 126, 128, 131,	1, 3, 5, 7, 8, 12, 26, 29, 30, 31, 32, 33, 34, 36, 37, 38, 41, 42, 43, 47, 48, 53, 57, 59, 62, 63, 64, 66, 69, 73, 76, 78, 85, 88, 89, 91, 96, 97, 99, 101, 104, 108, 109, 111, 116, 118, 119, 124, 127, 133, 134, 136, 138, 140	2, 4, 6, 10, 11, 13, 14, 20, 23, 28, 35, 40, 44, 50, 55, 56, 58, 60, 67, 70, 71, 72, 74, 77, 79, 80, 82, 83, 84, 86, 87, 92, 93, 94, 95, 98, 100, 102, 103, 105, 106, 107, 110, 112, 113, 114, 115, 117, 120, 121, 122, 123, 129, 130, 132, 135,137, 139

1.   **What is the proper sequential order of development for the acquisition of nonlocomotor skills?** *(Average Rigor) (Skill 1.1)*

A. Stretch, sit, bend, turn, swing, twist, shake, rock & sway, dodge; fall.
B. Bend, stretch, turn, twist, swing, sit, rock & sway, shake, dodge; fall.
C. Stretch, bend, sit, shake, turn, rock & sway, swing, twist, dodge; fall.
D. Bend, stretch, sit, turn, twist, swing, sway, rock & sway, dodge; fall.

Answer C: Stretch, bend, sit, shake, turn, rock & sway, swing, twist, dodge; fall.

Each skill in the progression builds on the previous skills.

2.   **What is the proper order of sequential development for the acquisition of locomotor skills?** *(Rigorous) (Skill 1.1)*

A. Creep, crawl, walk, jump, run, slide, gallop, hop, leap, skip; step-hop.
B. Crawl, walk, creep, slide, walk, run, hop, leap, gallop, skip; step-hop.
C. Creep, crawl, walk, slide, run, hop, leap, skip, gallop, jump; step-hop.
D. Crawl, creep, walk, run, jump, hop, gallop, slide, leap, skip; step-hop.

Answer D: Crawl, creep, walk, run, jump, hop, gallop, slide, leap, skip; step-hop.

LOCOMOTOR SKILL: A skill that utilizes the feet and moves you from one place to another.

CRAWL: A form of locomotion where the person moves in a prone position with the body resting on or close to the ground or on the hands and knees.

CREEP: A slightly more advanced form of locomotion in which the person moves on the hands and knees.

WALK: A form of locomotion in which body weight is transferred alternately from the ball (toe) of one foot to the heel of the other. At times one foot is on the ground and during a brief phase, both feet are on the ground. There is no time when both feet are off the ground.

RUN: A form of locomotion much like the walk except that the tempo and body lean may differ. At times one foot is on the ground and during a brief phase both feet are off the ground. There is no time when both feet are on the ground simultaneously.

JUMP: A form of locomotion in which the body weight is projected from one or two feet and lands on two feet. Basic forms: for height, from height, distance, continuous, and rebounding.

HOP: A form of locomotion in which the body is projected from one foot to the same foot.

GALLOP: A form of locomotion that is a combination of an open step by the leading foot and a closed step by the trailing foot. The same foot leads throughout. The rhythm is uneven.

SLIDE: The same action as the gallop except that the direction of travel is sideways instead of forward. The rhythm is uneven.

LEAP: An exaggerated running step. There is a transfer of weight from one foot to the other and a phase when neither foot is in contact with the ground.

SKIP: A locomotor skill that combines a hop and a step (walk or run). The rhythm is uneven.

3.   The two main categories of are knowledge of performance and information about the performance. *(Average Rigor) (Skill 1.2)*

A. Self assessment
B. Intrinsic feedback
C. Extrinsic feedback
D. Observational learning

Answer C: Extrinsic feedback

Extrinsic feedback, also known as augmented feedback, is information not inherent in the movement itself but which improves intrinsic feedback. There are two main categories: knowledge of performance and information about the technique and performance. The coach can provide extrinsic feedback verbally or visually via video. Extrinsic feedback enables the athlete to establish a kinesthetic reference for the correct movement.

4.   Which movement concept involves students making decisions about an object's positional changes in space? *(Rigorous) (Skill 1.3)*

A. Spatial Awareness
B. Effort Awareness
C. Body Awareness
D. Motion Awareness

Answer A: Spatial awareness

Spatial awareness is an organized awareness of objects in the space around us. It is also an awareness of our body's position in space. Without this awareness, we would not be able to pick food up from our plates and put it in our mouths. We would have trouble reading, because we could not see the letters in their correct relation to each other and to the page. Athletes would not have the precise awareness of the position of other players on the field and the movement of the ball, which is necessary to play sports effectively.

5.   Applying the mechanical principles of balance, time, and force describes which movement concept? *(Average Rigor) (Skill 1.3)*

A. Spatial Awareness
B. Effort Awareness
C. Body Awareness
D. Motion Awareness

Answer B: Effort awareness

Effort Awareness is the knowledge of balance, time, and force and how they relate to athletic movements and activities.

6.   There are two sequential phases to the development of spatial awareness. What is the order of these phases? *(Rigorous) (Skill 1.3)*

A. Locating more than one object in relation to each object; the location of objects in relation to one's own body in space.
B. The location of objects in relation to one's own body in space; locating more than one object in relation to one's own body.
C. Locating more than one object independent of one's body; the location of objects in relation to one's own body.
D. The location of objects in relation to one's own body in space; locating more than one object in relation to each object and independent of one's own body.

Answer D: The location of objects in relation to one's own body in space; locating more than one object in relation to each object and independent of one's own body.

The order of the two sequential phases to develop spatial awareness are as follows: the location of objects in relation to one's own body in space, and locating more than one object in relation to each object and independent of one's own body.

7.   Process assessment does not identify which of the following errors in skill performance. *(Average Rigor) (Skill 1.5)*

A. Style
B. Form
C. End result
D. Mechanics

Answer C: End result

Process assessment does not evaluate end results. Process assessment emphasizes analysis of style, form, and mechanics.

8.   Which of the following principles is not a factor to assess to correct errors in performance for process assessment? *(Average Rigor) (Skill 1.5)*

A. Inertia
B. Action/Reaction
C. Force
D. Acceleration

Answer C: Force

Force is not a factor to focus on in process assessment.

9. **Instructors can assess skill level achievement in bowling by:** *(Easy) (Skill 1.5)*

A. Calculating a student's average score.
B. Calculating how many gutter-balls the student threw.
C. Calculating how many strikes the student threw.
D. Calculating how many spares

Answer A: Calculating a student's average score.

Instructors can determine the skill level of a bowler by calculating the student's average game score. There is a possibility that some coincidences take place (e.g., bowling a strike). To check the consistency, we determine the average instead of looking at only the score from a single game.

10. **A subjective, observational approach to identifying errors in the form, style, or mechanics of a skill is accomplished by:** *(Rigorous) (Skill 1.5)*

A. Product assessment
B. Process assessment
C. Standardized norm-referenced tests
D. Criterion-referenced tests

Answer B: Process assessment

Process assessment is one way to identify errors in the skills of an individual. It is one way to know the limitations and skills that every individual possesses.

11. **What type of assessment objectively measures skill performance?** *(Rigorous) (Skill 1.5)*

A. Process assessment
B. Product assessment
C. Texas PE Test
D. Iowa Brace Test

Answer B: Product assessment

Product assessment measures the skills of an individual. This process is a methodical evaluation of the characteristics of your product or service in the eyes of potential users and customers. The two principle types of assessments are principle-based assessments and usability testing.

12. **Determining poor performance of a skill using process assessment can best be accomplished by:** *(Average Rigor) (Skill 1.5)*

A. Observing how fast a skill is performed.
B. Observing how many skills are performed.
C. Observing how far or how high a skill is performed.
D. Observing several attributes comprising the entire performance of a skill.

Answer D: Observing several attributes comprising the entire performance of a skill.

To determine the source of the error in the poor performance of an individual, we use observations of several attributes that compromise the entire performance of a skill. Instructors should observe limitations and mistakes and determine how to best address these problems to improve future performance.

13. **Which of the following methods measures fundamental skills using product assessment?** *(Rigorous) (Skill 1.5)*

A. Criterion-referenced tests
B. Standardized norm-referenced tests
C. Both A and B
D. Neither A nor B

Answer C: Both A and B

Criterion-referenced tests and standardized norm-referenced tests are both methods that can prove and measure skills in product assessment. They can help to prevent or lessen errors.

14. **Product assessment measures all of the following except:** *(Rigorous) (Skill 1.5)*

A. How the student performs the mechanics of a skill.
B. How many times the student performs a skill.
C. How fast the student performs a skill.
D. How far or high the student performs a skill.

Answer A: How the student performs the mechanics of a skill.

Product assessment evaluates student performance and gives insight into how students can correct errors. Product assessment measures results. Thus, how the student performs the mechanics of a skill is not relevant to product assessment.

15.   Having students pretend they are playing basketball or trying to catch a bus develops which locomotor skill? *(Easy) (Skill 2.1)*

A. Galloping
B. Running
C. Leaping
D. Skipping

Answer B: Running

Playing basketball involves near constant running up and down the court. In addition, chasing is a good example to use with children to illustrate the concept of running.

16.   Having students play Fox and Hound develops: *(Easy) (Skill 2.1)*

A. Galloping
B. Hopping
C. Stepping-hopping
D. Skipping

Answer A: Galloping
Fox and Hound is an activity that emphasizes rapid running. The form of the exercise most closely resembles a gallop, especially in rhythm and rapidity. It can develop or progress at an accelerated rate.

17.   Having students take off and land with both feet together develops which locomotor skill? *(Easy) (Skill 2.1)*

A. Hopping
B. Jumping
C. Leaping
D. Skipping

Answer B: Jumping

Jumping is a skill that most humans and many animals share. It is the process of getting one's body off of the ground for a short time using one's own power, usually by propelling oneself upward via contraction and then forceful extension of the legs. One can jump up to reach something high, jump over a fence or ditch, or jump down. One can also jump while dancing and as a sport in track and field.

18. **Which nonlocomotor skill entails movement around a joint where two body parts meet?** *(Easy) (Skill 2.1)*

A. Twisting
B. Swaying
C. Bending
D. Stretching

Answer C: Bending

Bending is a deviation from a straight-line position. It is also means to assume a curved, crooked, or angular form or direction, to incline the body, to make a concession, yield, to apply oneself closely, or to concentrate (e.g., *she bent to her task*).

19. **A sharp change of direction from one's original line of movement is which nonlocomotor skill?** *(Easy) (Skill 2.1)*

A. Twisting
B. Dodging
C. Swaying
D. Swinging

Answer B: Dodging

Dodging is the ability to avoid something by moving or shifting quickly aside.

20. **Which manipulative skill uses the hands to stop the momentum of an object?** *(Rigorous) (Skill 2.1)*

A. Trapping
B. Catching
C. Striking
D. Rolling

Answer B: Catching

The ability to use the hands to catch an object is a manipulative skill. Catching stops the momentum of an object. A successful catch harnesses the force of the oncoming object to stop the object's momentum.

21.   Activities such as pretending to pick fruit off a tree or reaching for a star develop which non-locomotor skill? *(Easy) (Skill 2.1)*

A. Bending
B. Stretching
C. Turning
D. Twisting

Answer B: Stretching

Stretching is the activity of gradually applying <u>tensile</u> force to lengthen, strengthen, and lubricate <u>muscles</u>, often performed in anticipation of <u>physical exertion</u> and to increase the range of motion within a <u>joint</u>. Stretching is an especially important accompaniment to activities that emphasize controlled muscular strength and flexibility. These include <u>ballet</u>, <u>acrobatics</u> or <u>martial arts</u>. Stretching also may help prevent <u>injury</u> to <u>tendons</u>, <u>ligaments</u>, and muscles by improving muscular <u>elasticity</u> and reducing the stretch reflex in greater ranges of motion that might cause injury to tissue. In addition, stretching can reduce <u>delayed onset muscle soreness</u> (DOMS).

22.   Picking up coins, tying shoes, and petting animals develop this nonlocomotor skill. *(Easy) (Skill 2.1)*

A. Bending
B. Stretching
C. Turning
D. Twisting

Answer A: Bending

Bending is the action of moving the body across a skeletal joint. In each of the sample activities, one must bend from the waist or knees to reach a low object.

23.   To enhance skill and strategy performance for striking or throwing objects, for catching or collecting objects, and for carrying and propelling objects, students must first learn techniques for: *(Rigorous) (Skill 2.1)*

A. Offense
B. Defense
C. Controlling objects
D. Continuous play of objects

Answer C: Controlling objects

For enhancing the catching, throwing, carrying, or propelling of objects, a student must learn how to control the objects. The control gives the player a sense of the object. Thus, offense, defense, and continuous play come naturally, as they are part of the controlling process.

24. **Coordinated movements that project a person over an obstacle is:** *(Easy)* *(Skill 2.1)*

A. Jumping
B. Vaulting
C. Leaping
D. Hopping

Answer B: Vaulting

Vaulting is the art of acrobatics on horseback. Vaulting is an internationally recognized, competitive sport that is growing in popularity. At the most basic level vaulting enhances riding skills. At any skill-level, this ancient dance between horse and rider deepens the sense of balance, timing, and poise for the rider, as well as a sensitivity to and respect for the horse-rider relationship. Participants can vault in competition individually or on a team of 8 people with up to 3 people on the horse at once.

25. **Using the same foot to take off from a surface and land is which locomotor skill?** *(Easy)* *(Skill 2.1)*

A. Jumping
B. Vaulting
C. Leaping
D Hopping

Answer D: Hopping

Hopping is a move with light, bounding skips or leaps. Basically, it is the ability to jump on one foot.

26.   All of the following are parts of the sequence of an overhand throw movement except: *(Average Rigor) (Skill 2.2)*

A. A stride
B. A hip rotation
C. A hyperextension
D. A trunk rotation

Answer C: A hyperextension

The overhand throw consists of a sequence of four movements: a stride, hip rotation, trunk rotation, and forward arm movement. The thrower should align his body sideways to the target (with opposite shoulder pointing towards the target). The overhand throw begins with a stride with the opposite foot (i.e. left foot for a right-handed thrower). As the stride foot contacts the ground, the pivot foot braces against the ground and provides stability for the subsequent movements. Hip rotation is the natural turning of the hips toward the target. Trunk rotation follows hip rotation. The hips should rotate before the trunk because the stretching of the torso muscles allows for stronger muscle contraction during trunk rotation. Following trunk rotation, the arm moves forward in two phases. In the first phase the elbow is bent. In the second phase, the elbow joint straightens and the thrower releases the ball

27.   Having students collapse in their own space or lower themselves as though they are a raindrop or snowflake develops this nonlocomotor skill. *(Easy) (Skill 2.3)*

A. Dodging
B. Shaking
C. Swinging
D. Falling

Answer D: Falling

Falling is a major cause of personal injury in athletics. Athletic participants must learn how to fall in such a way as to limit the possibility of injury.

28.   **Which is the proper sequential order of development for the acquisition of manipulative skills?** *(Rigorous) (Skill 2.3)*

A. Striking, throwing, bouncing, catching, trapping, kicking, ball rolling; volleying.
B. Striking, throwing, kicking, ball rolling, volleying, bouncing, catching; trapping.
C. Striking, throwing, catching, trapping, kicking, ball rolling, bouncing; volleying.
D. Striking, throwing, kicking, ball rolling, bouncing; volleying.

Answer B: Striking, throwing, kicking, ball rolling, volleying, bouncing, catching, and trapping.

This is the proper sequential order of development for the acquisition of manipulative skills. Each skill in this progression builds on the previous skill.

29.   **Having students hit a large balloon with both hands develops this manipulative skill.** *(Average Rigor) (Skill 2.3)*

A. Bouncing
B. Striking
C. Volleying
D. Trapping

Answer C: Volleying

In a number of ball games, a volley is the ball that a player receives and delivers without touching the ground. The ability to volley a ball back and forth requires great body control and spatial awareness.

30.   **Progressively decreasing the size of a target that balls are projected at develops which manipulative skill.** *(Average Rigor) (Skill 2.3)*

A. Throwing
B. Trapping
C. Volleying
D. Kicking

Answer A: Throwing

Children develop throwing skills (the ability to propel an object through the air with a rapid movement of the arm and wrist) by projecting balls at progressively smaller targets.

31. **Hitting a stationary object while in a fixed position, then incorporating movement, develops this manipulative skill.** *(Average Rigor) (Skill 2.3)*

A. Bouncing
B. Trapping
C. Throwing
D. Striking

Answer D: Striking

Striking is the process of hitting something sharply, as with the hand, the fist, or a weapon.

32. **Playing "Simon Says" and having students touch different body parts applies which movement concept?** *(Average Rigor) (Skill 2.5)*

A. Spatial Awareness
B. Effort Awareness
C. Body Awareness
D. Motion Awareness

Answer C: Body Awareness

Body Awareness is a method that integrates European traditions of movement and biomedical knowledge with the East Asian traditions of movement (e.g. Tai chi and Zen meditation).

33. **The ability to change rapidly the direction of the body is:** *(Average Rigor) (Skill 2.5)*

A. Coordination
B. Reaction time
C. Speed
D. Agility

Answer D: Agility

Agility is the ability of the body to change position quickly. Reaction time, coordination, and speed are not the right words to describe the ability to move quickly, as we always say that the goalkeeper is agile.

34. **Having students move on their hands and knees, move on lines, and/or hold shapes while moving develops which quality of movement?** *(Average Rigor) (Skill 3.1)*

A. Balance
B. Time
C. Force
D. Inertia

Answer A: Balance

Balance is one of the physiological senses. It allows humans and animals to walk without falling. Some animals are better at this than humans. For example, a cat (as a quadruped using its inner ear and tail) can walk on a thin fence. All forms of equilibrioception are essentially the detection of acceleration.

35. **Students that paddle balls against a wall or jump over objects with various heights are demonstrating which quality of movement?** *(Rigorous) (Skill 3.1)*

A. Balance
B. Time
C. Force
D. Inertia

Answer C: Force

Force is the capacity to do work or create physical change, energy, strength, or active power. It is a classical **force** that causes a free body with <u>mass</u> to <u>accelerate</u>. A net (or resultant) force that causes such acceleration may be the non-zero additive sum of many different forces acting on a body.

36. **Having students move in a specific pattern while measuring how long they take to do so develops which quality of movement?** *(Average Rigor) (Skill 3.1)*

A. Balance
B. Time
C. Force
D. Inertia

Answer B: Time

Time is a sequential arrangement of all events or the interval between two events in such a sequence. We can discuss the concept of time on several different levels: physical, psychological, philosophical, scientific, and biological. Time is the non-spatial continuum in which events occur, in apparently irreversible succession, from the past through the present to the future.

37. **Equilibrium is maintained as long as**: *(Average Rigor) (Skill 3.1)*

A. Body segments are moved independently.
B. The center of gravity is over the base of support
C. Force is applied to the base of support.
D. The center of gravity is lowered.

Answer A: The center of gravity is over the base of support.

Equilibrium is a condition in which all acting influences are canceled by others, resulting in a stable, balanced, or unchanging system. It allows humans and animals to walk without falling. An object maintains equilibrium as long as its center of gravity is over its base of support.

38. **Which of the following does not enhance equilibrium?** *(Average Rigor) (Skill 3.1)*

A. Shifting the center of gravity away from the direction of movement.
B. Increasing the base of support.
C. Lowering the base of support.
D. Increasing the base of support and lowering the center of support.

Answer A: Shifting the center of gravity away from the direction of movement.

Equilibrium is a state of balance. When a body or a system is in equilibrium, there is no net tendency toward change. In mechanics, equilibrium has to do with the forces acting on a body. When no force acts to make a body move in a line, the body is in translational equilibrium. When no force acts to make the body turn, the body is in rotational equilibrium. A body in equilibrium while at rest is in static equilibrium. Increasing the base of support, lowering the base of support, and increasing the base of support and lowering the center of support all enhance equilibrium by balancing forces.

39. **All of the following affect force except**: *(Easy) (Skill 3.1)*

A. Magnitude
B. Energy
C. Motion
D. Mass

Answer D: Mass

Mass is a property of a physical object that quantifies the amount of matter and energy it contains. Unlike weight, the mass of something stays the same regardless of location. Every object has a unified body of matter with no specific shape.

40. **For a movement to occur, applied force must overcome inertia of an object and any other resisting forces. What concept of force does this describe?** *(Rigorous) (Skill 3.1)*

A. Potential energy
B. Magnitude
C. Kinetic energy
D. Absorption

Answer B: Magnitude

Speaking of magnitude in a purely relative way states that nothing is large and nothing small. If everything in the universe increased in bulk one thousand diameters, nothing would be any larger than it was before. However, if one thing remained unchanged, all of the others would be larger than they had been. To a person familiar with the relativity of magnitude and distance, the spaces and masses of the astronomer would be no more impressive than those of the microscopist would. To the contrary, the visible universe may be a small part of an atom, with its component ions floating in the life-fluid (luminiferous ether) of some animal.

41. **The energy of an object to do work while recoiling is which type of potential energy?** *(Average Rigor) (Skill 3.1)*

A. Absorption
B. Kinetic
C. Elastic
D. Torque

Answer C: Elastic

In materials science, the word elastomer refers to a material that is very elastic (like rubber). We often use the word elastic colloquially to refer to an elastomeric material such as rubber or cloth/rubber combinations. It is capable of withstanding stress without injury. Elastic potential energy describes the energy inherent in flexible objects.

42.   Gradually decelerating a moving mass by utilization of smaller forces over a long period of time is: *(Average Rigor) (Skill 3.1)*

A. Stability
B. Equilibrium
C. Angular force
D. Force absorption

Answer D: Force absorption

Force absorption is the gradual deceleration of a moving mass by utilization of smaller forces over a long period of time.

43.   The tendency of a body/object to remain in its present state of motion unless some force acts to change it is which mechanical principle of motion? *(Average Rigor) (Skill 3.2)*

A. Acceleration
B. Inertia
C. Action/Reaction
D. Linear motion

Answer B: Inertia

Inertia is a term used in physics that describes the resistance of a body to any alteration in its state of <u>motion</u>. Inertia is a property common to all matter. Galileo first observed this property and Newton later restated it. Newton's first law of motion is sometimes called the law of inertia. Newton's second law of motion states that the external force required to affect the motion of a body is proportional to that acceleration. The constant of proportionality is the <u>mass</u>, which is the numerical value of the inertia. The greater the inertia of a body, the less acceleration is needed for a given, applied force.

44.   The movement response of a system depends not only on the net external force, but also on the resistance to movement change. Which mechanical principle of motion does this definition describe? *(Rigorous) (Skill 3.2)*

A. Acceleration
B. Inertia
C. Action/Reaction
D. Air Resistance

Answer A: Acceleration

Acceleration is the change in the velocity of a body with respect to time. Since velocity is a vector quantity involving both magnitude and direction, acceleration is also a vector. In order to produce acceleration, a force must on a body. The magnitude of the force (F) must be directly proportional to both the mass of the body (m) and the desired acceleration (a), according to Newton's second law of motion $(F=ma)$. The exact nature of the acceleration depends on the relative directions of the original velocity and force. A force acting in the same direction as the velocity changes only the speed of the body. An appropriate force, acting always at right angles to the velocity, changes the direction of the velocity but not the speed.

45.   Which of the following mechanical principles of motion states that every motion has a similar, contrasting response? *(Easy) (Skill 3.2)*

A. Acceleration
B. Inertia
C. Action/Reaction
D. Centripetal force

Answer C: Action/Reaction

The principle of action/reaction is an assertion about the nature of motion from which we can determine the trajectory of an object subject to forces. The path of an object yields a stationary value for a quantity called the action. Thus, instead of thinking about an object accelerating in response to applied forces, one might think of them as picking out the path with a stationary action.

46.   **Activities that enhance team socialization include all of the following except:** *(Easy) (Skill 4.1)*

A. Basketball
B. Soccer
C. Golf
D. Volleyball

Answer C: Golf

Golf is mainly an individual sport. Though golf involves social interaction, it generally lacks the team element inherent in basketball, soccer, and volleyball.

47.   **Some students practicing basketball are having difficulty with "free throws," even though the shots make it to and over the hoop. What adjustment will improve their "free throws?"** *(Average Rigor) (Skill 4.1)*

A. Increasing the height of release (i.e. jump shot).
B. Increasing the vertical path of the ball.
C. Increasing the velocity of the release.
D. Increasing the base of support.

Answer B: Increasing the vertical path of the ball

In this case, increasing the vertical path of the ball will help the students make more free throws. Increased vertical path provides greater margin for error, allowing the ball to drop more easily through the hoop. Increasing the velocity cannot work due to common sense. Finally, increasing the height of release and base of support are not viable options in this case because the students are having no problem getting the ball to the basket.

48.   **An archery student's arrow bounced off the red part of the target face. What is the correct ruling?** *(Average Rigor) (Skill 4.1)*

A. No score.
B. Re-shoot arrow.
C. 7 points awarded.
D. Shot receives same score as highest arrow shot that did not bounce off the target.

Answer C: 7 points awarded

When an arrow bounces off the red area of a target, the archer receives 7 points, the value of the shot had the arrow stuck in the target.

49.   A student playing badminton believed that the shuttlecock was going to land out-of-bounds. The shuttlecock landed on the line. What is the correct ruling? (*Easy*) (*Skill 4.1*)

A. The shuttlecock is out-of-bounds.
B. The shuttlecock is in-bounds.
C. The point is replayed.
D. That player is charged with a feint.

Answer B: The shuttlecock is in-bounds.

If a shuttlecock lands on the line, it is inbounds by the rules of badminton.

50.   A mechanical pinsetter accidentally knocked down the only bowling pin left standing for a spare attempt after clearing all the other pins knocked down by the first ball thrown. What is the correct ruling? (*Rigorous*) (*Skill 4.1*)

A. Foul
B. Spare
C. Frame is replayed
D. No count for that pin

Answer D: No count for that pin

When the mechanical pin setter touches a pin and knocks it down, there is no count for the pin because the pin fell because of mechanical fault and the player had nothing to do with it. The other pins count and there is no foul for the player.

51.   The ball served in racquetball hits the front line and lands in front of the short line. What is the ruling? (*Easy*) (*Skill 4.1*)

A. Fault
B. Reserve
C. Out-of-bounds
D. Fair ball

Answer A: Fault

If a served ball falls in front of the short line, it is a fault according to a rule that states that a ball must fall within the short line frame at the time of serving. It is not out-of-bounds, as it is still within the limits of the pitch. However, it is also not a fair ball due to the service rule.

52. Two opposing soccer players are trying to gain control of the ball when one player "knees" the other. What is the ruling? *(Easy) (Skill 4.1)*

A. Direct free kick
B. Indirect free kick
C. Fair play
D. Ejection from the game

Answer A: Direct free kick

Assuming that the soccer player didn't intentionally hit the other player's knee, the result would be a direct free kick. If the foul was intentional, the referee can eject the offender from the game. Minor offenses and offenses not involving contact result in indirect free kicks.

53. Two students are playing badminton. When receiving the shuttlecock, one student consistently stands too deep in the receiving court. What strategy should the server use to serve the shuttlecock? (Average Rigor) (Skill 4.1)

A. Smash serve
B. Clear serve
C. Overhead serve
D. Short serve

Answer D: short serve

The short serve would give land short in the court so the opponent would not be able to reach the shuttlecock. Therefore, the short serve would win the point. A clear or overhead serve enables the opponent to hit the shuttlecock and continue the game. A smash serve runs a higher risk of falling out-of-bounds. Neither of these scenarios are goals of the server.

54. A basketball team has an outstanding rebounder. In order to keep this player near the opponent's basket, which strategy should the coach implement? *(Easy) (Skill 4.1)*

A. Pick-and-Roll
B. Give-and-Go
C. Zone defense
D. Free-lancing

Answer C: Zone defense

A zone defense, where each player guards an area of the court rather than an individual player, allows an outstanding rebounder to remain near the basket. The give-and-go, pick-and-roll, and free-lancing are offensive strategies that do not affect rebounding.

55. When a defensive tennis player needs more time to return to his position, what strategy should he apply? *(Rigorous) (Skill 4.1)*

A. Drop shot
B. Dink shot
C. Lob shot
D. Down-the-line shot

Answer C: Lob shot

When a tennis player is off the court and needs time to return to his position, the player should play a lob shot. Down-the-line shots and drop shots are offensive shots and are too risky in this situation. The dink shot would allow the opponent to take control of the point.

56. An overhead badminton stroke used to hit a fore-hand-like overhead stroke that is on the backhand side of the body is a(n): *(Rigorous) (Skill 4.1)*

A. Around-the-head shot
B. Down-the-line shot
C. Lifting the shuttle
D. Under hand shuttle

Answer A: Around-the-head shot

A shot played from the backhand side and over the head is known as an around-the-head shot. It is played when the shuttlecock is high and cannot be reached any other way.

57. A maneuver when an offensive player passes to a teammate and then immediately cuts in toward the basket for a return pass is: *(Average Rigor) (Skill 4.1)*

A. Charging
B. Pick
C. Give-and-go
D. Switching

Answer C: Give-and-go

In the game of basketball, a give-and-go is an offensive play where a player passes to a teammate and immediately cuts toward the basket for a return pass. Charging is an offensive foul, a pick is a maneuver to free up a teammate for a pass or shot, and switching is a defensive maneuver.

58. A bowling pin that remains standing after an apparently perfect hit is a: *(Rigorous) (Skill 4.1)*

A. Tap
B. Turkey
C. Blow
D. Leave

Answer A: Tap

A bowling pin that remains standing, even after a perfect shot, is known as a tap. Other options, like turkeys and blows, are not relevant to the standing pin.

59. A soccer pass from the outside of the field near the end line to a position in front of the goal is a: *(Average Rigor) (Skill 4.1)*

A. Chip
B. Settle
C. Through
D. Cross

Answer D: Cross

Any long pass from the sides of the field toward the middle is a cross, since the hitter hits it across the field. A chip is a high touch pass or shot. A through pass travels the length of the field through many players. Finally, settling is the act of controlling the ball after receiving a pass.

60. Although they are still hitting the target, the score of some students practicing archery has decreased as the distance between them and the target has increased. Which of the following adjustments will improve their scores? *(Rigorous) (Skill 4.1)*

A. Increasing the velocity of their arrows.
B. Increasing the students' base of support.
C. Increasing the weight of the arrows.
D. Increasing the parabolic path of the arrows.

Answer D: Increasing the parabolic path of the arrows.

Increasing the parabolic path of the arrows will increase accuracy and precision at greater distances.

61.   A volleyball that opponents simultaneously contact and momentarily hold above the net is a(n): *(Easy) (Skill 4.1)*

A. Double fault
B. Play over
C. Overlap
D. Held ball

Answer D: Held ball

In volleyball, if two players simultaneously contact the ball above the net, the ball is a held ball.

62.   Volleyball player LB on team A digs a spiked ball. The ball deflects off LB's shoulder. What is the ruling? *(Average Rigor) (Skill 4.1)*

A. Fault
B. Legal hit
C. Double foul
D. Play over

Answer B: Legal hit

Since the spiked ball does not touch the ground and instead deflects off LB's shoulder, it is a legal hit. In order for a point

63.   Instructors can evaluate skill level of achievement in archery by: *(Average Rigor) (Skill 4.1)*

A. Giving students a written exam on terminology.
B. Having students demonstrate the correct tension of arrow feathers.
C. Totaling a student's score obtained on the target's face.
D. Time how long a student takes to shoot all arrows.

Answer C: Totaling a student's score obtained on the target's face.

Archery is the practice of using a bow to shoot arrows. Totaling a student's score is the only method, of the possible choices, that evaluates skill level. Choices A and B test knowledge and choice D is an arbitrary measure.

TEACHER CERTIFICATION STUDY GUIDE

64. **Instructors can determine skill level achievement in golf by:** (*Average Rigor*) (*Skill 4.1*)

A. The number of "birdies" that a student makes.
B. The number of "bogies" a student makes.
C. The score obtained after several rounds
D. The total score achieved throughout the school year.

Answer C: The score obtained after several rounds

Instructors can determine skill level in golf by evaluating a golfer's score after several rounds. The number of bogies or birdies is not necessarily indicative of skill level because they are isolated events (i.e. the score on one hole). The player who consistently scores the lowest likely has the most impressive golf skills. Therefore, a player's score is the best way to determine his/her skill level. Finally, several rounds are a sufficient sample to determine skill level. An entire year's worth of scores is not necessary.

65. **Social skills and values developed by activity include all of the following except:** (*Easy*) (*Skill 4.2*)

A. Winning at all costs
B. Making judgments in groups
C. Communicating and cooperating
D. Respecting rules and property

Answer A: Winning at all costs

Winning at all costs is not a desirable social skill. Instructors and coaches should emphasize fair play and effort over winning. Answers B, C, and D are all positive skills and values developed in physical activity settings.

PHYSICAL EDUCATION   259

66. **The sense of the relative position of neighboring parts of the body is/are called:** (*Average Rigor*) (*Skill 4.3*)

A. Proprioception
B. Spatial orientation
C. Hand-eye coordination
D. Movement skills

Answer A: Proprioception

Proprioception is the sense of the relative position of neighboring parts of the body. Unlike the six external senses (sight, taste, smell, touch, hearing, and balance), proprioception is an internal sense that provides feedback solely on the status of the body internally. Spatial orientation refers to the process of aligning or positioning oneself with respect to a specific direction or reference system, while hand eye coordination is the ability of the visual perception system to coordinate the information received through the eyes to control, guide, and direct the hands in the accomplishment of a given task (examples include handwriting or catching a ball). Finally, movement skills center on the integration of balance and proprioceptive skills to produce movement that effectively manages the weight distribution of the body.

67. _____ **education should always accompany the _____ practice of the activity.** (*Rigorous*) (*Skill 4.4*)

A. Affective; practical
B. Cognitive; physical
C. Metacognitive; physical
D. Cognitive; practical

Answer B: Cognitive, physical

Cognitive education should always accompany the physical practice of the activity. Students should understand the correct and incorrect process of technique execution as well as why the correct way is biomechanically correct and why the incorrect way is biomechanically incorrect. This will make it possible for the students to focus on their weaknesses and to self-monitor their progress.

68.   Modern, jazz, ballet, hip-hop, and ballroom are just some of the types of
_____ students can physically study. (*Easy*) (*Skill 5.1*)

A. Theatre
B. Dance
C. Music
D. Art

Answer B: Dance

Modern, jazz, ballet, hip-hop, and ballroom are all types of dance that can be
physically studied. These also could be types of music; however, students would not
physically study those.

69.   Instructors can determine skill level achievement in swimming by:
(*Average Rigor*) (*Skill 5.2*)

A. How long a student can float
B. How many strokes it takes a student to swim a specified distance.
C. How long a student can stay under the water without moving.
D. How many times a student can dive in five minutes.

Answer B: How many strokes it takes a student to swim a specified distance.

Instructors can determine skill level in swimming by counting the strokes a swimmer
takes when covering a certain distance. The arm movement, the strength, and the
tactic to move quickly give the swimmer an ability to swim faster. The ability to float,
stay under water, and dive quickly is not relevant to swimming ability.

70.   An instructor notices that class participation is much lower than
expected. By making changes in equipment and rules, the instructor
applied which of the following concepts to enhance participation?
(*Rigorous*) (*Skill 5.4*)

A. Homogeneous grouping
B. Heterogeneous grouping
C. Multi-activity designs
D. Activity modification

Answer D: Activity modification

Activity modification involves changing rules and equipment to fit the needs of
students of different ability levels and physical development levels. Activity
modification can encourage participation by making games and activities more
enjoyable and allowing for more student success.

71. A teacher who modifies and develops tasks for a class is demonstrating knowledge of which appropriate behavior in physical education activities. (*Rigorous*) (*Skill 5.4*)

A. Appropriate management behavior
B. Appropriate student behavior
C. Appropriate administration behavior
D. Appropriate content behavior

Answer D: Appropriate content behavior

In this case, the teacher is demonstrating knowledge of a behavior in reference to physical activity. It is known as appropriate content behavior. The other options are not related to physical activities.

72. Using tactile clues is a functional adaptation that can assist which type of students? (*Rigorous*) (*Skill 5.4*)

A. Deaf students
B. Blind students
C. Asthmatic students
D. Physically challenged students

Answer B: Blind students

Blind people use tactile clues to identify colors. Instructors should use tactile clues to help students see or hear targets by adding color, making them larger, or moving them closer. It will help cooperation in a creative way.

73. Physiological benefits of exercise include all of the following except: (*Average Rigor*) (*Skill 6.1*)

A. Reducing mental tension
B. Improving muscle strength
C. Cardiac hypertrophy
D. Quicker recovery rate

Answer A: Reducing mental tension

Physical exercises can help improve muscle strength by making the body move and they can help provide quicker recovery between exercise sessions and from injuries. However, physical activity does not directly relieve mental tension. It might reduce tension temporarily, but chances are the tension will persist.

74. **Psychological benefits of exercise include all of the following except:** *(Rigorous) (Skill 6.1)*

A. Improved sleeping patterns
B. Improved energy regulation
C. Improved appearance
D. Improved quality of life

Answer B: Improved energy regulation

The psychological benefits of exercise include improved sleeping patterns, improved appearances, and an improved quality of life. Improved energy regulation is a physical benefit, not a psychological one.

75. **The most important nutrient the body requires, without which life can only be sustained for a few days, is:** *(Easy) (Skill 6.2)*

A. Vitamins
B. Minerals
C. Water
D. Carbohydrates

Answer C: Water

Although the body requires vitamins, minerals, and carbohydrates to achieve proper growth and shape, water is essential. Without it, the body gets dehydrated and death is a possibility. Water should be pure, as seawater can cause kidney failure and death.

76. **Which of the following conditions is not associated with a lack of physical activity?** *(Average Rigor) (Skill 6.3)*

A. Atherosclerosis
B. Longer life expectancy
C. Osteoporosis
D. Certain cancers

Answer B: Longer life expectancy

A lack of physical activity can contribute to atherosclerosis, osteoporosis, and certain cancers. Conversely, regular physical activity can contribute to longer life expectancy.

77. Data from assessing _____ identifies an individual's potential of developing musculoskeletal problems and an individual's potential of performing activities of daily living. *(Rigorous) (Skill 6.4)*

A. Flexibility
B. Muscle endurance
C. Muscle strength
D. Motor performance

Answer A: Flexibility

Level of flexibility is the factor most likely to indicate future problems and quality of daily living.

78. The ability for a muscle(s) to repeatedly contract over a period of time is: *(Average Rigor) (Skill 6.4)*

A. Cardiovascular endurance
B. Muscle endurance
C. Muscle strength
D. Muscle force

Answer B: Muscle endurance

Muscle endurance gives the muscle the ability to contract over a period of time. Muscle strength is a prerequisite for the endurance of muscle. Cardiovascular endurance involves aerobic exercise.

79. Working at a level that is above normal is which exercise training principle? *(Rigorous) (Skill 6.5)*

A. Intensity
B. Progression
C. Specificity
D. Overload

Answer D: Overload

Overloading is exercising above normal capacities. Intensity and progression are supporting principles in the process of overload. Overloading can cause serious issues within the body, either immediately or after some time.

80.	Students on a running program to improve cardio-respiratory fitness apply which exercise principle. (*Rigorous*) (*Skill 6.5*)

A.	Aerobic
B.	Progression
C.	Specificity
D.	Overload

Answer C: Specificity

Running to improve cardio-respiratory fitness is an example of specificity. Specificity is the selection of activities that isolate a specific body part or system. Aerobics is also a good option, but it deals with the entire body, including areas not specific to cardio-respiratory fitness.

81.	Prior to activity, students perform a 5-10 minute warm-up. Which is not recommended as part of the warm-up? (*Easy*) (*Skill 6.5*)

A.	Using the muscles that will be utilized in the following activity.
B.	Using a gradual aerobic warm-up.
C.	Using a gradual anaerobic warm-up.
D.	Stretching the major muscle groups to be used in the activity.

Answer C: Using a gradual anaerobic warm-up.

Warm-up is always necessary, but it should not be an anaerobic warm-up. The muscle exercises, the stretching, and even the aerobics are all helpful and athletes should complete these exercises within the normal breathing conditions. In fact, athletes should focus more closely on proper breathing. Athletes should engage in anaerobic stretching after activity, when muscles are loose and less prone to injury.

82.	Which is not a benefit of warming up? (*Rigorous*) (*Skill 6.5*)

A.	Releasing hydrogen from myoglobin.
B.	Reducing the risk of musculoskeletal injuries.
C.	Raising the body's core temperature in preparation for activity.
D.	Stretching the major muscle groups to be used in the activity.

Answer A: Releasing hydrogen from myoglobin.

Warm-up can reduce the risk of musculoskeletal injuries, raise the body's temperature in preparation for activity, and stretch the major muscle groups. However, a warm-up does not release hydrogen from myoglobin. Myoglobin binds oxygen, not hydrogen.

83. Which is not a benefit of cooling down? *(Rigorous) (Skill 6.5)*

A. Preventing dizziness.
B. Redistributing circulation.
C. Removing lactic acid.
D. Removing myoglobin.

Answer D: Removing myoglobin.

Cooling down helps the body to regain blood circulation and to remove lactic acid. It also prevents dizziness, which may occur after extensive exercises. The only thing that cooling down does not support is removing myoglobin. However, it can help myoglobin get a strong hold in the muscles.

84. Activities to specifically develop cardiovascular fitness must be: *(Rigorous) (Skill 6.5)*

A. Performed without developing an oxygen debt
B. Performed twice daily.
C. Performed every day.
D. Performed for a minimum of 10 minutes.

Answer A: Performed without developing an oxygen debt

The development of cardiovascular fitness is not dependent on specific time limits or routine schedules. Participants should perform aerobic activities without developing an oxygen debt.

85. Which of following overload principles does not apply to improving body composition? *(Average Rigor) (Skill 6.5)*

A. Aerobic exercise three times per week.
B. Aerobic exercise at a low intensity.
C. Aerobic exercise for about an hour.
D. Aerobic exercise in intervals of high intensity.

Answer A: Aerobic exercise three times per week.

To improve body composition, a person should engage in aerobic exercise daily, not three times per week. However, an individual can do aerobics for at least half an hour daily, he/she can exercise at a low intensity, or he/she can train with intervals of high intensity.

86. **Which of the following principles of progression applies to improving muscle endurance?** *(Rigorous) (Skill 6.5)*

A. Lifting weights every day.
B. Lifting weights at 20% to 30% of assessed muscle strength.
C. Lifting weights with low resistance and low reps.
D. Lifting weights starting at 60% of assessed muscle strength.

Answer B: Lifting weights at 20% to 30% of assessed muscle strength.

To improve muscle endurance, a person should lift weights at 20 to 30% of the assessed muscle strength. Lifting weights daily is counterproductive because it does not allow for adequate rest. In addition, lifting at 60% of the assessed muscle strength can damage the muscle.

87. **Overloading for muscle strength includes all of the following except:** *(Rigorous) (Skill 6.5)*

A. Raising heart rate to an intense level.
B. Lifting weights every other day.
C. Lifting with high resistance and low reps.
D. Lifting 60% to 90% of assessed muscle strength.

Answer A: Raising heart rate to an intense level.

Overloading muscle strength is possible by lifting the weights every other day or by lifting weights with high resistance and low repetition. Overloading does not cause or require an intense increase in heart rate. However, overloading has many other possibilities.

88. **Adding more reps to a weightlifting set applies which exercise principle.** *(Average Rigor) (Skill 6.5)*

A. Anaerobic
B. Progression
C. Overload
D. Specificity

Answer B: Progression

Adding more repetitions (reps) to sets when weightlifting is an example of progression. Adding reps can result in overload, but the guiding principle is progression.

89.   Cardiovascular fitness refers to: (*Average Rigor*) (*Skill 6.6*)

A. the ability to perform moderate to high intensity exercise for a prolonged period.
B. how much force a muscle group can generate and how effectively the muscle group can sustain that force over a period of time.
C. the physical makeup of the body.
D. ability of a joint to move through its range of motion.

Answer A: the ability to perform moderate to high intensity exercise for a prolonger period

Answer A defines cardiovascular fitness. Answer B defines muscular fitness; Answer C defines body composition; and Answer D defines flexibility.

90.   Instructors can encourage students to self-assess their physical education progress by employing: (*Easy*) (*Skill 6.7*)

A. Reflection
B. Journal writing
C. Interdisciplinary study
D. All of the above

Answer D: All of the above

Reflection/questioning, journal writing, and relating physical education topics with other content areas through interdisciplinary study are just some of the ways teachers can promote students' ability to assess their own physical fitness which encourages life-long fitness.

91.   All of the following are elements of a quality cardiovascular fitness program except: (*Average Rigor*) (*Skill 7.1*)

A. Mode
B. Frequency
C. Progression
D. Endurance

Answer D: Endurance

Mode is the type of aerobic activity such as jogging or swimming. Frequency refers to the amount of time each week spent exercising (recommended 3-5 times per week), and progression refers to adjustments made to accelerate an individual's fitness program. All of these elements, in addition to time (length of time spent exercising) and intensity (60% - 90% of maximum oxygen intake) make up a quality cardiovascular fitness program. Endurance is the individual's ability to perform a task for an extended period of time, and the goal of a good cardiovascular program is to increase a person's endurance.

92. **Swimming does not improve which health or skill related component of fitness?** *(Rigorous) (Skill 7.2)*

A. Cardio-respiratory function
B. Flexibility
C. Muscle strength
D. Foot Speed

Answer D: Foot speed

Swimming involves every part of the body. It works on the cardio-respiratory system and it develops flexibility because of the intense body movement in the water. It also improves muscle strength as swimmers must move their bodies against the force of water. Increased foot speed is not an outcome of swimming.

93. **Which of the following does not modify overload?** *(Rigorous) (Skill 7.3)*

A. Frequency
B. Perceived exertion
C. Time
D. Intensity

Answer B: Perceived exertion

Time extension, frequency of movement, and intensity are all indicators of overload. However, exertion is not a good indicator of overload, because measuring exertion is subjective and difficult to monitor.

94. **Using the Karvonean Formula, compute the 60% - 80% THR for a 16-year old student with a RHR of 60.** *(Rigorous) (Skill 7.3)*

A. 122-163 beats per minute
B. 130-168 beats per minute
C. 142-170 beats per minute
D. 146-175 beats per minute

Answer D: 146-175 beats per minute

220 – 16 (age) = 204, 204 – 60 (RHR) = 144, 144 x .60 (low end of heart range) = 86, 86 + 60 (RHR) = **146 (bottom of THR)**

220 – 16 (age) = 204, 204 – 60 (RHR) = 144, 144 x 0.80 (high end of heart range) = 115, 115 + (RHR) = **175 (top of THR)**

146-175 beats per minute is the 60%-80% THR.

95.   **Using Cooper's Formula, compute the THR for a 15 year old student.** (*Rigorous*) (*Skill 7.3*)

A. 120- 153 beats per minute
B. 123-164 beats per minute
C. 135-169 beats per minute
D. 147-176 beats per minute

Answer B: 123 – 164 beats per minute

Cooper's Formula to determine target heart range is: THR
= (220 - AGE) x .60 to (220 - AGE) x .80.

So, (220 – 15) x .6 to (220 – 15) x.8 = 123 - 164

96.   **Freehand front lunges will help an individual target muscle endurance in which of the following muscle groups:** (*Average Rigor*) (*Skill 8.1*)

A. Trapezoids and lateral muscles
B. Thighs and hamstrings
C. Triceps and biceps
D. Obliques and thighs

Answer B: Thighs and hamstrings

Freehand front lunges emphasize large muscle groups in the lower body, more specifically the legs. Trapezoids and lateral muscles are located in the middle and upper back. Triceps and biceps are located in the arms, and obliques are located in the mid-section. Thighs and hamstrings are the muscles targeted by the exercise pictured below.

Freehand Front Lunge
Thighs and Hamstrings

97. **Students are performing trunk extensions. What component of fitness does this activity assess?** (*Average Rigor*) (*Skill 8.2*)

A. Balance
B. Flexibility
C. Body Composition
D. Coordination

Answer B: Flexibility

The core component of trunk extensions is flexibility. Trunk extensions also indicate the body's capacity for full expansion and emphasizes areas such as the stomach, arms, and shoulder joints.

98. **Which of the following applies the concept of progression?** (*Rigorous*) (*Skill 8.2*)

A. Beginning a stretching program every day.
B. Beginning a stretching program with 3 sets of reps.
C. Beginning a stretching program with ballistic stretching.
D. Beginning a stretching program holding stretches for 15 seconds and work up to holding stretches for 60 seconds.

Answer D: Beginning a stretching program holding stretches for 15 seconds and work up to holding stretches for 60 seconds.

Progression is the process of starting an exercise program slowly and cautiously before proceeding to more rigorous training. Answer D is the only answer that exemplifies progression.

99. **A tendon is:** (*Average Rigor*) (*Skill 8.4*)

A. contractile tissue.
B. the location at which two bones make contact.
C. a tough band of fibrous connective tissue that connects muscle to bone or muscle to muscle.
D. a short band of tough fibrous connective tissue composed mainly of long, stringy collagen fibers.

Answer C: a tough band of fibrous connective tissue that connects muscle to bone or muscle to muscle.

Answer C defines tendons correctly as touch bands of fibrous connective tissue that connects muscle to bone or muscle to musde. Answer A defines muscles are contractile tissue. Answer B defines joints, the locations at which two bones make contact. Finally Answer D defines ligaments short bands of tough fibrous connective tissue composed mainly of long, stringy collagen fibers.

100. This form of workout promotes muscular endurance development, but it more taxing than average workout programs. (*Rigorous*) *(Skill 8.5)*

A. Weight training
B. Circuit training
C. Partner-resistance exercise
D. Technique training

Answer B: Circuit training

Athletes use circuit training to increase the efficiency and intensity of a training routine by alternating exercises that target different muscle groups instead of alternating exercises with rest-periods. This form of workout promotes muscular endurance development, but is more taxing on the students. Only those students who already exercising regularly and have proven their ability to remain disciplined and follow directions should attempt circuit training.

101. With regard to protein content, foods from animal sources are usually: (*Average Rigor*) *(Skill 9.1)*

A. Complete
B. Essential
C. Nonessential
D. Incidental

Answer A: Complete

Animal protein is complete, meaning it provides all of the amino acids that the human body requires. Although animal meat is not essential to a person's diet, it is an excellent source of protein.

102. Fats with room for two or more hydrogen atoms per molecule-fatty acid chain are: (*Rigorous*) *(Skill 9.1)*

A. Monounsaturated
B. Polyunsaturated
C. Hydrosaturated
D. Saturated

Answer B: Polyunsaturated

Polyunsaturated fatty acids contain multiple carbon-carbon double bonds. Thus, there is room for two or more hydrogens. Polyunsaturated fats are healthier than saturated fats.

103. **An adequate diet to meet nutritional needs consists of:** *(Rigorous) (Skill 9.1)*

A. No more than 30% caloric intake from fats, no more than 50 % caloric intake from proteins, and at least 20% caloric intake from carbohydrates.
B. No more than 30% caloric intake from fats, no more than 40% caloric intake from proteins, and at least 30% caloric intake from carbohydrates.
C. No more than 30% caloric intake from fats, no more than 15% caloric intake from proteins, and at least 55% caloric intake from carbohydrates.
D. No more than 30 % caloric intake from fats, no more than 30% caloric intake from proteins, and at least 40% caloric intake from carbohydrates.

Answer C: No more than 30% caloric intake from fats, no more than 15% caloric intake from proteins, and at least 55% caloric intake from carbohydrates.

General guidelines for nutritionally sound diets are 30% caloric intake from fats, no more than 15% caloric intake from proteins, and at least 55% caloric intake from carbohydrates.

104. **Maintaining body weight is best accomplished by:** *(Average Rigor) (Skill 9.1)*

A. Dieting
B. Aerobic exercise
C. Lifting weights
D. Equalizing caloric intake relative to output

Answer D: Equalizing caloric intake relative to output

The best way to maintain a body weight is by balancing caloric intake and output. Extensive dieting (caloric restriction) is not a good option as this would result in weakness. Exercise is part of the output process that helps balance caloric input and output.

105. **Electronic impedance, a technique that estimates body fat percentage, uses this tool to measure the conductive potential of the body.** *(Rigorous) (Skill 9.2)*

A. Bioimpedance meter
B. Calipers
C. Individual's height and weight
D. All of the above

Answer A: Bioimpedance meter

Answer A is the tool used when using the technique of electronic impedance. Calipers are used for skinfold tests, and an individual's height and weight are used when computing BMI (body mass index).

106.   Which is not a sign of stress? (*Rigorous*) *(Skill 9.5)*

A. Irritability
B. Assertiveness
C. Insomnia
D. Stomach problems

Answer B: Assertiveness

Assertiveness is not a sign of stress. Irritability, insomnia, and stomach problems are all related to stress.

107.   Which is not a common negative stressor? (*Rigorous*) *(Skill 9.5)*

A. Loss of significant other.
B. Personal illness or injury.
C. Moving to a new state.
D. Landing a new job.

Answer D: Landing a new job.

Landing a new job is generally not a cause of worry or stress. In fact, it is a positive event. Personal illness, loss of a significant other, or moving to a strange state can cause negative stress.

108.   Which of the following is a negative coping strategy for dealing with stress? (*Average Rigor*) *(Skill 9.5)*

A. Recreational diversions
B. Active thinking
C. Alcohol use
D. Imagery

Answer C: Alcohol use

The use of alcohol is a negative coping strategy for dealing with stress. Alcohol causes the brain to lose the stressful data thus soothing the individual, but it can be highly detrimental in the long run. Positive ways to deal with stress include active thinking, imagery, and recreational diversions.

109.   Most high-protein diets: *(Average Rigor) (Skill 9.6)*

A. Are high in cholesterol
B. Are high in saturated fats
C. Require vitamin and mineral supplements
D. All of the above

Answer D: All of the above

High-protein diets are high in cholesterol, saturated fats, and they require vitamin and mineral supplements.

110.   Which one of the following statements about low-calorie diets is false? *(Rigorous) (Skill 9.6)*

A. Most people who "diet only" regain the weight they lose.
B. They are the way most people try to lose weight.
C. They make weight control easier.
D. They lead to excess worry about weight, food, and eating.

Answer C: They make weight control easier.

People who participate in low-calorie diets do not control their weight easily. They must work more and utilize their bodies in many other ways (e.g., walking) to keep themselves fit.

111.   The local health food store is sponsoring a "Health Watch Day" with the local high school's physical education department where students, teachers, and local citizens can come in to receive a free BMI rating and information on a balance diet. This event is a good example of: *(Average Rigor) (Skill 9.7)*

A. Interdisciplinary study
B. Consumer education
C. Stress management
D. Marketing diet plans

Answer B: Consumer education

We can find services for promoting consumer awareness skills in relation to physical activity, recreation, fitness, and wellness online in the local community. For example, health food stores may also offer seminars on fitness and wellness. Physical education professionals can work to build ties between these publicly offered services and their own curriculums. Interdisciplinary study typically takes place within the school and is implemented when teachers of various content areas relate one area of study through their multiple subject areas. Stress management refers to strategies used to reduce high levels of stress. Marketing diet plans refers to strategies used to market fad diet plans.

112. **Through physical activities, John has developed self-discipline, fairness, respect for others, and new friends. John has experienced which of the following?** *(Rigorous) (Skill 10.1)*

A. Positive cooperation psycho-social influences
B. Positive group psycho-social influences
C. Positive individual psycho-social influences
D. Positive accomplishment psycho-social influences

Answer B: Positive group psycho-social influences

Through physical activities, John developed his social interaction skills. Social interaction is the sequence of social actions between individuals (or groups) that modify their actions and reactions due to the actions of their interaction partner(s). In other words, they are events in which people attach meaning to a situation, interpret what others mean, and respond accordingly. Through socialization with other people, John feels the influence of the people around him.

113. **Which of the following psycho-social influences is <u>not</u> negative?** *(Rigorous) (Skill 10.1)*

A. Avoidance of problems
B. Adherence to exercise
C. Ego-centeredness
D. Role conflict

Answer B: Adherence to exercise

The ability of an individual to adhere to an exercise routine due to her/his excitement, accolades, etc. is not a negative psycho-social influence. Adherence to an exercise routine is healthy and positive.

114. **Aerobic dance develops or improves each of the following skills or health components except:** *(Rigorous) (Skill 10.1)*

A. Cardio-respiratory function
B. Body composition
C. Coordination
D. Flexibility

Answer D: Flexibility

Aerobic dance does not develop flexibility, as flexibility results from stretching and not aerobic exercise. Ballet dancing, however, does develop flexibility. Aerobic dance develops cardio-respiratory function due to the unusual body movements performed. It also improves body composition and coordination due to the movement of various body parts.

115. The most effective way to promote the physical education curriculum is to: (*Rigorous*) (*Skill 10.1*)

A. Relate physical education to higher thought processes
B. Relate physical education to humanitarianism
C. Relate physical education to the total educational process
D. Relate physical education to skills necessary to preserve the natural environment

Answer C: Relate physical education to the total educational process

The government treats the physical education curriculum as one of the major subjects. Because of all of the games that we now participate in, many countries have focused their hearts and set their minds on competing with rival countries. Physical education is now one of the major, important subjects and instructors should integrate physical education into the total educational process.

116. This method refers to instructional method when teachers address the whole class through lecture, demonstration, or questioning. (*Average Rigor*) (*Skill 10.3*)

A. Large-group skill instruction
B. Small-group skill instruction
C. Individual skill instruction
D. Cognitive structuring

Answer D: Cognitive structuring

Cognitive structuring refers to when teachers the instructional method when teachers address the whole class. Large-group skill instruction involves all the students in the class completing one related activity, while small-group skill instruction is when the teacher divides students into groups, each of which works on a different skill or activity. Finally, in the individual skill instruction format, the instructor asks each student to select a skill on which to work. The students independently decide when they are ready to progress to the next skill.

117. **Rowing develops which health or skill related component of fitness?** (*Rigorous*) (*Skill 10.4*)

A. Muscle endurance
B. Flexibility
C. Balance
D. Reaction time

Answer A: Muscle endurance

Rowing helps develop muscle endurance because of the continuous arm movement against the force of the water. However, flexibility, balance, and reaction time are not important components of rowing. Rowing also develops the lower abdominal muscles while the individual is in the sitting position when rowing.

118. **Calisthenics develops all of the following health and skill related components of fitness except:** (*Average Rigor*) (*Skill 10.4*)

A. Muscle strength
B. Body composition
C. Power
D. Agility

Answer C: Power

Calisthenics is a sport that actually helps to keep a body fit in by combining gymnastic and aerobic activities. Calisthenics develop muscle strength and agility and improves body composition. However, calisthenics do not develop power because they do not involve resistance training or explosiveness.

119. **Which health or skill related components of fitness are developed by rope jumping?** (*Average Rigor*) (*Skill 10.4*)

A. Muscle Force
B. Coordination
C. Flexibility
D. Muscle strength

Answer B: Coordination

Rope jumping is a good mental exercise and it improves coordination. Many athletes (e.g. boxers, tennis players) jump rope to improve coordination and quickness. Muscle strength is secondary to that.

120. Educators can evaluate the cognitive domain by all of the following methods except: (*Rigorous*) (*Skill 10.6*)

A. Norm-Referenced Tests
B. Criterion Referenced Tests
C. Standardized Tests
D. Willis Sports Inventory Tests

Answer D: Willis Sports Inventory Tests

The Willis Sports Inventory Test is the tally of all wins and losses of the popular basketball player, Willis.

121. Students are performing the vertical jump. What component of fitness does this activity assess? (*Rigorous*) (*Skill 10.8*)

A. Muscle strength
B. Balance
C. Power
D. Muscle endurance

Answer C: Power

Vertical jumping assesses the power of the entire body. It shows the potential of the legs to hold the upper body and the strength in the joints of the legs. Balance and muscle strength are secondary requirements. Power automatically ensures these secondary requirements.

122. Which of the following body types is the most capable of motor performance involving endurance? (*Rigorous*) (*Skill 11.1*)

A. Endomorph
B. Ectomorph
C. Mesomorph
D. Metamorph

Answer B: Mesomorph

Characteristically, ectomorphs are lean and slender with little body fat and musculature. Ectomorphs are usually capable of performing at high levels in endurance events.

123. Movement activities promote fairness, equity, and diversity because they consider this type of individual development. (*Rigorous*) (*Skill 11.5*)

A. Psychological
B. Human growth
C. Aesthetic
D. Both A and B

Answer D: Both A and B

Movement activities promote personal growth and development physically, by way of stimulating muscular development, and emotionally, by raising personal confidence levels among children and by allowing them to explore concepts of inter-group equity that may at first seem threatening. To the insecure child, the concept that another group may be equal to his own may seem to 'demote' his group and the child by extension.

124. An instructor used a similar movement from a skill learned in a different activity to teach a skill for a new activity. The technique used to facilitate cognitive learning was: (*Average Rigor*) (*Skill 11.6*)

A. Conceptual thinking
B. Transfer of learning
C. Longer instruction
D. Appropriate language

Answer B: Transfer of learning

Using a previously used movement to facilitate a new task is a transfer of learning. The individual relates the past activity to the new one, enabling him/her to learn it more easily. Conceptual thinking is related to the transfer of learning, but it does not give the exact idea. Rather, it emphasizes the history of all learning.

125. Long-term planning is essential for effective class management. Identify the management techniques not essential to long-term planning. (*Easy*) (*Skill 12.1*)

A. Parental observation
B. Progress evaluation
C. Precise activity planning
D. Arrangements for line markings

Answer A: Parental observation

While it is important that a child have support from his/her parents, parental observation is not an essential consideration in long-term planning. Progress evaluation, precise activity planning, and arranging line markings are all essential management techniques for long-term planning.

126. Which of the following is not a class-management technique? *(Easy)* *(Skill 12.1)*

A. Explaining procedures for roll call, excuses, and tardiness
B. Explaining routines for changing and showering
C. Explaining conditioning
D. Promoting individual self-discipline

Answer C: Explaining conditioning

Explaining conditioning is not a class management technique. It is an instructional lesson.

127. The physical education philosophy based on experience is: *(Average Rigor) (Skill 12.2)*

A. Naturalism
B. Pragmatism
C. Idealism
D. Existentialism

Answer B: Pragmatism

Pragmatism, as a school of philosophy, is a collection of different ways of thinking. Given the diversity of thinkers and the variety of schools of thought that have adopted this term over the years, the term pragmatism has become almost meaningless in the absence of further qualification. Most of the thinkers who describe themselves as pragmatists indicate some connection with practical consequences or real effects as vital components of both meaning and truth.

128. The modern physical education philosophy that combines beliefs from different philosophies is: *(Easy) (Skill 12.2)*

A. Eclectic
B. Humanistic
C. Individualism
D. Realism

Answer A: Eclectic

Eclectics are so-called philosophers who attach themselves to no system in particular. Instead, they select what, in their judgment, is true out of the other philosophies. In antiquity, the Eclectic philosophy is that which sought to unite into a coherent whole, the doctrines of Pythagoras, Plato, and Aristotle. There is eclecticism in art as well as philosophy. The term was applied to an Italian school which aimed at uniting the excellence of individual intellectual masters.

129. A physical education teacher emphasizes healthy attitudes and habits. She conducts her classes so that students acquire and interpret knowledge and learn to think/analyze, which is necessary for physical activities. The goals and values utilized and the philosophy applied by this instructor is: *(Rigorous) (Skill 12.2)*

A. Physical Development Goals and Realism Philosophy
B. Affective Development Goals and Existentialism
C. Motor Development Goals and Realism Philosophy
D. Cognitive Development Goals and Idealism Philosophy

Answer D: Cognitive Development Goals and Idealism Philosophy

Educators use cognitive development goals to describe the act of teaching children in a manner that will help them develop as personal and social beings. Concepts that fall under this term include social and emotional learning, moral reasoning/cognitive development, life-skills education, health education, violence prevention, critical thinking, ethical reasoning, and conflict resolution and mediation. This form of education involves teaching children and teenagers such values as honesty, stewardship, kindness, generosity, courage, freedom, justice, equality, and respect. Idealism is an approach to philosophical inquiry that asserts direct and immediate knowledge can only be had as ideas or mental pictures. We can only know the objects that are the basis of these ideas indirectly.

130. The affective domain of physical education contributes to all of the following except: *(Rigorous) (Skill 12.2)*

A. Knowledge of exercise, health, and disease
B. Self-actualization
C. An appreciation of beauty
D. Good sportsmanship

Answer A: Knowledge of exercise, health, and disease

The affective domain encompasses emotions, thoughts, and feelings related to physical education. Knowledge of exercise, health, and disease is part of the cognitive domain.

131. An obese student's fitness assessments were poor for every component of fitness. Which would you recommend first? (*Easy*) (*Skill 12.4*)

A. A jogging program.
B. A weight lifting program.
C. A walking program.
D. A stretching program.

Answer C: A walking program

An obese person should begin by walking and then progress to jogging. Weightlifting and stretching are not as important initially. They are also dangerous because the student may not have the ability to complete such strenuous tasks safely.

132. All of the following are Systematic Observational Evaluations except: (*Rigorous*) (*Skill 12.4*)

A. Reflective Recording
B. Event Recording
C. Duration Recording
D. Self Recording

Answer A: Reflective Recording

Reflective recording is not a type of systematic observational evaluation. Event, duration, and self recordings are all methods used in systematic observational evaluations.

133. While studying the social science, students might: (*Average Rigor*) (*Skill 12.6*)

A. examine the relationship between physical activity and health.
B. study the physical science that stands behind bodily movements.
C. examine the interactions between groups in competitive team-based games.
D. Both A and C.

Answer C: examine the interactions between groups in competitive team-based games

When studying social sciences, students will examine the interactions between groups and team-based games. Answer A describes what students examine when studying the health sciences, and answer B describes what students learn when studying life/physical sciences.

134. **A legal wrong resulting in a direct or an indirect injury is:** *(Average Rigor)* *(Skill 13.1)*

A. Negligence
B. A Tort
C. In loco parentis
D. Legal liability

Answer B: A Tort

A tort is damage, injury, or a wrongful act done willfully, negligently, or in circumstances involving strict liability, but not involving breach of contract, for which the injured party can bring a civil suit.

135. **Although Mary is a paraplegic, she wants to participate in some capacity in the physical education class. What federal legislative act entitles her to do so?** *(Rigorous) (Skill 13.2)*

A. PE 94-142
B. Title IX
C. PL 94-142
D. Title XI

Answer C: PL 94-142

It is the purpose of Act PL 94-142 to assure that all handicapped children have available to them, within the time periods specified in section 612(2), (B.), a free, appropriate public education that emphasizes special education and related services designed to meet their unique needs, to assure that the rights of handicapped children and their parents/guardians are protected, to assist states and localities to provide for the education of all handicapped children, and to assess and assure the effectiveness of efforts to educate handicapped children.

136. **A physical education instructor anticipates and prevents potential injuries, watches for hidden injuries, and takes an injury evaluation of the entire class. Which of the following strategies to prevent injuries is the teacher demonstrating?** *(Average Rigor) (Skill 13.3)*

A. Maintaining hiring standards
B. Proper use of equipment
C. Proper procedures for emergencies
D. Participant screening

Answer D: Participant screening

In order for the instructor to know each student's physical status, she takes an injury evaluation. Such surveys are one way to know the physical status of an individual. It chronicles past injuries, tattoos, activities, and diseases the individual may have or had. It helps the instructor to know the limitations of each individual. Participant screening covers all forms of surveying and anticipation of injuries.

137. **Which of the following is not a consideration for the selection of a facility?** *(Rigorous) (Skill 13.5)*

A. Community involvement
B. Custodial staff
C. Availability to women, minorities, and the handicapped
D. Bond issues

Answer A: Community involvement

While community involvement positively impacts the communities where individuals live and work, it is not a major consideration in facility selection. Factors that are more important are staffing, accessibility, and financial considerations.

138. **All of the following actions help avoid lawsuits except:** *(Average Rigor) (Skill 13.5)*

A. Ensuring equipment and facilities are safe
B. Getting exculpatory agreements
C. Knowing each students' health status
D. Grouping students with unequal competitive levels

Answer D: Grouping students with unequal competitive levels

Grouping students with unequal competitive levels is not an action that can help avoid lawsuits. Such a practice could lead to injury because of the inequality in skill, size, and strength.

139. **Which of the following actions does not promote safety?** (*Rigorous*) (*Skill 13.6*)

A. Allowing students to wear the current style of shoes
B. Presenting organized activities
C. Inspecting equipment and facilities
D. Instructing skill and activities properly

Answer A: Allowing students to wear the current style of shoes

Shoes are very important in physical education and the emphasis on current shoe styles does not promote safety because they focus more on the look of the clothing, rather than functionality.

140. **Which of the following sequences displays the correct order for performing CPR?** (*Average Rigor*) (*Skill 13.6*)

1. **Give two breaths**
2. **Firmly push down two inches on the chest 15 times**
3. **Call 911**
4. **Position hands in the center of the chest**
5. **Tilt head, lift chin, and check breathing**

A. 1, 5, 3, 4, 2
B. 3, 5, 1, 4, 2
C. 5, 3, 1, 4, 2
D. 3, 5, 4, 2, 1

Answer B: 3, 5, 1, 4, 2

Answer B displays the correct CPR sequence.

XAMonline, INC. 21 Orient Ave. Melrose, MA 02176

Toll Free number 800-509-4128

TO ORDER Fax 781-662-9268 OR www.XAMonline.com

TEXAS EXAMINATION OF EDUCATOR STANDARD-EXAMINATION FOR THE CERTIFICATION OF EDUCATORS   - TEXES/EXCET - 2008

PO#   Store/School:

Address 1:

Address 2 (Ship to other):

City, State Zip

 Credit card number_____-_____-_____-_____   expiration_____

EMAIL _____

PHONE   **FAX**

ISBN	TITLE	Qty	Retail	Total
978-1-58197-925-1	ExCET ART SAMPLE TEST (ALL-LEVEL-SECONDARY) 005 006			
978-1-58197-926-8	ExCET FRENCH SAMPLE TEST (SECONDARY) 048			
978-1-58197-723-3	ExCET SPANISH (SECONDARY) 047			
978-1-58197-580-2	TExES PRINCIPAL 068			
978-1-58197-929-9	TExES PEDAGOGY AND PROFESSIONAL RESPONSIBILITIES 4-8 110			
978-1-58197-899-5	TExES PEDAGOGY AND PROFESSIONAL RESPONSIBILITIES EC-4 100			
978-1-58197-271-9	TExES GENERALIST 4-8 111			
978-1-58197-945-9	TExES GENERALIST EC-4 101			
978-1-58197-948-0	TExES MATHEMATICS-SCIENCE 4-8 114			
978-1-58197-295-5	TExES MATHEMATICS 4-8 114-115			
978-1-58197-297-9	TExES SCIENCE 4-8 116			
978-1-58197-931-2	TExES SCIENCE 8-12 136			
978-1-58197-772-1	TExES ENGLISH LANG-ARTS AND READING 4-8 117			
978-1-58197-771-4	TExES ENGLISH LANG-ARTS AND READING 8-12 131			
978-1-58197-661-8	TExES SOCIAL STUDIES 4-8 118			
978-1-58197-621-2	TExES SOCIAL STUDIES 8-12 132			
978-1-58197-339-6	TExES MATHEMATICS 8-12 135			
978-1-58197-618-2	TExES LIFE SCIENCE 8-12 138			
978-1-58197-949-7	TExES CHEMISTRY 8-12 140			
978-1-58197-939-8	TExES MATHEMATICS-PHYSICS 8-12 143			
978-1-58197-940-4	TExES SCHOOL LIBRARIAN 150			
978-1-58197-941-1	TExES READING SPECIALIST 151			
978-1-58197-719-6	TExES SCHOOL COUNSELOR 152			
978-1-58197-620-5	TExES PHYSICAL EDUCATION EC-12 158			
978-1-58197-262-7	TExES SPECIAL EDUCATION EC-12 161			
978-1-58197-606-9	THEA TEXAS HIGHER EDUCATOR ASSESSMENT			
			SUBTOTAL	
			Ship	$8.25
			TOTAL	